SHIPPING ONLY

Critical Studies Series

SAMUEL JOHNSON:
New Critical Essays

SAMUEL JOHNSON:
New Critical Essays

edited by

Isobel Grundy

VISION
and
BARNES & NOBLE

Vision Press Limited
Fulham Wharf
Townmead Road
London SW6 2SB

and

Barnes & Noble Books
81 Adams Drive
Totowa, NJ 07512

ISBN (UK) 0 85478 485 3
ISBN (US) 0 389 20534 6

First published in the U.S.A. 1984

Printed and bound in Great Britain by
Unwin Brothers Ltd.,
Old Woking, Surrey.
Phototypeset by Galleon Photosetting,
Ipswich, Suffolk.
MCMLXXXIV

Contents

		page
	Preface	7
	Abbreviations	11
1	Samuel Johnson: Man of Maxims? by *Isobel Grundy*	13
2	That Man's Scope by *Robert Folkenflik*	31
3	Johnson and the Scholars by *Paul J. Korshin*	51
4	Johnson on 'The Rise of the Novel' by *Mark Kinkead-Weekes*	70
5	The Fall of Orgilio: Samuel Johnson as Parliamentary Reporter by *Robert Giddings*	86
6	The Political Character of Samuel Johnson by *Howard Erskine-Hill*	107
7	The Essayist, 'Our Present State', and 'The Passions' by *J. S. Cunningham*	137
8	*Rasselas* and the Traditions of 'Menippean Satire' by *James F. Woodruff*	158
9	Johnson and Commemorative Writing by *Mary Lascelles*	186
	Index	203

Preface

Two hundred years have now passed since the death of Samuel Johnson left his friends feeling the total lack of any 'next best'. During those years no figure has appeared (as none appeared before) to dominate the field of English letters in quite his manner. Frontiers have been charted and formally regulated to divide topical and polemical journalism from poetry, drama, essays, sermons, fiction, criticism, bibliography, lexicography, travel books, private letters, and lectures expounding the laws of the land, making it virtually certain that no writer will ever range so widely again. Yet there are few whose work is more consistent or characteristic. Johnson's importance to our own day is repeatedly evidenced not only by respected studies and bestselling biographies, but also by quotation and misquotation, by reproduction of visual likenesses and unlikenesses, in every branch of the media. Our impressions of him, it seems, are disparate and incompatible enough to need some attention.

Like Oliver Goldsmith, we have none of us travelled over Johnson's mind. It continues to beckon, though, as few mental regions do; it is still being rediscovered and reassessed. This group of essays constitutes another file of travellers' tales. They are, the editor hopes and believes, such as meet Johnson's own stringent requirements for that genre, of whose difficulties of both observation and reporting Johnson was well aware. He often stressed the way travellers tend in observation to ignore whatever they do not expect or cannot accommodate, and in reporting to exaggerate in hopes of producing surprise and wonderment. He might have foreseen—indeed, his penetrating comments on the relation of man and image as he wrote of his great poetic predecessors makes it inconceivable that he did not foresee—the way that the myth of his mind would flourish, and that typical travellers' versions of it would tend to take precedence over careful and scrupulous explorations and charting of the complex truth.

It is too late in the day now to offer one's aid against any of the well-known Johnson heresies. Even Dick Minim understands by now that there used to be a wrong way of interpreting him that must now be avoided. We have learned, thank goodness, not to see him as either humourless, authoritarian, long-winded, or prone to evade imagination and stick to statement. I have myself heard a group of six persons unanimously pick the word 'succinct' as best to describe his style; they were graduate students with a perhaps unusual readiness to think for themselves, but in their freedom from the old prejudices they were none the less symptomatic.

This collection, then, does not claim to be revolutionary, but it hopes to be revisionary. It sets out from the assumptions that Johnson is easy to love but hard to understand; that there is always some further angle we have not yet grasped; that his readers undergo a persistent experience of having, not without effort, to rethink; and that having made such an effort they may then find themselves in a position to offer new information or new insight. We have tried in this volume, while bearing in mind the wealth of his achievement, to set before our readers some aspects of his writing which have been least well recognized and which have strongest contemporary interest.

The editor opens the collection from the starting-point of Johnson's inveterate habit of stating that which everybody knows (this feature of his style is itself something that everybody knows) and proceeds from there to comment on his attitude to the wisdom of the past in its most general manifestation. Robert Folkenflik follows with a discussion of Johnson's 'scope', the extraordinary and unequalled breadth and variety of his contributions to letters, and the position of literary dictator as it was thrust upon him in his own time and since. Paul Korshin considers his relationship to the polymaths of the past and the manner in which his work continued theirs. Mark Kinkead-Weekes re-opens the vexed question of Johnson and a modern field of literature, that of fiction and more specifically the new and as yet uncodified novel. These essays move over a broad selection of Johnson's written work and to some extent his oral pronouncements, and seek to trace his relations with other minds.

Each of the remaining essays focuses more directly on some particular piece or pieces of writing, though these contributors also have moved in many directions far beyond Johnson's work, in order to set it into its place in that complex web which makes up the writer's mental environment. Robert Giddings and Howard Erskine-Hill are both concerned with Johnson's political views. Reconsideration of this issue leads the former through an account of the parliamentary debates which Johnson wrote for the *Gentleman's Magazine*, with their powerful dramatic presentation of the issues and personalities surrounding the fall of Sir Robert Walpole. The latter proceeds by way of the clouded maze of Jacobite shades of opinion to a re-reading of *The Vanity of Human Wishes* which, without any interference with those aspects of the poem already established in our minds, adds a transforming topical dimension. J. S. Cunningham looks at the picture presented chiefly in the *Rambler* essays of the nature of our 'present state', with special reference to the passions as instruments of both good and evil. James Woodruff offers a wealth of learned and persuasive evidence to maintain that we can learn a better comprehension of *Rasselas* through seeing it in relation to the long and various tradition of Menippean satire. Finally, Mary Lascelles discusses Johnson's contribution to commemorative writing, in his criticism of epitaphs and in his 'opportunistic' or occasional celebration of dead friends. She sets him into another continuous chain: one which he himself began, of meditation and re-meditation on his own thoughts, and of learning from his transmutation of experience into literature.

Johnson thought of commemoration as an act, in a religious context: a definition which precludes the classification of a book like this one as commemorative. Johnson is being commemorated in 1984, in religious, literary, and purely social contexts. It is worthwhile to remember him in a year which has become so universally linked in the public mind with George Orwell and with the notion of humanity as facing a threat of transformation in its very nature. For Johnson, any 'present alarming crisis' was suspect, as a likely exaggeration or even hoax, yet the actual unremarkable minute was pregnant with frightening potential for good or evil. To simplify our situation is to run the risk of impoverishment of understanding; to follow Johnson through the almost unprecedentedly rich trade routes of his mind, to examine the unusually complex structures and procedures out of which his works are composed, is to develop our capacity for understanding and enjoyment of, and for nourishment by, diversity and interrelatedness as they are found in all human environments and human behaviour.

I.M.G.

London, 1984

Abbreviations

Heritage	Johnson, *The Critical Heritage*, ed. James T. Boulton (London: Routledge and Kegan Paul, 1971)
Letters	Johnson, *Letters*, collected and edited by R. W. Chapman, 3 vols. (Oxford: Clarendon Press, 1952)
Life	James Boswell, *The Life of Samuel Johnson, LL.D.*, ed. George Birkbeck Hill, revised by L. F. Powell, 6 vols. (Oxford: Clarendon Press, 1934)
Lives	Johnson, *Lives of the English Poets*, ed. George Birkbeck Hill, 3 vols. (Oxford: Clarendon, 1905)
Yale	*The Yale Edition of the Works of Samuel Johnson* (New Haven, Oxford and London) 1 *Diaries, Prayers, and Annals*, ed. E. L. McAdam, Jr., with Donald and Mary Hyde, 1958 2 *The Idler* and *The Adventurer*, ed. W. J. Bate, John M. Bullitt and L. F. Powell, 1963 3–5 *The Rambler*, ed. W. J. Bate and Albrecht B. Strauss, 1969 6 *Poems*, ed. E. L. McAdam, Jr., with George Milne, 1964 7, 8 *Johnson on Shakespeare*, ed. Arthur Sherbo, introduction Bertrand H. Bronson, 1968 9 *A Journey to the Western Islands of Scotland*, ed. Mary Lascelles, 1971 10 *Political Writings*, ed. Donald J. Greene, 1977 14 *Sermons*, ed. Jean Hagstrum and James Gray, 1978

1

Samuel Johnson: Man of Maxims?

by ISOBEL GRUNDY

Johnson's predominant position in the recent *Oxford Book of Aphorisms*, duly noted by reviewers, can have surprised no one.[1] That Johnson dealt in axioms is itself axiomatic. The talking Johnson of legend had always an aphorism on his lips ('when a man is tired of London, he is tired of life'; 'no man is a hypocrite in his pleasures'). A listener exclaimed, ' "How he does talk! Every sentence is an essay." ' In this matter there appears to be no discrepancy between the spontaneous talker, the lexicographer, and the premeditating moralist ('Marriage has many pains, but celibacy has no pleasures'; 'Sorrow is a kind of rust of the soul'), or the critic ('Nothing can please many, and please long, but just representations of general nature'; 'Poetry is the art of uniting pleasure with truth, by calling imagination to the help of reason'; or again 'To circumscribe poetry by a definition will only shew the narrowness of the definer').[2] In every kind of expression, it seems, Johnson's mind struck off, freely and magisterially, a continual succession of these freshly-minted, portable specimens from the store of wisdom within.

Everybody can recognize these still current coins; to give them their right name is harder. *Axiom*, as Johnson defines it, suggests too strongly a proposition in logic; *epigram* for him implies verse as well as 'terminating in a point'. *Adage* and *saw*, like *proverb*, suggest the triteness of something inherited, not coined[3]; *precept* (a 'rule authoritatively given; a mandate; a commandment; a direction') suggests the dead hand of dogmatism: all these smack of Polonius rather than Socrates. *Generalization* (absent from the *Dictionary*) has been generally disapproved, from Blake through Virginia Woolf (quoted below) to rearguard actions mounted by various scholars to defend Johnson from the charge of generalizing. *Apophthegm*, which the *Dictionary* applies to something not only 'remarkable' and 'valuable' but also 'uttered on some sudden occasion', would do for his conversational sallies but not his written ones, unless by a very unwarrantable assumption about his methods of composition. Writers on Johnson have mostly preferred *aphorism* to *maxim*, probably because it sounds more dignified. The *Dictionary* refers from *aphorism* to *maxim*, from *maxim* to *axiom*. Although Johnson's definitions recognize shades of difference between *maxim* ('a general principle; a leading truth') and *aphorism* ('a precept contracted in a short sentence; an unconnected position'), the varying shades are all embraced in the stylistic habit which I mean to discuss. It involves distilling much thought into a small space; it carries with it an assumption of authority or an air of being the last word on the subject; it risks shading into truism, and also risks antagonizing instead of edifying its audience: from instruction, as Johnson wrote of Milton, we may 'retire harassed and overburdened, and look elsewhere for recreation'.[4]

Several causes have conspired since Johnson's day to increase readers' resistance to this habit. The prevalence of naturalism in fiction, of the romantic or the confessional in poetry, of professionalism and of theory in criticism, and of pluralism in all kinds of thought, have made the voices of the preacher and the wit alike uncongenial to us, and the combination of the two in aphorism something which we find hard to take seriously. Maxims are for advertising, for lapel buttons, for graffiti, not for imaginative literature. Writers who have little else in common are united in a hostile or sardonic attitude to axiomatic wisdom.

During Johnson's lifetime the plays of Goldsmith and Sheridan consistently mocked the fashionable sententia: in *She Stoops to Conquer* Goldsmith makes it a staple of tavern talk. 'The genteel thing is the genteel thing at any time', pronounces one 'fellow' at the Three Jolly Pigeons, and another replies admiringly, 'I like the maxum of it, Master Muggins.' Blake turned common precepts upside down in 'Proverbs of Hell', and was perhaps the most memorable, though neither the first nor the last , to generalize himself as he attacked the practice: 'To generalize is to be an idiot.' Hazlitt thought to damn *The Rambler* by calling it 'a splendid and imposing common-place book of general topics'.[5] George Eliot addressed the question more ruminatively but no less firmly:

> All people of broad, strong sense have an instinctive repugnance to the men of maxims; because such people early discern that the mysterious complexity of our life is not to be embraced by maxims, and that to lace ourselves up in formulas of that sort is to repress all the divine promptings and inspirations that spring from growing insight and sympathy. And the man of maxims is the popular representative of the minds that are guided in their moral judgment solely by general rules, thinking that these will lead them to justice by a ready-made patent method, without the trouble of exerting patience, discrimination, impartiality, without any care to assure themselves whether they have the insight that comes from a hardly-earned estimate of temptation, or from a life vivid and intense enough to have created a wide fellow-feeling with all that is human.[6]

As Eliot traces the effects of aphoristic wisdom in straitlaced moral judgement, Virginia Woolf traces them in straitlaced social habit:

> these generalizations are very worthless. The military sound of the word is enough. It recalls leading articles, cabinet ministers—a whole class of things indeed which, as a child, one thought the thing itself, the standard thing, the real thing, from which one could not depart save at the risk of nameless damnation. Generalizations bring back somehow Sunday in London, Sunday afternoon walks, Sunday luncheons, and also ways of speaking of the dead, clothes, and habits—like the habit of sitting all together in one room until a certain hour, although nobody liked it. There was a rule for everything.

Such rules, she says, prescribed an accepted pattern for tablecloths as well as the social hierarchies charted by Whitaker's Table of Precedency.[7]

The common reader, I believe, still associates Johnson with dogmatism as to moral and critical rules, if not social ones. It is worth asking how his use of maxims differs from reliance on ready-made patent methods, and from the tone of the leading article, which undoubtedly, in the long run, stems from a tradition begun in his essays.

As subject-matter for all his varied writings, Johnson chooses the moral and psychological relationships of one human being with another, and of the conscious, choosing self to the recalcitrant material of inclination and circumstance. This subject-matter is George Eliot's too, and there is a significant overlap in method between the narratives in which she evokes the inner experience of individuals and the discursive writing in which he analyses that of humanity in general. Now Johnson supplies particular detail (like the old curate and the lieutenant of dragoons who alone among all the acquaintance of the newly impoverished Melissa in *Rambler* 75 retain their courtesy to her); now George Eliot resorts to maxims, as in the 'Conclusion' to *The Mill on the Floss*, with its successive 'leading truths': 'Nature repairs her ravages—repairs them with her sunshine, and with human labour. . . . Nature repairs her ravages—but not all. . . . To the eyes that have dwelt on the past, there is no thorough repair' (p. 656). Eliot's use of generalization here, first succinctly struck off, then expanded, then modified, and finally exchanged for another generalization of different and even opposite tendency, is strikingly Johnsonian. Indeed, sharing with him her desire to make sense of her human material in its 'mysterious complexity', she also uses his methods. Regularly in her work we alight on passages like that about the 'men of maxims', in which she distils as much of her own understanding as she can conscientiously give the name of truth: passages cast in the form of general statement, so that any portion which can stand alone is potentially an aphorism, as is 'All people of broad, strong sense have an instinctive repugnance to the men of maxims.'

George Eliot's thought, however, is not completed in this sentence, but must be developed through a paragraph. In this too she resembles Johnson. Although he defines *aphorism* as 'an unconnected position', his positions are seldom unconnected;

even the 'sudden occasions' to which he confines apophthegm do not disrupt the powerful current of his thought, which, like Eliot's 'Conclusion', is constantly unmaking and remaking its propositions. His characteristic method in discursive essays is to lay down at first the foundation of an axiom (that is, according to the *Dictionary*, a 'proposition evident at first sight' and 'to be granted without new proof'—even though his own axioms, unlike those of his first definition, usually can 'be made plainer by demonstration'), and then to work from that. Many *Idlers* particularly (whose style is in general more condensed than that of earlier essays) open with a pure aphorism of a dozen words or fewer. Nos. 23, 102, 87, 58, for instance, sound from their opening sentences as if they will surely consist of a sermon on a text, a simple expansion of a statement which does not appear designed to admit of any modification. In fact, however, 'Life has no pleasure higher or nobler than that of friendship' stands in ironic relationship to an essay on the vulnerability of friendship to all sorts of unworthy and self-defeating impulses. 'It very seldom happens to man that his business is his pleasure' sympathetically introduces a plea to authors to write their own lives, no matter how disinclined to it they may feel. 'Of what we know not we can only judge by what we know' makes an incongruously philosophical opening to a rather whimsical account of travellers' tall tales, especially those of states governed by women, which are contrasted with 'the ladies of England', satirically considered. 'Pleasure is very seldom found where it is sought' differs from the other opening gambits I have mentioned in that Johnson does spend the body of his essay elaborating and expanding it; he closes, however, with a sentence embodying two counter-aphorisms: 'Yet it is necessary to hope, tho' hope should always be deluded, for hope itself is happiness, and its frustrations, however frequent, are yet less dreadful than its extinction.' Johnson has not here contradicted his initial aphorism, but he has contradicted its tendency, and countermanded the precept which his readers might be expected to draw from it.[8]

Johnson is less fond of lacing himself up in a formula than of trying it on experimentally: sometimes he then endorses it; sometimes he demonstrates its limitations, or goes on to offer a means of escape. Our most cherished familiar formulas, he maintains, often have the status of the persistent though unfounded beliefs which he evokes in the opening sentence of *Rasselas*. To be guided to the throne of Truth, he suggests in *The Vanity of Human Wishes* (line 142ff.), is a difficult undertaking beset by manifold risks of different kinds of failure. He often employs his virtuoso skill at dialectic, sharpened on the parliamentary debates he composed for the *Gentleman's Magazine*, in submitting generally accepted maxims to a fiery trial from which they may or may not emerge as valid currency. To vary the metaphor, he mounts a demonstration in geometry, where every proposition follows on the preceding one, or a climb on a rock face, where each hold must be established before the next can be essayed. It is a method demanding intellectual agility in the writer and offering intellectual suspense to the reader.

Rambler 2 opens with a favourite observation of Johnson's own, which he here presents as having been frequently made by others before him: that 'the mind of man is never satisfied with the objects immediately before it, but is always breaking away from the present moment. . . .' A reader with a preconception about Johnson's use of axioms, or with a personal taste for aphorism, may be tempted to set a mental frame around this statement and take it as the writer's own direct offering. Johnson, however, goes on to enumerate the various methods and tones in which this observation has been so frequently made: as 'raillery to the gay . . . declamation to the serious', with 'all the amplifications of rhetoric'. This survey detaches the writer more and more distinctly from the earlier observers, and itself provides new material for a resounding aphorism ('Censure is willingly indulged, because it always implies some superiority') to stand at the head of the second paragraph, which makes observations on the observers. This presents a tissue of further potential aphorisms ('men please themselves with imagining that they have made a deeper search, or wider survey, than others . . . the pleasure of wantoning in common topicks is so tempting to a writer, that he cannot easily resign it'), and concludes with a statement which is general, authoritative and not aphoristic only because of its length and complexity:

> It affords such opportunities of triumphant exultation, to exemplify the uncertainty of the human state, to rouse mortals from their dream, and inform them of the silent celerity of time, that we may believe authors willing rather to transmit than examine so advantageous a principle, and more inclined to pursue a track so smooth and so flowery, than attentively to consider whether it leads to truth.

What was so frequently remarked has not been contradicted, but the tone of the remarks and the conclusions drawn from them have been completely undermined, the remarkers deprived of any claim to disinterestedness and therefore to authority.[9]

Rambler 2 presents the acceptance and transmission of received maxims as a writer's temptation: flowery, delightful, but erroneous. It goes on to suggest (contradicting what is implied in the maxims) that to look to futurity may be a *good* thing, and (wounding the *amour propre* of the maxim-makers) that they as writers are peculiarly liable to the harmful effects of what they have so much enjoyed lambasting. Johnson turns to aphorism whenever in the course of his complex argument he needs to make some point beyond risk of cavil. 'The natural flights of the human mind are not from pleasure to pleasure, but from hope to hope', or 'no man turns up the ground but because he thinks of the harvest', he writes in opposition to the 'widely received', 'long retained'—even, he says, true and natural—maxims that warn against obsessive attention to the future.

Johnson, of course, has a general principle to offer, through the mouth of Imlac, to cover himself from the charge of self-contradiction: 'Inconsistencies . . . cannot both be right, but, imputed to man, they may both be true. Yet diversity is not inconsistency.'[10] Aphoristic wisdom is well suited to such diversity. We all know that proverbs tend to come in antithetical pairs (great minds think alike, fools seldom differ; many hands make light work, too many cooks spoil the broth).

Johnson often goes beyond the questioning or testing of established precepts and our eager assent to them, to actual mockery. This is not, of course, a practice peculiar to himself. Dryden had opened his celebration of triumphant stupidity with his monarch's discovery of the pompous, resounding and undeniable truth that

All humane things are subject to decay,
And, when Fate summons, Monarchs must obey.

Jane Austen was to open a celebration of beleaguered intelligence by presenting a crude and shrewd tenet of matrimonial opportunists as 'a truth universally acknowledged'.[11] Neither technique was foreign to Johnson, who loved to make fun of oracular wisdom inappropriately applied. His letters to Mrs. Thrale make endless play with the great truths deducible from the trivia of daily life, or pretentiously expressed by writers with whom he has nothing in common.[12] 'This was obvious', he writes in deadpan style when his hero, having reached his twenty-eighth year in ignorance 'that what cannot be repaired is not to be regretted', discovers this general truth by eavesdropping on a philosophic housemaid. *Idler* 40 ridiculously applies the maxim 'Genius is shewn only by invention' to the inventor of the small-ad, and 'Whatever is common is despised' to the world's lack of respect for the art of 'puffing'.[13] (A footnote in the Yale edition tells us that Johnson was to use the maxim about genius and invention again in his life of Milton, but does not distinguish the serious use from the burlesque.) Johnson's fictional characters use maxims to dignify foolish aims or deplorable conduct. 'Delay in great affairs is often mischievous', writes the lottery-addict in *Rambler* 181, who has missed a ticket-number of occult personal significance; 'any business is better than idleness', maintains the heartless mother in *Idler* 13 to justify her keeping her daughters at mind-destroying and valueless labour; 'Every heart ought to rejoice when true merit is distinguished with publick notice', says Johnson the Idler, celebrating a Guinness-Book-of-Records heroine who has, for a bet, ridden the same horse 1000 miles in 1000 hours.[14]

Even when he is writing in his own person, even when his intentions are earnest, Johnson, says Emrys Jones, uses epigrammatic formulations

> in such a way that one is made to see, even while enjoying them, how comically insufficient to the true purposes of life such rhetorical devices really are. If they seem, often, to lead us into a baffling cul-de-sac, this is their precise intention; they lead us there because we follow too innocently.[15]

But when we have repudiated the charge of using aphorisms restrictively, and shown how for Johnson they are a versatile tool for wit, scepticism, and the personal involving of the reader in a learning process, we still have not enumerated all the reasons for the uniquely high proportion of his utterance which they make up. Again and again his opening, closing and intermediate sentences, and subordinate clauses besides, attain the condition of aphorism; instead of either narrating or describing, they either enunciate some established truth, or they put forward a statement about some abstract quality or about some person who is representative rather than particular; and they do so with epigrammatic terseness. There is nothing aphoristic in

> Here falling houses thunder on your head,
> And here a female atheist talks you dead.
> (*London*, lines 17–18)

Two incidents are here made stylized, compressed, almost emblematic, but still simply narrative. Elsewhere in the poem, however, each couplet supplies an aphorism:

> Of all the griefs that harass the distress'd,
> Sure the most bitter is a scornful jest;
> Fate never wounds more deep the gen'rous heart,
> Than when a blockhead's insult points the dart. (166–69)

Here Johnson only alludes to, instead of narrating, the incident (the jest, the insult), but also delivers a judgement on each (as hyperbolical, by the way, as the incidents narrated in the earlier couplet), which relates the event to the moral character of the persons concerned and to the whole possible scale of human suffering. *London*, the first major effort of Johnson's English muse, teems with such aphoristic statements: 'unrewarded science toils in vain', 'All crimes are safe, but hated poverty', 'The groom retails the favours of his lord' (38, 159, 181). They *sound* like general principles, leading truths, though they are put forward as true of the social organization of the capital city rather than of human life in general. The poem centres on one particular leading truth, 'SLOW RISES WORTH, BY POVERTY DEPRESS'D' (line 177), which is marked out as crucial by succinctness (Juvenal's line and a half condensed to a line), by capitals, by its position exactly two-thirds of the way through the poem (half-way through in Juvenal), by its congruence with the other aphoristic formulations just quoted, and by a specific pointer to its universality and trustworthiness: 'This mournful truth is ev'ry where confess'd.' Even this, though, is far from unconnected with Johnson's developing discourse. Its generality and tone of gloomy acceptance give way at once to the particularity and resentment of 'But here more slow . . .'. In *London* as in later works, Johnson draws on his stock of knowledge about the constants of human behaviour to relate the uniquely competitive, insecure and anti-social conditions of the city to the universal tendencies which produce them—though he finds his awareness of the wider situation quite without power to console or reconcile. It is *London*'s generalizations, the sense that the individual case exemplifies psychological constants, which marks it off from other cityscapes presented in Swift's 'Description of a City Shower', Gay's *Trivia* and Pope's *Dunciad*.

Although only a few of Johnson's essays outside the *Idler* open in the Baconian manner with a pure maxim, nearly all lay down at the outset some base position whose structural rôle is that of an axiom; even some imaginary letters from correspondents open in this way. Johnson takes some axiomatic starting-points from earlier writers: Horace opens *Rambler* 9, Periander of Corinth's 'Be master of thy anger' opens No. 11, and other classical maxims open Nos. 6, 17, and 24. Many openings which cannot be defined as maxims or aphorisms because they are too much expanded with qualifications or further developments nevertheless make a claim to general or universal statement which gives them a similar effect. 'Every man is prompted by the love of himself to imagine, that he possesses some qualities, superior, either in kind or in degree, to those which he sees allotted to the rest of the world' opens *Rambler* 21 with a maxim's air of unassailability, though 'either in kind or in degree' achieves precision at the expense of brevity, and the sentence does not end there but proceeds to mocking elaboration of the ways in which this prompting works. *Rambler* 5 sets out from a single well-defined proposition, though a complex one:

> Every man is sufficiently discontented with some circumstances of his present state, to suffer his imagination to range more or less in quest of future happiness, and to fix upon some point of time, in which, by the removal of the inconvenience which now perplexes him, or acquisition of the advantage which he at present wants, he shall find the condition of his life very much improved.[16]

These two openings, like those of the first and second *Ramblers*, deliberately avoid the brevity of aphorism, but in evoking 'every man' they claim both authority and universality—in fact, omniscience.

When he does not assume such authority himself, Johnson often ascribes it to the general voice of humanity, which he cites in just the same way as a published source. This general voice opens very many of his essays, beginning, as we have seen, with *Rambler* 2. No. 14 then opens, 'Among the many inconsistencies which folly produces, or infirmity suffers in the human mind, there has often been observed . . .'. No. 18, two weeks later, goes further: 'There is no observation more frequently made by such as employ themselves in surveying the conduct of mankind, than . . .'. Nos. 29 and 189 follow suit: 'There is nothing recommended with greater frequency among the gayer poets of antiquity, than . . .' and 'The world scarcely affords opportunities of making any observation more frequently, than . . .'. Johnson is still doing the same thing in the *Adventurer*: 'That familiarity produces neglect, has been long observed', begins No. 67.[17] Such openings, as we have seen with *Rambler* 2, may prove susceptible to modification in the later course of the argument. But though they may be challenged, and though they may not introduce a maxim as such, they contribute importantly to the way the essays emphasize the existence and persistence of aphoristic wisdom.

If we put these openings, which acknowledge the familiarity of what they are saying, alongside those which consist either of a pure aphorism, or of a longer or more complex formulation which would easily lend itself to quarrying for aphorisms, or of an aphoristic quotation, or of reference to the experience of 'every man', we find that an overwhelming majority of Johnson's essays begin by staking out a position which has already been occupied, and by drawing attention to this fact.

It is positively amusing to note the various twists and turns of phrasing by which he claims *greatest* frequency or antiquity, now for that observation, now for this. The reader forms the impression of a mind abnormally well-stocked with precedent, like a legal text-book; Macaulay's gibe about his thinking like a lawyer not a legislator, in terms of precedent and authority, has some basis in observable fact, though Macaulay is badly mistaken in thinking that he leaves such precedent unchallenged.[18] Johnson may seem to be taking a high risk when in *Rambler* 109 he invents a correspondent who jokes at the surprise which Mr. Rambler will feel at the discovery of a *new* facet of human experience, and speculates 'that you imagine none but yourself able to discover what I suppose has been seen and felt by all the inhabitants of the world'. Readers who are happy to admire many Johnsonian aphorisms as coming under the heading of 'What oft was *Thought*, but ne'er so well *Exprest*' may nevertheless grow restive at being told how this or that truth, mournful or otherwise, is 'universally experienced, and almost universally confessed'— in the words of *Idler* 80, which opens by echoing with remarkable fidelity, given the different medium and twenty intervening years, *London* line 176.[19]

Again Hazlitt has effectively voiced the objection to Johnson on this head. Of *The Rambler* he writes:

> there is hardly a reflection that had been suggested on [the conduct and business of human life] which is not to be found in this celebrated work, and there is, perhaps, hardly a reflection to be found in it which had not been already suggested and developed by some other author, or in the common course of conversation. The mass of intellectual wealth here heaped together is immense, but it is rather the result of gradual accumulation, the produce of the general intellect, labouring in the mine of knowledge and reflection, than dug out of the quarry, and dragged into the light by the industry and sagacity of a single mind.[20]

Hazlitt's image here is astonishingly, I suppose unwittingly, Johnsonian. Behind all Johnson's writings stands the concept of the communal source into which generations of human thinkers follow each other's footsteps to labour at the increase of knowledge. He rejoices at the 'successive labours of innumerable minds' which have contributed to 'the hereditary stock devolved to them from ancient times, the collective labour of a thousand intellects',[21] and he takes this stock to include not only scientific knowledge but also hard-won understanding of truths about the human condition. The human race has its intellectual history to offer to its constantly renewed recruits of the untaught and the inexperienced. Johnson's learning bars him from over-estimating his own originality; when he thinks what oft was thought, he does not suppose himself the first. George Eliot, despite her low opinion of maxims, seems to share these views when she makes Maggie Tulliver long for 'her inherited share in the hard-won treasures of thought, which generations of painful toil have laid up for the race of men'. Laid up for her, Maggie hopes to find 'effectual wisdom', 'some explanation of this hard, real life', 'some key that would enable her to understand and, in understanding, endure'.[22]

Johnson might doubt the existence of a single key, but it is for such readers as Maggie that he writes his essays and *Rasselas*. He makes the point at the outset of each essay series. He heads the first *Rambler* with a quotation from Juvenal declaring his willingness to explain, as Elphinston translated it,

> Why to expatiate in this beaten field,
> Why arms, oft us'd in vain, I mean to wield.

Johnson reminds us in the last paragraph of the second *Rambler* that 'it is not sufficiently considered, that men more frequently require to be reminded than informed', in the first sentence of the third that the 'task of an author is, either to teach what is not known, or to recommend known truths, by his manner of adorning them', and at the beginning of the second *Idler* that 'Many positions are often on the tongue, and seldom in the mind; there are many truths which every human being acknowledges and forgets.'[23]

'In poems,' Coleridge was to write,

> equally as in philosophic disquisitions, genius produces the strongest impressions of novelty while it rescues the most admitted truths from the impotence caused by the very circumstance of their universal admission.[24]

Johnson performs such rescues as dazzlingly as he performs the demolition of unexamined *idées reçus*. His second great poem uses a maxim as crown or keystone even more notably than *London*: 'Nor think the doom of man revers'd for thee' (line 156) is of course an instruction to avoid what 'every man' thinks or feels; though it is addressed by the poet to a particular character, the scholar, it is advice which every person in the poem needs and ignores.

The life of Savage opens, like *Rambler* 2 and so many others, with a statement of something which 'has been observed in all ages', here 'that the advantages of nature or of fortune have contributed very little to the promotion of happiness'. Still in his first sentence Johnson rephrases this observation, which amounts to a cliché, in an extended form which emphasizes that people of meaner rank or ability have little cause for envy, and introduces a metaphor of splendour shining from 'the summits of human life' on those below. He then goes on to adduce two possible alternative reasons for the observation: 'whether it be that' superiority induces 'great designs' and therefore failure, 'or that' the failures of superior people are not more severe or common but merely more conspicuous than those of others. The second alternative smuggles into the argument, as hypothesis not fact, the potential aphorism 'that the general lot of mankind is misery'; it also suggests that the frequently observed maxim is less universal and unprejudiced than it might seem: it is made from a specific point of view, that of those who look up 'from a lower station'.

The printer of the first edition mistakenly placed a full stop before these clauses beginning 'Whether . . .', apparently supposing that the thought would have moved on. Johnson, however, has not yet finished meditating his opening proposition, branching out from the unhappiness of the great to the *particular* unhappiness of the great, whether as fact or as mere appearance. His second paragraph draws a distinction between greatness of situation and greatness of mind, and develops at some length the reasons why the latter might be expected to be altogether excluded from the opening proposition. His third paragraph again appeals to precedent to crush the hopes aroused by the second ('But this expectation, however plausible, has been very frequently disappointed') and includes the life he is just beginning among instruments of the disappointment.[25] This opening foreshadows the biography's delicate poise between admiration and condemnation, the sympathetic and the judicial. Savage as Johnson presents him certainly receives little benefit from his talents or his dubiously elevated rank, and gives no reader cause for envy; the observations of the opening clauses are vindicated in the life as a whole, but their inadequacy, the way they set the baffled mind vainly seeking explanation or interpretation, is also repeated at large in the work after being set out in brief in the introductory paragraphs. Savage the unique individual is trammelled at every turn by general facts about human nature which he had not supposed to apply to himself. His extraordinary story becomes one more piece of evidence proving the banality of the doom of man.

Johnson made his fullest statement about aphorisms in the sombre, vehement opening paragraphs of *Rambler* 71, which deals, as so many of his other essays do, with the shortness of life:

> Many words and sentences are so frequently heard in the mouths of men, that a superficial observer is inclined to believe, that they must contain some primary principle, some great rule of action, which it is proper always to have present to the attention, and by which the use of every hour is to be adjusted. Yet, if we consider the conduct of those sententious philosophers, it will often be found, that they repeat these aphorisms, merely because they have somewhere heard them, because they have nothing else to say, or because they think veneration gained by such appearances of wisdom, but that no ideas are annexed to the words, and that, according to the old blunder of the followers of Aristotle, their souls are mere pipes or organs, which transmit sounds, but do not understand them.
>
> Of this kind is the well known and well attested position, 'that life is short,' which may be heard among mankind by an attentive auditor, many times a day, but which never yet within my reach of observation left any impression upon the mind; and perhaps if my readers will turn their thoughts back upon their old friends, they will find it difficult to call a single man to remembrance, who appeared to know that life was short till he was about to lose it.[26]

As so often, Johnson's reasonable tone softens a most extreme attitude: 'never yet within my reach of observation' has this most obvious of all truisms left any impression. This is a staggeringly defeatist position for a moralist to take, yet it is comparable to a point made with great delicacy in *The Mill on the Floss*. To Maggie, even at 9 years old, '*Mors omnibus est communis*' would have been 'jejune' in her own language; yet the reader receives a shock when the novelist, comparing the 19-year-old Maggie's hidden destiny to an unmapped river, reminds us 'that for all rivers there is the same final home'.[27] It is of course as commonplace to be shocked at the brevity of one particular life as inured to the brevity of life as axiom; as Johnson writes in another of the many essays he devoted to this subject, 'nothing can so much disturb the passions, or perplex the intellects of man, as the disruption of his union with visible nature.'[28] With his every reference to the 'well attested position, "that life is short"', Johnson aims to break through the maxim's inefficacy, to create the disturbing effect of the thought behind the words. He does not seriously and consistently believe his readers to be invincibly ignorant, mere pipes to transmit sound without understanding, but he would agree with Keats that 'axioms in philosophy are not axioms until they are proved upon our pulses: We read fine things but never feel them to thee full until we have gone the same steps as the author.'[29] In Johnson's opinion a writer needs all his skill to reach the readers' pulses, to make them tread by his own steps.

Johnson aims at 'subtlety of disquisition' as well as 'the stability of truth'.[30] The units of his thought tend naturally to aphorism, formulations or more often re-formulations of basic positions, but he takes care that the units shall be closely interconnected in a manner which gives the most simple proposition an immensely complex set of qualifications and implications. In so far as his epigrammatic sentences can be disconnected from the thread of his discourse, they fall now one side, now the other, of the careful line he is tracing. They become maxims only as the reader detaches them, in which condition they retain the value only of whatever forcefulness and ingenuity we ourselves can find for applying them to new contexts. In so far as they remain embedded in their original sequence of reasoning, they function not as conclusions but as part of a process—in Yeats's terms, perhaps, not stone but living stream.[31] The weightiness of Johnson's style, and his concision in phrase-making, constantly press the reader to make that pause at the end of a general statement which will disconnect it from the progress of the argument, and make it permanent: a stone, an aphorism. On the other hand the momentum of that argument converts the individual nuggets of truth into incomplete steps in the movement to comprehend complex questions. It is noticeable that Johnson's conclusions (which are no longer susceptible to modification) are on the whole less aphoristic than his openings.

So Johnson's use of aphorism presents us with at least two paradoxes. A habit which has its root in humility (the writer's realization that his own insights are not unique, but shared with a community of thinkers, past and present) produces an effect of authority, as of an individual speaking for the race, or for some undefined succession of authoritative voices; and the epigrammatic brevity which makes a maxim seem impregnable also makes it cry out for that explication and interpretation which will inevitably reveal it as ambiguous or incomplete, and so lead back into the process which will arrive at a new maxim. Johnson's phrases and sentences often sound more assured, but his paragraphs and whole essays more tentative, than those of other writers.

He draws lavishly on the stores offered him by other thinkers, but constantly tests and tries their conclusions. Obloquy heaped on 'men of maxims' passes him by, for his are under constant, sensitive re-evaluation. From his base in aphorism he sets sail on his voyage of exploration; in the concision and solidity of aphorism he often brings his chain of argument to rest. The natural flights of his mind are both from maxim to maxim, and from test to test.

NOTES

1. He contributes more aphorisms than anyone else, and figures largely in the introduction (ed. John Gross, Oxford: Oxford University Press, 1983).
2. *Life*, Vol. 3, p. 178; Vol. 4, pp. 316, 284; *Rasselas*, Chap. xxvi; *Rambler* 47 (Yale, Vol. 3, p. 258); preface to Shakespeare (Yale, Vol. 7, p. 61); *Lives* Vol. 1, p. 170; Vol. 3, p. 251.
3. Johnson certainly did not scorn proverbial expression. See Pat Rogers, 'Johnson and the Diction of Common Life', in *Transactions* of the Johnson Society of Lichfield (1982), pp. 8–19.

4. *Lives*, Vol. 1, pp. 183–84.
5. *She Stoops to Conquer*, 1773, Act I (Goldsmith, *Collected Works*, ed. Arthur Friedman, Oxford: Clarendon, 1966, Vol. 5, p. 117); Blake, *Complete Writings*, ed. Geoffrey Keynes (London: Oxford University Press, 1966), pp. 150ff., 451; Hazlitt, *Lectures on the English Comic Writers*, 1819, in *Heritage*, p. 86.
6. *The Mill on the Floss*, 1860, Book VII, Ch. 2: ed. A. S. Byatt (Harmondsworth: Penguin, 1979), p. 628. Feminist critics, using this passage among others, have singled out as important this opposition to constricting and institutionalized *ideés reçus* (e.g. Mary Jacobus, 'The Question of Language: Men of Maxims and *The Mill on the Floss*' in *Critical Inquiry*, 8 (1981–82), 207–22).
7. 'The Mark on the Wall' in *A Haunted House* (London: Hogarth, 1944, repr. 1978), p. 44.
8. Yale, Vol. 2, pp. 72, 311, 269, 180, 182.
9. Yale, Vol. 3, pp. 9–10.
10. *Rasselas*, Chap. viii.
11. *MacFlecknoe*, 1684 (*Poems and Fables*, ed. James Kinsley (London: Oxford University Press, 1958), p. 238; *Pride and Prejudice*, 1813.
12. E.g. *Letters*, nos. 233, 256, 262, 293, 408.
13. *Rasselas*, Chap. iv; Yale, Vol. 2, p. 125.
14. Yale, Vol. 5, p. 188; 2, pp. 45, 19 (no. 6).
15. 'The Artistic Form of *Rasselas*' in *R.E.S.*, n. s. XVIII (1967), 398; cf. Leopold Damrosch, 'Johnson's Manner of Proceeding in the *Rambler*' in *E.L.H.* 40 (1973), 70–89.
16. Yale, Vol. 3, pp. 115, 25.
17. Ibid., pp. 74, 97, 158; Vol. 5, p. 224; Vol. 2, p. 383.
18. Review of Croker's ed. of Boswell's *Life*, 1831 (*Heritage*, p. 424).
19. Yale, Vol. 4, p. 215; Pope, *An Essay on Criticism*, 1711, line 298; Yale, Vol. 2, p. 249.
20. *Heritage*, p. 86.
21. *Ramblers* 9, 121: Yale, Vol. 3, p. 49; Vol. 4, p. 282.
22. *The Mill on the Floss*, Book IV, Chap. 3 (pp. 379–81).
23. Yale, Vol. 3, pp. 3, 14–15; Vol. 2, p. 6.
24. *Biographia Literaria*, 1817, Chap. 4.
25. *Lives*, Vol. 2, p. 321; *Early Biographical Writings*, ed. J. D. Fleeman (Farnborough: Gregg, 1973), p. 199.
26. Yale, Vol. 4, pp. 7–8.
27. Book II, Chap. 1, p. 217; Book III, Ch. 6, pp. 514–15. In *Middlemarch*, Eliot addresses the reader directly to mark Mr. Casaubon's arrival at 'one of those rare moments of experience when we feel the truth of a commonplace'—which is, of course, the commonplace 'We must all die' (Book IV, Ch. 42: Boston: Houghton Mifflin, 1956, p. 311).
28. *Rambler* 78 (Yale, Vol. 4, p. 47).
29. To John Hamilton Reynolds, 3 May [1818] (*Letters*, ed. Hyder Edward Rollins, Cambridge, Mass.: Harvard, 1958).
30. *Life*, Vol. 2, p. 147 (of *The False Alarm*); Yale, Vol. 7, p. 62.
31. 'Easter 1916' in *Collected Poems* (London: Macmillan, 1965, p. 204).

2

That Man's Scope

by ROBERT FOLKENFLIK

In 1974 a striking exhibition opened in the Queen's Gallery, Buckingham Palace, celebrating the favourite ancestor of the present Prince of Wales: George III, as collector and patron. In the introduction to the catalogue of the exhibition, panegyrics to the king in dedications of books on science, music and art are quoted to show that specific references to the king's knowledge and taste go beyond the 'hyperbolic effusions' expected of a dedicator. Some of the seven quotations come from John Kennedy's *A Complete System of Astronomical Chronology* (1762), John Gwynn's *London and Westminster Improved* (1766), Sir Joshua Reynolds's *Discourses on Art* (1778) and Charles Burney's *An Account of the Musical Performances in Westminster-Abbey . . . in Commemoration of Handel* (1784).[1] What the unnamed author of the catalogue has not realized, however, is that a majority of his quotations, those from the four books I have named, were not written by the authors of those books, but by Samuel Johnson. And of those three which he mentions as particularly perceptive, two were written by Johnson. (I do not believe that Johnson had anything to do with Alexander Cumming's *The Elements of Clock and Watch-work*.)

What I hope to show by this citation of Johnson's ability to make a modern art historian believe that he was four other men is that if we desire, in the words of Shakespeare's 'Sonnet 29' (which T. S. Eliot borrowed for *Ash Wednesday*) 'this man's art and that man's scope', one of the things that makes

Johnson most humanly admirable is the sheer range of his interests, as the Sale Catalogue of his library reflects it.

Appropriately, range or scope provides themes and metaphors in his work. His greatest poem begins with a god-like perspective on the world:

> Let Observation with Extensive View,
> Survey Mankind from China to Peru.

He believed that 'the true Genius is a mind of large general powers, accidentally determined to some particular direction.' The context of this remark in the *Life of Cowley* shows that he is thinking of Sir Joshua Reynolds as well as Cowley. Yet if we think for a moment of Johnson attempting to equal Reynolds or Rembrandt with a brush, we recognize that genius cannot always take any course it wishes. Johnson's pronouncement serves a number of purposes. It is an expression, despite the emphasis on accidental determination, of the freedom of the will and the breadth of human possibility. It emphasizes the importance of experience. As a definition, it turns away from the notion of genius as a 'bent', or, as Johnson puts it, 'that particular designation of mind and propensity for some certain science or employment, which is commonly called Genius'.[2] How characteristic of him to praise Goldsmith in his epitaph as a man 'Qui nullum ferè scribendi genus/non tetegit' (who almost none of the kinds of writing did not touch). He certainly could have written this for his own tombstone.

Consider the variety of rôles he played as a writer: poet, playwright, essayist, satirist, novelist (at least many in his own time thought of his philosophical tale, *Rasselas*, as a novel), lexicographer, bibliographer, biographer, autobiographer and diarist (though the products of these last two activities were not intended for publication), journalist, book reviewer, editor (in several senses of the term), scholar, translator, travel writer, political writer, sermon writer, and—hardly least—critic.

The achievement of the *Dictionary* was remarkable. In France and Italy whole academies went to work to produce dictionaries for their nations. Once when Dr. William Adams, who had been a junior fellow at Oxford when Johnson was a student, found him at work on the Dictionary, he commented:

> This is a great work, Sir, How are you to get all the etymologies? JOHNSON. Why, Sir, here is a shelf with Junius, and Skinner, and others; and there is a Welch gentleman who has published a collection of Welch proverbs who will help me with the Welch. ADAMS. But, Sir, how can you do this in three years? JOHNSON. Sir, I have no doubt that I can do it in three years. ADAMS. But the French Academy, which consists of forty members, took forty years to compile the Dictionary. JOHNSON. Sir, thus it is. This is the proportion. Let me see; forty times forty is sixteen hundred. As three to sixteen hundred, so is the proportion of an Englishman to a Frenchman.[3]

Johnson did not complete it in three years, but David Garrick caught the spirit of his enterprise in a poem celebrating the completion of the *Dictionary* as a heroic exploit:

> And Johnson, well arm'd like a hero of yore,
> Has beat forty French, and will beat forty more![4]

Following the completion of the *Dictionary*, Johnson planned to start a *Bibliothèque*, a review of foreign and domestic books on all subjects. Thomas Percy tells of the scheme in a letter to Shenstone, 24 November 1757:

> He talks of undertaking a kind of Monthly Review upon a New Plan: which shall only extend to the choicest and most valuable Books that are publish'd not in England only but throughout Europe: something like the Acta Eruditorum Leipsiensia, &c.[5]

When his friend Dr. Adams again protested: 'How, Sir . . . can you think of doing it alone? All branches of knowledge must be considered in it. Do you know Mathematics? Do you know Natural History?', Johnson's answer was 'Why, Sir, I must do as well as I can.'[6] He would emphasize Continental literature (meaning by 'literature' something far broader than we mean now) and he would have the choice of books. Although this scheme, for which his work on the *Preceptor* and the *Gentleman's Magazine* had prepared him, came to nothing, it is typical of Johnson to move from the accomplishment of one vast scheme hardly thought credible for a single man to another.

Johnson might have answered less modestly, for he knew a good deal about science. Unlike Pope and Swift, he was generally respectful of the search for scientific knowledge and even conducted his own experiments. When that medical man of revolutionary America, Dr. Benjamin Rush, Professor of Chemistry in Philadelphia and later first Professor of Medicine at the University of Pennsylvania, was at dinner with Johnson, someone brought up the question of whether the sea anemone was animal or vegetable:

> 'It is an animal', said Dr. Johnson, 'for its ashes have been analized and they yield a *Volatile* alkali, and this we know is the criterion of animal matter, as distinguished from the vegetable, which yields a *fixt* alkali'. I was much struck with this remark, for I did not expect to hear a man, whose studies appeared from his writings, to have been confined to moral and religious subjects, to decide so confidently upon a controversy in Natural History and Chymistry.[7]

The answer was that thought at the time to be right, according to the best opinions. Johnson's knowledge of medicine probably dated from the early '40s when he worked on the *Medicinal Dictionary* of Dr. Robert James. Many of his good friends were doctors, and he did not hesitate to prescribe remedies in his letters to his mother and to Hill Boothby, the pious woman whom he probably intended as his second wife.

Boswell quotes Johnson as saying that he founded his style on Sir William Temple's and on that of Ephraim Chambers in his proposals for his *Cyclopaedia: or, an Universal Dictionary of Arts and Sciences*. Thomas Tyers, another biographer of Johnson, claims that it was the Preface, but the modern scholars who have examined the problem find little Johnsonian in the Preface and the Proposals are not extant. I think, however, that Johnson may have found in Chambers not his style but his ideal. The first paragraph of the preface calls attention to the human achievement in terms similar to those we have encountered in Johnson's discussion of his *Dictionary*:

> It is not without some concern that I put this work in the reader's hands; a work so seemingly disproportionate to any single person's experience, and which might have employed an academy. What adds to my apprehensions is the scanty measure of time that could be employed in a performance, which a man's whole life scarce appears equal to. The Vocabulary of the della Crusca was above forty years in compiling, and the Dictionary of the French Academy much longer; and yet the present work will be found more extensive

> than either of them in its subject and design, as much as it falls short of them in respect of years, or of hands employed in it.[8]

Johnson would have admired the attempt carried out by one man to present what Chambers elsewhere calls 'universal science' (that is, universal knowledge).

He was not, of course, a cloistered academic, and he respected tradesmen. This has its risible side. Following the death of his friend Henry Thrale, the wealthy brewer, Johnson is portrayed in an anecdote told by Lord Lucan as

> bustling about, with an ink-horn and pen in his button-hole, like an excise man; and on being asked what he really considered to be the value of the property which was to be disposed of, answered, 'We are not here to sell a parcel of boilers and vats, but the potentiality of growing rich, beyond the dreams of avarice.'[9]

This sounds as though Johnson, the brewmaster's executor, was in search of Sir Epicure Mammon.

Johnson had been brought up to a trade. When I was a graduate student, I was invited to use Mary Hyde's magnificent Johnson collection at Four Oaks Farm. There, among other things, I read the bound copy of Johnson's proofs for the *Life of Pope*. But I handled the copy very carefully, because Johnson had bound it himself, a feat learned from his bookseller father, Michael.

Johnson always seemed to be interested in the processes of making and manufacturing. In part this was an interest in applied science. He enthusiastically discusses the wonders of glassmaking in *Rambler* 36. On his trip to France he observed with interest the making of the Gobelin tapestries and china at Sèvres. In Wales he visited brass, copper and iron works.[10] Johnson's letter to Susannah Thrale of 25 March 1784 contains a miniature educational treatise which begins by recommending that she get to know the astronomer Herschel 'for he can show you in the sky what no man before him has ever seen . . .'. He then characteristically draws back from some of the implications:

> What he has to show is indeed a long way off, and perhaps concerns us but little [the astronomer in *Rasselas* confuses

> himself by being more concerned with star-knowledge than self-knowledge], but all truth is valuable and all knowledge is pleasing in its first effects, and may be subsequently useful.

Speaking as a former schoolteacher himself he comments in the *Life of Milton* on Milton's curriculum as teacher: 'we are perpetually moralists, but we are geometricians only by chance.'[11] In the letter he emphasizes knowledge of all sorts:

> Take . . . all opportunities of learning that offer themselves, however remote the matter may be from common life or common conversation. Look in Herschel's telescope; go into a chymist's laboratory; if you see a manufacturer at work, remark his operations. By this activity of attention, you will find in every place diversion and improvement.[12]

Pleasure and instruction are not found in poetry alone. Despite his own poor eyesight, he makes Herschel's telescope his point of departure for the recommendation of the kinds of knowledge in which he himself found 'diversion and improvement'.

Johnson believed in intellectual ambition while recognizing human frailty. He once told Reynolds,

> There are two things which I am confident I can do very well: one is an introduction to any literary work, stating what it is to contain, and how it should be executed in the most perfect manner; the other is a conclusion, shewing from various causes why the execution has not been equal to what the authour promised to himself and to the publick.[13]

This is a joke on himself. Yet the moving personal side of the Preface to his *Dictionary* presents just such an ironic vision of his task:

> When first I engaged in this work, I resolved to leave neither words nor things unexamined, and pleased myself with a prospect of the hours which I should revel away in feasts of literature, the obscure recesses of northern learning, which I should enter and ransack, the treasures with which I expected every search into those neglected mines to reward my labour, and the triumph with which I should display my acquisitions to mankind.[14]

This passage gives us the dictionary-maker, that 'harmless drudge', as an intellectual explorer and conqueror; yet after detailing his intentions, he is constrained to confess that 'these were the dreams of a poet doomed at last to wake a lexicographer.' This awareness of the magnitude of intellectual tasks followed by the realization of the impossibility of their ideal attainment forms the diastole and systole of his thought. In *Rasselas* Imlac's account of the requirements of the poet, which I have characterized elsewhere as employing a 'rhetoric of aggrandizement', stresses universal knowledge:

> 'To a poet nothing can be useless. Whatever is beautiful, and whatever is dreadful, must be familiar to his imagination: he must be conversant with all that is awfully vast or elegantly little. . . .
>
> 'All the appearances of nature I was therefore careful to study, and every country which I have surveyed has contributed something to my poetical powers. . . .
>
> 'But the knowledge of nature is only half the task of a poet; he must be acquainted likewise with all the modes of life. . . .
>
> 'His labour is not yet at an end: he must know many languages and many sciences. . . .'[15]

Certainly this build-up calls out for Rasselas's retort: 'Enough! Thou hast convinced me that no human being can ever be a poet.' But it is important to stress that Imlac's view is not wrong; it is only impossible for a human to achieve. Like the preface telling what is to be done and the conclusion detailing how it has fallen short, both sides have to be given weight. Although Johnson sees the irony of such poetic dreams, he unironically expresses similar intentions in related images elsewhere. A few years earlier in *Rambler* 137 he claimed that 'It is the proper ambition of the heroes in literature to enlarge the boundaries of knowledge by discovering and conquering new regions of the intellectual world.'[16]

Johnson was strongly aware of both his abilities and his potentialities. When Sir William Scott, upon the death of Lord Lichfield, told Johnson,

> 'What a pity it is, Sir, that you did not follow the profession of the law. You might have been Lord Chancellor of Great Britain, and attained to the dignity of the peerage; and now that the title of Lichfield, your native city, is extinct, you might have had it.'[17]

Johnson's angry and exasperated reply was quick in coming: 'Why will you vex me by suggesting this, when it is too late?'

Johnson was interested in the law. When he was around 30, he tried to get himself admitted to practice: 'I am . . . a total stranger to these studies; but whatever is a profession, and maintains numbers, must be within the reach of common abilities, and some degree of industry.'[18] The 'degree of industry' could not compensate for his lack of a law degree. Later, at the height of his fame, he helped Robert Chambers, the successor to the great Sir William Blackstone, prepare his long series of Vinerian law lectures at Oxford. Just how much help Johnson provided among those 1,600 manuscript pages is still a problem, but it was certainly substantial.[19] In a sense Johnson may be said to have earned his honorary LL.D.

Johnson was often characterized in his own time as a philosopher, meaning a moral philosopher rather than someone in the tradition of Aristotle, Descartes, Locke and Hume. This was how he was memorably addressed when late in life he met his old schoolfellow, Edwards: 'You are a philosopher, Dr. Johnson. I have tried too in my time to be a philosopher; but I don't know how, cheerfulness was always breaking in.'[20] When Bennet Langton first went to meet Johnson

> From perusing his writings, he fancied he should see a decent, well-drest, in short, a remarkably decorous philosopher. Instead of which, down from his bed-chamber, about noon, came, as newly risen, a huge uncouth figure. . . .[21]

The notion of Johnson as moral philosopher is the root sense of Macaulay's patronizing conclusion to his essay on Johnson:

> The old philosopher is still among us in the brown coat with the metal buttons and the shirt which ought to be at wash, blinking, puffing, rolling his head, drumming his fingers, tearing his meat like a tiger, and swallowing his tea in oceans.[22]

That overcharged portrait, a concentrated version of details from Boswell, gives us 'Oddity' Johnson with a vengeance, and modern scholars are still trying to eradicate the damage done to Johnson's reputation by Macaulay's clever rhetoric, which turns the 'old philosopher' into fit company for Sir Roger de Coverley (another Whig portrait of an amiable, eccentric and politically insignificant Tory), a comic fiction rather than a peer of Reynolds, Hume and Burke. Macaulay's use of 'philosopher' has nothing to do with ideas.

But what, if anything, can we make of Johnson as a philosopher in the most important sense? His philosophical acuteness has been denied frequently enough on the basis of the famous (some would say infamous) kicking of the stone to refute Berkeley's immaterialism: 'I refute it *thus*.'[23] One modern philosopher, H. F. Hallett, has ingeniously defended Johnson's action by noting that Johnson's foot 'rebounded from the stone' and suggesting that the key to what Johnson was doing is contained not in the action but in the reaction: 'the Johnsonian refutation of Berkeley . . . required . . . that the stone should show itself capable of *doing* something to establish its reality independent of being perceived.' (Boswell earns an assist here for accurate observation.) Therefore Johnson's refutation is 'a genuine contribution to philosophy and not the mere humorous exemplification of vulgar misunderstanding that it has generally been represented to be'. He goes on to find Johnson's conclusion 'radiant with a philosophical acuity transcending his powers of general analysis'.[24] Move over, Heidegger and Wittgenstein, Johnson seems to have arrived as a philosopher.

It is tempting to leave things here, but the article to which I refer is more a celebration of Hallett's philosophical acuity than of Johnson's. If Hallett had bothered to examine Johnson's writings, he would have found that the positions taken there indicate a misunderstanding of Berkeley. In *Idler* No. 10, for example, Johnson links the disciples of Descartes and Malebranche with 'the follower of Berkley, who, while he sits writing at his table, declares he has neither table, paper, nor fingers', as thinkers who 'have all the honour at least of being deceived by fallacies not easily detected . . .'.[25] There is no question here of a reality which asserts itself in response. Yet the kicking of the stone has not, as far as I know, been defended in its context. Boswell, as he reports it, relates it to Common Sense philosophy: 'This was a stout exemplification of the *first truths* of *Père Bouffier*, or the original principles of Reid and of Beattie.' (Trust him to bring in the Scottish School.) I think rather, however, that Johnson's action is a *refutatio* which derives from Diogenes the Cynic's way of dispatching a philosopher who attempted to prove that motion does not exist: 'he got up and walked about.'[26] The anecdote appears in Diogenes Laertius's *Lives of the Philosophers*, which Johnson owned, and he himself had planned to write a series of such biographies. His grudging admiration for the Cynic can be found in the anecdotes he recounts in *Ramblers* 203 and 206, *Idler* 14 and *Adventurer* 119. (The story of Alexander's visit to Diogenes, which Johnson repeats in *Rambler* 203 and *Idler* 14, occurs in the same paragraph as the Cynic's refutation.) Hence, Johnson's action, for all its spontaneity, is meant to be seen as a viable statement in a philosophical tradition (or at least as a philosophical allusion) and not simply as Johnsonian recalcitrance. He is applying a philosophical solution, the *solvitur ambulando*, to a philosophical problem.

If at times I have made Johnson sound like the last Renaissance man (or at least a full-fledged member of the Enlightenment), such an intention is not altogether foreign to me. Yet there are significant differences. Although Johnson admired curiosity as an intellectual virtue, he is far from Faustian man, nor could he quote, as could so typical an Enlightenment figure as Diderot, the resonant line from Terence, '*Homo sum, humani a me nihil alienum puto*' (I am a man, I think nothing human alien to me). There were many things, both for better and worse, that were alien to him, and distinct areas—especially the religious—in which he refused to allow others to meddle. He was a great admirer of Raphael's speech to Adam in *Paradise Lost* on the proper limits of human knowledge.

All the same, even when we examine things he disliked or thought unimportant, we frequently find that he took an interest of some sort. Johnson's dislike of music is notorious. When Boswell told him that music

> affected me to such a degree, as often to agitate my nerves painfully, producing in my mind alternate sensations of pathetick dejection, so that I was ready to shed tears; and of daring resolution, so that I was inclined to rush into the thickest part of the battle. 'Sir, (said he,) I should never hear it, if it made me such a fool.'[27]

Of course, when this passage is quoted, it is usually forgotten that the conversation follows on Johnson's asking for a tune on a fiddle to be played again. Johnson's general insensibility to music did not stop him from assisting his musical friends. In addition to the Dedication to Burney's *Commemoration of Handel*, mentioned earlier, he had also written the Dedication to Burney's *History of Music* and even a dedication for 'some music for the German flute'. Perhaps it is worth quoting the passage supposed to be by Burney singled out for perceptivity in the Introduction to *George III Collector & Patron*, for it is more revealing of Johnson than of George. He claims that the King is 'a judge . . . who hears [music] not merely with instinctive emotion, but with rational approbation, and whose praise of Handel is not the effusion of credulity . . .'.[28] Johnson strongly prefers intellectual claims to others. Towards the end of his life at a Freemason's funeral procession he heard solemn music played on French horns, which led him to exclaim, 'This is the first time that I have ever been affected by musical sounds.'[29] He was now 71 years old. It was typical of him to notice this 'first', and typical too that some years before when the eldest Thrale child was playing the harpsichord and Johnson called out 'Why don't you dash away like Burney?', and Burney responded 'I believe, Sir, we shall make a musician of you at last', Johnson replied, 'Sir, I shall be glad to have a new sense given to me.'[30] Look at Johnson's limitations long enough, and you often come once again upon breadth of spirit.

This openness to new experience is characteristic—Johnson was in his 60s when he first travelled out of his own country. He made his journey to the Hebrides (or, as he puts it in the title of his travel book, the Western Islands of Scotland) in 1773. He visited Wales in 1774. He went to France with the Thrales and would have gone with them to Italy in the following year, but for the death of their son. Near the end of his life there was a plan afoot, of which he was aware, to send him to Italy for his health. It is worth remembering that in 1762, upon hearing that he had been granted a pension, he remarked 'Had this happened twenty years ago, I should have gone to Constantinople to learn Arabick, as Pococke did.'[31] The portion of the journal in France which was preserved (about a third of the whole) shows such a responsiveness to art and architecture that a nineteenth-century editor of Boswell's *Life* thought it a forgery. In the summer of 1773, Johnson, aged

64, started to learn Dutch. Nine years later he took it up again (that comment on Pococke's study of Arabic is not atypical).

Johnson objected to Fenton's suggestion that Waller's genius 'passed the zenith' at 55:

> That natural jealousy which makes every man unwilling to allow much excellence in another always produces a disposition to believe that the mind grows old with the body, and that he whom we are now forced to confess superior is hastening daily to a level with ourselves. By delighting to think this of the living, we learn to think it of the dead. . . .[32]

Johnson thought that the *Sacred Poems*, written when Waller was 82, show no loss of power. And he himself was 70 when he expressed his strong disagreement with Fenton in the *Lives of the Poets*. Johnson remained open to new experience throughout his life and argued for the lifelong possibility of human accomplishment.

Johnson had notoriously poor eyesight and could on occasion snort contemptuously at those who saw much in art. One anecdote, told by Hawkins, even has him confessing that he could not see much of a correspondence between a painting and its subject; another has him telling Reynolds that since the materials of painting are perishable, he would be better off using Henry Thrale's copper brewing vats instead of canvas.[33] Frequently enough in his letters he refers to paintings as 'trifles'. Presumably, one could expect that the topic of Johnson and art could be inscribed on the head of a pin with room left over for all those dancing angels. Yet in addition to the help he gave Reynolds on the *Discourses*, which went beyond the Dedication and the stylistic aid in the body of the work, he had a hand in some of the most important developments in mid-eighteenth century English art. It was Johnson who wrote the 'Address of the Painters, Sculptors and Architects to George III on his Accession to the Throne'. He also wrote the letter to the Society of Arts (of which he was a member) to obtain the use of its Great Room for the exhibition by the group which would later become known as the Society of Artists—a major step on the way to the founding of the Royal Academy of Arts, in which Johnson held the honorary post of Professor of Ancient Literature. When the Society of

Artists shifted their Exhibition from the Society of Arts to Spring Gardens (Vauxhall), Johnson wrote the Preface to the Catalogue of 1762. But most important of all his art-connected writings is *Idler* 45, long-ignored and only recently recognized as playing a part in the first award for a topic on English history-painting. This pioneering essay considers a series of possible subjects for a history painting and may have had some influence on the decision of the Society of Arts to award the first premium for English History Painting. The topic of Johnson and art, which I discuss elsewhere at length, has some unexpectedly interesting aspects.[34]

With all his interests and his willingness to find new ones, it is not surprising that in the year before Johnson's death, when Goldsmith suggested that the Club ought to take in new members, 'for . . . there can now be nothing new among us: we have travelled over one another's minds', Johnson angrily responded, 'Sir, you have not travelled over *my* mind, I promise you.'[35]

If we consider the range of Johnson's literary achievement in conjunction with the authoritativeness of his utterance, we will encounter a version of Johnson with both positive and negative overtones that needs examination. As England had its poet laureate from the seventeenth century on, it also tended to have its unofficial literary ruler. (Infrequently they were even the same person.) Ben Jonson at the Mermaid Tavern like John Dryden after him at Will's Coffee House settled, as Johnson put it speaking of Dryden, 'the appeal upon any literary dispute'. Addison, in Pope's words, gave his little senate laws, Gibbon claimed in his *Memoirs* that William Warburton 'reigned the Dictator and tyrant of the World of Litterature' in his day.[36] Matthew Arnold played a similar rôle through his touchstones and witty sloganeering. In our own century T. S. Eliot began his essay 'Dryden the Poet' by investigating 'what I may call the "literary dictator", that is, in our history, Ben Jonson, Dryden, Samuel Johnson and in his way, Coleridge'.[37] At mid-century Delmore Schwartz, recognizing the logic of Eliot's formula, expanded the tradition in 'The Literary Dictatorship of T. S. Eliot' (Schwartz explains what he at least means by the term):

> One can hardly use such a term as dictatorship without suggesting unfortunate political associations. A literary dictator-

> ship, however, is quite unlike a political one because you cannot force people to like poets or poetry, although you can persuade them. The remarkable thing about most literary dictators is that they succeeded in persuading at least one generation of readers to accept their taste.[38]

Schwartz too includes Johnson in the line of poet-critics whom he designates literary dictators. If this view of Johnson does not reach from China to Peru, it has at least extended from Paris to Buenos Aires—the relevant articles are 'Un Dictateur littéraire: Samuel Johnson et ses critiques' (1880) and 'Johnson: un dictador literario' (1949; the same year Schwartz was speaking in similar terms of Eliot).[39] The French essay may have taken its cue from Leslie Stephen's *Samuel Johnson* (1878), in which Chapter 4 is entitled 'Johnson as a Literary Dictator'. This phrase or similar ones had been used of Johnson by some of his contemporaries (generally with pejorative intentions—few of them would have agreed with the notion of T. S. Eliot that a literary dictatorship is likely to be a good thing).

Those who did not like Johnson had their own ways of recognizing that he occupied a special position in English literary life. In 1762, the year before Boswell met Johnson, Charles Churchill portrays Johnson in his satire *The Ghost* as

> Pomposo insolent and loud,
> Vain idol of a *scribbling* crowd,
> Whose very name inspires an awe,
> Whose ev'ry word is Sense and Law,
> For what his Greatness hath decreed,
> Like Laws of PERSIA and of MEDE,
> Sacred thro' all the realm of *Wit*,
> Must never of Repeal admit.[40]

William Cowper attacked him as 'King Critic', the traducer of Milton and Prior. Robert Potter argues that Gray's 'The Bard' warns 'literary tyrants to bear their faculties meekly'. This idea was related to an opposed conception, that of the 'republic of letters'. William Kenrick claims that the

> Republic of letters is a perfect democracy, where, all being equal, there is no respect of persons, but every one hath a right to speak the truth of another, to censure without fear and to comment without favour or affection.

Yet Johnson he finds is treated differently:

> Graduated by universities, pensioned by his prince, and surrounded by pedagogues and poetasters, he finds a grateful odour in the incense of adulation; while admiring booksellers stand at a distance, and look up to him with awful reverence, bowing the knee to Baal, and holding in fearful remembrance the exemplary fate of Tom Osborne; presumptuous Tom Osborne! who braving the vengeance of this paper-crowned idol, was, for his temerity, transfixed to his mother-earth by a thundering folio![41]

Kenrick begins by a characterization close to those Johnson suggests of the praise-loving, clique-forming Addison, and presents a bumptious mock-heroic version of Johnson. (We may also detect in Churchill's Pomposo overtones of *MacFlecknoe.*)

In responding to a similar metaphor in Sir Walter Scott's account of Johnson, James T. Boulton suggests a number of the causes behind it: envy of Johnson's rise from poverty and of his status, 'jealousy of his social renown', displeasure with the 'stylistic revolution' he instituted, dislike of his 'alleged approval of authoritarianism in politics'.[42] Boulton also suggests that the term must be seen in the context of eighteenth-century fear of 'absolute power' in order to be fully understood.

But there are other reasons closer to our theme that need exploration. As far as I know the first use of the term 'dictator' to describe Johnson was in praise of him and came from a source one might not suspect, his would-be patron Chesterfield. Because Johnson's letter rebuking Chesterfield is so famous, it is easy to forget that Johnson was replying to Chesterfield's puffing essays in *The World* (1754) for the *Dictionary*:

> Toleration, adoption, and naturalization have run their lengths. Good order and authority are now necessary. But where shall we find them, and at the same time the obedience due to them? We must have recourse to the old Roman expedient in times of confusion, and choose a dictator. Upon this principle, I give my vote for Mr. Johnson to fill that great and arduous post. And I hereby declare that I make a total surrender of all my rights and privileges in the English

> language, as a free-born British subject, to the said Mr. Johnson during the term of his dictatorship.[43]

Chesterfield was having fun with the fact that 'dictionary' and 'dictator' both stem from the same root, which translates as 'say' or 'speak'. I think that annoying as Johnson must have found these flippant essays, the connection goes beyond etymology. Johnson was best known in his own day as 'Dictionary' Johnson—it is the phrase that James L. Clifford used in the title of his account of Johnson's middle years—and there seems to be an almost unconscious belief that the master of words is also the master of what the words mean. Boswell plays with a similar notion in the *Life*. When Johnson was proposed to act as secretary for The Club and write a letter requesting another hogshead of claret, Boswell broke out, 'He will be our Dictator', to which Johnson answered, 'No, the company is to dictate to me.'[44] But in the case of the *Dictionary*, the production of a single man, the mastery of the words required an encyclopedic education. And Johnson, whose reading had been prodigious, acquainted himself with an extraordinary range of books to carry out his task.

A crude engraving by George Townshend, entitled 'The Secret Counsel [sic] of the Heads' depicts Johnson as a talking head atop his 'Dictionary of Hard Words' telling the assembled artists who hope to start an academy

> Sirs I have givn you as fine words as your plan would admit of. and when you are all ready I will unite you & from you shall spring a Tale[,] a Tale which (like the Tail of the Rattle snake) shall jingle in every ear from Pole to Pole.[45]

The intention is satiric, but the caricature pays tribute to that combination of knowledge and scope which we have been examining.

The connection between words and authority is very clear, to take an example involving Johnson, when at the beginning of Thackeray's *Vanity Fair*, Becky Sharp throws her school-mistress's present, an edition of Johnson's *Dictionary* (obviously not the two folio volumes of the early editions) out of the window of the carriage that takes her from school. We are in no doubt that Becky's gesture is against authority in general, as well as Johnsonian morality in particular.

Although Johnson neither chose the poets for his *Lives*, nor persuaded his generation to adopt his implied canon, he certainly stands in that line of authoritative critics dubbed literary dictators by Eliot. But in view of what Johnson himself has had to say about literary authority using this metaphor the notion is ironical. In *Rambler* 156, an essay anticipating his remarks on the unities in the 'Preface to Shakespeare', he says

> It ought to be the first endeavour of a writer to distinguish nature from custom, or that which is established because it is right, from that which is right only because it is established; that he may neither violate essential principles by a desire of novelty, nor debar himself from the attainment of beauties within his view by a needless fear of breaking rules which no literary dictator had authority to enact.[46]

In the 'Preface to Shakespeare' itself he explains his cursory mention of 'beauties and faults': 'Judgement, like other faculties, is improved by practice, and its advancement is hindered by submission to dictatorial decisions, as the memory grows torpid by the use of a table book.'[47] Again, in *Rambler* 92 he claims that 'Criticism reduces those regions of literature under the dominion of science, which have hitherto known only the anarchy of ignorance, the caprices of fancy, and the tyranny of prescription.'[48] No writer of the time does more to make the reader aware of the dangers of the literary dictator. Yet he did recognize in himself a tendency in this direction, and in the last *Rambler* essay claims with some self-mockery that 'scarcely any man is so steadily serious, as not to complain, that the severity of dictatorial instruction has been too seldom relieved . . .'.[49] The first person to call Johnson 'dictatorial' in print was Johnson himself. The important point is that Johnson is aware of the dangers of dogmatism and the dictatorial in both himself and others, and he strenuously argues for the individual's freedom to decide for himself. Even where he puts things most powerfully, as in the case of his attack on the unities, he is aware of the other side's strength. Conversely, his first essay on Milton, *Rambler* 86, begins with the hope that 'however, I may fall below the illustrious writer who has so long dictated to the commonwealth of learning [he has Addison in mind], my attempt may not be wholly useless'. But by the end of the essay, though he brings in classical practice, he insists that 'where the senses are to judge, authority is not necessary. . . .'[50]

I have sometimes complained that the value of books on Johnson varies inversely with the number of references to the 'Great Cham', 'Ursa Major' and so forth. Yet many of these nicknames given to Johnson by contemporaries—like Dr. Major (as opposed to Goldsmith's Dr. Minor)—point to his superiority, even if, as in the case of Smollett's dubbing him 'The Great Cham', the intention is to some extent ironic.

Carlyle sensed in Johnson a big man who could have been even bigger, and in 'The Hero as Man of Letters', the fifth chapter of *On Heroes, Hero-Worship, and the Heroic in History*, he rhapsodizes on this theme: 'A strong and noble man! so much left undeveloped in him to the last: in a kindlier element what might he not have been,—Poet, Priest, sovereign Ruler!'[51] To this we can hear Johnson responding, 'Why will you vex me by suggesting this, when it is too late?' (Or perhaps, 'Clear your mind of Cant.')

Yet Carlyle's response to the image of potentiality represented by Johnson's life and works, while over-inflated, is far from unfair. I hardly wish to leave the impression that I think I have travelled over Johnson's mind. In the *Life of Savage* Johnson recounts the story of Savage's friends, knowing his improvidence, sending a tailor to Savage instead of letting him order his own clothes. When he visited a friend (undoubtedly Johnson) in 'violent agonies of rage', he explained 'with the utmost Vehemence of Indignation, "That they had sent for a Taylor to measure him" '.[52] No one is very likely to take Johnson's measure.

NOTES

1. *George III, Collector & Patron* (London: The Queen's Gallery, Buckingham Palace, 1974), pp. 14–15. A version of this essay was originally delivered at the invitation of The Associates of the Stanford University Libraries.
2. *Lives*, Vol. 1, p. 2.
3. *Life*, Vol. 1, p. 186.
4. 'On Johnson's *Dictionary*', in *Life*, Vol. 1, p. 301.
5. Cleanth Brooks and A. F. Falconer (eds.), *The Percy Letters* (New Haven and London: Yale University Press, 1977), Vol. 1, p. 2.

6. The account appears in the *Life*, but I have preferred Boswell's original account, *The Correspondence and Other Papers of James Boswell Relating to the Making of the Life of Johnson* ed. Marshall Waingrow (London: Heinemann, 1969), pp. 23–4. Cf. *Life*, Vol. 1, p. 284. Boswell quotes some of Johnson's notes for this project.
7. Ibid., p. 535. In *Samuel Johnson and the New Philosophy*, Richard Schwartz investigates Johnson's scientific interests and demonstrates that they are more extensive than was previously thought. Neither he nor Boswell quotes this passage, however.
8. *Cyclopaedia: or, an Universal Dictionary of Arts and Sciences* (London, 1791), Vol. 1, p. i (second series), originally published 1728. W. Jackson Bate discusses Cornelius Ford's rôle in leading Johnson to a very broad conception of what he should know and a dislike of scholarly narrowness. See his biography, *Samuel Johnson* (New York and London: Harcourt Brace Jovanovich, 1977), pp. 51–2.
9. *Life*, Vol. 4, p. 87.
10. Yale, Vol. 1, pp. 231, 248, 186–87.
11. *Lives*, Vol. 1, p. 100.
12. *Letters*, #944; Vol. 3, p. 144.
13. *Life*, Vol. 1, p. 292.
14. 'Preface to the English Dictionary', *Johnson: Prose and Poetry*, ed. Mona Wilson [and John Crow] (London: Rupert Hart-Davis, 1950), p. 316.
15. G. B. Hill (ed.), *Rasselas* (Oxford: Clarendon Press, 1954), pp. 62–3. I have followed the punctuation of the first edition of 1759.
16. Yale, Vol. 4, p. 362.
17. *Life*, Vol. 3, pp. 309–10.
18. *Life*, Vol. 1, p. 134.
19. Thomas Curley is at work on this question, see 'Johnson's Secret Collaboration', *The Unknown Samuel Johnson*, ed. John J. Burke and Donald Kay (Madison, Wis.: University of Wisconsin Press, 1983), pp. 91–112. At an M.L.A. meeting in December 1983 during which he discussed his progress on a biography of Chambers, he indicated that his forthcoming edition of the law lectures will not take a stand on the issue.
20. *Life*, Vol. 3, p. 305.
21. *Life*, Vol. 1, p. 247.
22. Macaulay, *Life of Johnson*, ed. Albert Perry Walker (Boston: D. C. Heath & Co., 1909), pp. 53–4. I have purposely cited an American school text by the then Master, and teacher of English and History in the English High School, Boston, for it gives a sense of the survival of this view into the twentieth century. For the classic account, see Bertrand H. Bronson, 'The Double Tradition of Dr. Johnson' in *Johnson Agonistes and Other Essays* (Berkeley and Los Angeles: University of California Press, 1965), pp. 156–76.
23. *Life*, Vol. 1, p. 471.
24. 'Dr. Johnson's Refutation of Bishop Berkeley', *Mind*, 56 (1947), 132–47.
25. Yale, Vol. 2, p. 33.
26. Diogenes Laertius, *Lives of the Philosophers*, trans. R. D. Hicks (Cambridge, Mass.: Harvard University Press, 1957), Vol. 2, p. 41. Johnson was

compared explicitly to the Cynic in 'A Parallel between Diogenes the Cynic and Doctor J—n', a scurrilous essay in *Town and Country*, 7 (March, 1775), 115–18 ('Diogenes flourished and stunk in the days of Philip and Alexander; doctor J—n in those of George II and III', etc.). Johnson's friend Baretti draws on him for his character of Diogene Mastigoforo.

27. *Life*, Vol. 3, p. 197.
28. *George III, Collector & Patron*, p. 14.
29. *Life*, Vol. 4, p. 22.
30. *Life*, Vol. 2, p. 409.
31. *Life*, Vol. 4, pp. 27–8.
32. *Lives*, Vol. 1, p. 290.
33. Sir John Hawkins, *The Life of Samuel Johnson, LL.D.* (London, 1787), pp. 318–19; James Northcote, *Supplement to the Memoirs of . . . Sir Joshua Reynolds* (London: Henry Colburn, 1815), p. lvii.
34. 'Johnson and Art' in *Samuel Johnson: Pictures and Words* (Los Angeles: William Andrews Clark Memorial Library, forthcoming).
35. *Life*, Vol. 4, p. 183.
36. Georges A. Bonnard (ed.) *Memoirs of my Life* (London: Thomas Nelson and Sons, 1966), pp. 144–45.
37. *John Dryden: The Poet, the Dramatist, the Critic* (New York: Terence and Elsa Holliday, 1932), p. 5.
38. *The Partisan Review*, 16 (1949), 119–37; rev. in *Literary Opinion in America*, ed. Morton Dauwen Zabel (New York: Harper & Brothers, 1951), p. 573.
39. Léon Boucher in *Revue des Deux Mondes*, 3rd ser. 37 (1880), 674–97; Alberto Franco Diaz in *Aquí Está*, 14 (14 November 1949), 12–13.
40. For a number of these responses to Johnson I have used for ease of reference *Heritage*. For Churchill see p. 357.
41. Cowper, Letter to William Unwin, 17 January 1782, in *Heritage*, p. 274; Potter, *Inquiry into some passages in Dr. Johnson's Lives of the Poets* (1783), in *Heritage*, p. 302; Kenrick, *Review of Johnson's Shakespeare* (1765), in *Heritage*, p. 183.
42. 'Introduction', *Heritage*, pp. 17–18.
43. *Heritage*, p. 97.
44. *Life*, Vol. 3, p. 238.
45. [George Townshend, 1st Marquess], 'The Secret Counsel [sic] of the Heads' (London, 1768). See No. 4217, *British Museum Catalogue* of *Political and Personal Satires*. I quote from a copy in the Yale Center for British Art.
46. Yale, Vol. 5, p. 70.
47. Yale, Vol. 7, p. 104.
48. Yale, Vol. 4, p. 122.
49. Yale, Vol. 5, p. 319.
50. Yale, Vol. 4, pp. 88, 93.
51. *On Heroes, Hero-Worship and the Heroic in History* (New York: Doubleday & Co., n. d.), p. 173. Boulton includes selections from Carlyle's earlier essay on Johnson.
52. Clarence Tracy (ed.), *Life of Savage* (Oxford: Clarendon Press, 1971), p. 112.

3

Johnson and the Scholars

by PAUL J. KORSHIN

1

Johnson's lifelong involvement with scholars and scholarship was as thorough and intense as has been the association of his works and reputation with scholars and scholarship in the 200 years since his death. The 19-year-old boy who could quote from the fifth-century grammarian Macrobius during his interview at Pembroke College clearly was already acquainted with the best of Renaissance Continental scholarship, for to read such a late author Johnson could not have relied upon a schoolboy's edition.[1] And we know from the collection of books that he selected from his father's shop to take to Oxford that he had already been exposed to both Scaligers, Nicholas Heinsius, Jean LeClerc, Claudius Salmasius, Theodore Beza, and the neo-Latin poet-scholars George Buchanan and Girolamo Vida.[2] Since in this essay I shall be concerned mainly with Johnson and the scholars during his lifetime, it will be useful to begin with a few examples of what Johnson thought about scholarly work and its perpetrators. My first example is a note that Johnson wrote for the catalogue of the Harleian Library in 1743. With his collaborator William Oldys Johnson annotated hundreds of lots for the five-volume *Catalogus*, occupying himself almost exclusively with books of classical interest. The comment that I have in mind is one that he made on a sixteenth-century history of Italy by the jurist Carlo Sigonio:

> *Sigonius* was a Native of *Modena* eminently skilled in History and *Roman* Antiquities. He was so great a Master of the Stile of *Cicero*, that he wrote a Treatise *de Consolatione*, and published it as a Piece of *Cicero*'s Works newly discovered; many were in Reality deceived by the Counterfeit which was performed with great Dexterity, but *Lipsius*, having read only ten Lines, threw it away, crying, *Vah! non est Ciceronis.*[3]

My second example is from the anecdotes of Johnson that Bennet Langton gave Boswell and that Boswell assigned to 1780 because he was short of firsthand material for that year: 'Mr. Langton happening to mention his having read a good deal in Clenardus's Greek Grammar, "Why, Sir, (said he,) who is there in this town who knows any thing of Clenardus but you and I?" '[4] My final example is from *Rasselas*, Chapter VIII: 'To talk in publick, to think in solitude, to read and hear, to inquire, and answer inquiries, is the business of a scholar. He wanders about the world without pomp or terrour, and is neither known nor valued but by men like himself.'[5]

These examples, which come from different periods in Johnson's career and which do not by any means exhaust his statements about scholars and their work, are nevertheless significant, for they show how broad the scope of his scholarly interests was. His note about Sigonio exemplifies one of the principal occupations of the scholar in Renaissance Europe, the detection of inauthentic works or, if you will, the determination of canonicity. It is a topic with which Johnson himself was often concerned in his scholarly inquiries. Langton's anecdote shows a different side of Johnson's scholarship, his interest in philology, for Nicholas Clenardus's Greek grammar, a work of the 1530s, was, with its numerous scholia by other authors, the most important scholarly Greek grammar of the sixteenth and seventeenth centuries, appearing in scores of editions. Yet Johnson could tell Langton that the two of them were alone, in London, in even knowing the book. The statement from *Rasselas*, finally, shows that Imlac is scholar first and poet afterwards, and describes, not without poignance, the solitariness of the scholar in Johnson's time. We need not be concerned that Imlac fails to mention such chores as commentary and publication; his description of the scholar is a general, romanticized one suitable to a novel like

Rasselas. However, it does concern us to know exactly what scholarship did involve in Johnson's time, so that we may ascertain what he thought of his scholarly contemporaries and what effect they had upon him.

2

Scholarship, in Johnson's time, consists of perhaps as many as seven distinct kinds of endeavour. Eighteenth-century scholarship, many critics would urge, is really only a continuation of the studies of the late Renaissance, more copious but less original. Although such an assessment may be defensible in an area like classical scholarship, it would not be true of the century as a whole, for certain important changes in attitude and degree take place that elevate or depress certain kinds of studies. For instance, *canonicity*, or the establishment of the authenticity of a text, was of tremendous importance from the fourteenth to sixteenth centuries, as scholars tried to determine what works authors of antiquity had actually written and what people had falsely attributed to them. The canon of the books of the Bible had been under scrutiny for a millennium before the Renaissance, and was largely settled by the end of the sixteenth century.[6] But while canonicity was no longer the central business of scholarship in the eighteenth century, some of the most famous works of the period, like Richard Bentley's *Dissertation on the Epistles of Phalaris* (1697; 2nd rev. edn., 1699), which Johnson's friend Samuel Parr called the most learned book ever published, dealt with authenticity and forgery. Johnson would be involved with such matters, too, as with the charges by William Lauder of Milton's alleged plagiarisms in *Paradise Lost*, and the controversies over the authenticity of the Ossianic and Rowley poems, while Edmond Malone, another scholarly contemporary, was responsible for detecting the Shakespeare forgeries of the 1790s.[7] And canonicity (with its related subjects, plagiarisms and forgery) continues to be of interest even today, as the 'discovery' of the so-called Hitler Diaries in 1983 shows (a case of forgery), or the old accusations of plagiarism against Mikhail Sholokhov, revived at his death in 1984, but never conclusively proved, suggest.[8]

The *editing of texts*, mainly those of classical antiquity and, as the eighteenth century progressed, of more recent periods, is the second major endeavour of the period's scholarship. Relatively sophisticated studies of manuscripts—palaeography—, paper, fragmentary writings such as inscriptions, and other ancient remains became significant by the end of the seventeenth century, so that the vast classical compilations of Graevius, Gronovius and Montfaucon are early encyclopediae of a sort. Perhaps these works are closer to the syntagmata of the late Renaissance than to the modern reference book, but this kind of work, whatever its internal arrangement, makes possible the rich commentaries and scholia of eighteenth-century editions of the classics. Following the examples of these models, eighteenth-century editors of more recent English texts—Shakespeare, Spenser, Milton, Samuel Butler—usually included their commentaries as an integral part of the work that they edited. However, an important change takes place during the century, as the commentary and the scholium gradually develop into the scholarly book unconnected to an edition of an author's text. Hence Lewis Theobald's *Shakespeare Restored* (1726), John Upton's *Critical Observations upon Shakespeare* (1746), Richard Farmer's *An Essay on the Learning of Shakespeare* (1767), and Joseph Warton's *An Essay on the Writings and Genius of Mr. Pope* (1756–82)—and scores of other books less well known—represent an eighteenth-century English tradition of scholarship. In this area, too, Johnson had close ties, as editor of texts, commentator on them, and author of brief scholarly pieces on the importance of certain genres.

Philological studies in the eighteenth century include grammars, treatises on linguistic origins, studies of universal language and grammar, lexicons, and pioneering scholarly efforts to understand languages that no one had ever subjected to formal analysis before (most of the Oriental and Indian languages fell into this group). Grammars and dictionaries are highly imitative works, as we can see from Johnson's own *Dictionary* and the 'Grammar of the English Language' that he published with it. But while eighteenth-century scholars could keep using sixteenth-century grammars like that of Clenardus and lexica like those of Stephanus—usually in relatively recent editions—they also had available much contemporary linguistic theory on universal and comparative grammar, and a number of strictly eighteenth-century lexica devoted to previously unstudied languages like the works of George Hickes, Edward Lye and William Shaw.[9] We know that Johnson was personally acquainted with some of these scholars (not with Hickes, of course, whose study of the languages of Northern Europe appeared in 1703–5) and that he savoured the appearance of their works as keenly as a scholar of the later twentieth century would be likely to applaud the completion of the new *Oxford Latin Dictionary* (1968–82) or the completion of another letter in the *Middle English Dictionary*.

A fourth—and practically endless—avenue of eighteenth-century scholarship is the *historical compilation*. Antiquarian studies, collections of historical documents like Rymer's *Foedera* and many other similar predecessors of the reports of the Historical Manuscripts Commission, compilations of biographies of people in specialized pursuits (popes, philosophers, pickpockets, and so on), historical antiquities of regions of England and Europe, bibliographies of early printing, catalogues and lists of various kinds, historical studies of countries, wars, battles, and the like, and the vast genre that we loosely call 'chronology' only begin to list the main headings of this aspect of learning. Johnson himself produced one of his century's most influential such compilations—the *Lives of the Poets*, in its collected form, is in the tradition of biographical collections—and contributed to several others, beginning with the *Catalogus Bibliothecae Harleianae* and including James's *Medicinal Dictionary* (1743–45) and Burney's *General History of Music* (1776). Many eighteenth-century historical compilations are really popularizations of complicated subjects, scarcely worthy of the name of scholarship, but any agency that makes learning better known deserves some credit. While Johnson himself is hardly a popularizer of scholarship, he was certainly acquainted with many men and a few women who were and he surely knew their works.

The field of *theological scholarship*, even by the eighteenth century, had already been subjected to considerable specialization and classification. Discussions of the canon and authenticity of the Bible and of the sacred books of religions other than Judaism and Christianity; philological guides to the languages of different sacred books; editions of and commentaries on the Bible; liturgy and hymnology; theological controversy; and the origins of different religions: all these subjects were well established by the middle of the seventeenth century. Biblical criticism, in the modern sense, would be established before the end of the century through the works of the French Oratorian Richard Simon, the father of this branch of theology. A man or woman of letters who was no theologian would inevitably have been acquainted with some of this scholarship, through editions of the Bible, editions of important Christian writers, handbooks to homiletics and other branches of study, guides to prayer and Church fasts, and important contemporary treatises on religious subjects. A quarter of all eighteenth-century English publishing was associated with religious topics and so, too, was a proportional quantity of the scholarship.

Philosophical and scientific studies are probably the most difficult aspect of eighteenth-century scholarship to define, for they include science, pseudo-science, certain mystical speculations, pure scientific and philosophical treatises or speculation, and much applied learning in many branches of study. Writers on the natural sciences like Aldrovandus and the early members of the Royal Society are part of this category, but so are mystical speculators like Paracelsus and Kircher. Medical treatises and textbooks form an important part of scientific scholarship, yet the numerous abridgements and popularizations of such works are often little more than hackwork. A scientific classifier like Linnaeus we would readily define as a scholar, although we would be likely to regard authors like Buffon and Goldsmith as popularizers. A typical scholar's library usually contains a generous sampling of scientific scholarship, although the books owned by non-scientific scholars like Johnson tend to be quite mixed. Johnson, for example, owned a number of medical works by Boerhaave and a few others, but his books on metallurgy, mineralogy and chemistry are scattered. No doubt his medical interests—which his copies of books by Stephen Hales and Fallopius imply—were stronger than his interest in the pure and applied sciences. It is important to note, however, that the field of scientific scholarship was so broad that nearly every eighteenth-century man or woman of letters touched upon it at some time.[10]

A final category of contemporary scholarship consists of *books on method* that do not necessarily pertain to one of the foregoing six categories. Descartes' *Discours sur la méthode*, books of logic or rhetoric, handbooks of scholarly terminology like Faber's *Thesaurus eruditionis scholasticae* or guides to a particular kind of knowledge like the elder Scaliger's *Poetices*, and approaches to scholarly method like Daniel Morhof's *Polyhistor* fall into this category. So, too, do works dealing with the classification of all learning as exemplified in Diderot's famous typology of the arts and sciences in *L'Encyclopédie*, guides to bibliography, and synopses of scholarship. These specialized aids to learning are hardly popularizations, but they were—and always have been—popular with students. We know that Johnson owned a few such books, but he undoubtedly was acquainted with a great many more that he never mentions, for the methodological guide to scholarship has been the common coin of all advanced knowledge since the late middle ages.

3

Johnson's contemporaries would not be likely to think of him as a scholar in the same sense that they would have regarded the people who engaged in scholarship in their own age and in the previous three centuries. No matter how well qualified he was for the title, Johnson did not specialize in one particular branch of knowledge as did virtually all scholars by the middle of the eighteenth century. One of his early biographers, for instance, listing the 'multifarious characters' that he assumed as an author, described him as 'a *philologist*, a *biographer*, a *critic*, an *essayist*, a *bibliographer*, a *commentator*, a *novelist*, a *journalist of travels*, a *political writer*, an *epistolary writer*, a *theologian*, and a *poet*'.[11] At least three of these 'characters'—philologist, bibliographer and commentator—are rôles that the contemporary scholar customarily filled, yet the diversity of Johnson's interests seems to disqualify him for the title of scholar, at least in the eyes of Robert Anderson.

Despite the tendency of his contemporaries to classify his writings from many points of view, Johnson's association with scholars and scholarship was lifelong, so it will be appropriate for me to outline what those relationships were. Johnson's first acquaintance with scholarship, as I noted earlier, started before he left for Oxford, through the scholarly works that he encountered in Michael Johnson's bookshop. His undergraduate books, indeed, are little short of extraordinary, not only because of their breadth as to subject matter, but also because they show how thoroughly prepared he was in languages other than English, perhaps the most essential tool of the eighteenth-century scholar. During the 1730s and his early London years, until perhaps 1745, Johnson started to meet and become friendly with contemporary scholars, mostly antiquarians like Thomas Birch, William Oldys and Michael Maittaire. He also undertook scholarly chores, of which the translation of Lobo's *Voyage to Abyssinia* (1735) was one (all Renaissance scholars spent some time, usually while still young, as translators). Another was cataloguing the Harleian Library, an enormous collection that put Johnson in touch with every scholarly movement since the invention of printing. His miscellaneous writings of the 1740s are unquestionably scholarly. To mention only a few of them, I would suggest that Johnson's introduction to *The Harleian Miscellany* (1744) is among the first, if not the first, scholarly comments on the importance of printed ephemera; his 'Preface' to *The Preceptor* (1748) provides an extraordinary twelve-point scheme of learning for 'the young student', complete with a reading list that includes such recondite authors as Aristotle, Baronius, Hooker, Scaliger, Wolfius and Zouch; and the *Miscellaneous Observations on the Tragedy of Macbeth* (1745) actually opens with allusions to Olympiodorus, St. Chrysostom and Photius. Throughout this period, Johnson writes of his scholarly and antiquarian sources with a sense of intimate rather than casual acquaintance.

During the years when he was working on the *Dictionary*, from 1747 to 1755, Johnson continued to devote time now and then to various scholarly tasks, among them a number of brief biographies of distinguished, often learned, men and a scattering of prefaces. But during this period, his foremost scholarship, other than his philological work, is *The Rambler*, a work that, in its collected editions, closely resembles some of the scholarly miscellanies of the previous two and a half centuries with which Johnson had become familiar in the 1730s and '40s. Many *Rambler* essays, of course, are contrived letters and oriental fictions, but we tend to slight the scholarly qualities of the collection as a whole. The essays on pastoral, on Milton's versification and on *Samson Agonistes* differ very little from the learned scholia that the eighteenth-century reader would normally have found as part of a learned edition. And a great number of essays begin with scholarly reflections that Johnson takes from well known classical authors like Euclid, Plutarch, Herodotus and Epictetus, from lesser known authors like Quintus Curtius, Diodorus Siculus and Diogenes Laertius, and somewhat obscure writers like Periander of Corinth, Chilo of Lacedemon and Cleobolus the Lindian (these last three from the *Anthologia Graeca*).[12] Johnson's lexicographical scholarship is too well known to require much comment now, but here, too, his originality is notable. The *Dictionary* for instance, is the first English work of its kind to use illustrative quotations, a practice that all major lexica since have observed. While we know that Johnson borrowed this device from the many Continental dictionaries that he used, he is radically different from his sources in that he uses quotations from a particular chronological period,[13] with the announced intention of establishing a clear and uncorrupted speech.

In the decade that he was occupied—at least part of the time—with his edition of Shakespeare, Johnson's other scholarly efforts continued, among them an outpouring of learned reviews in the short-lived *Literary Magazine* (1756–58), including, in three issues of 1757, his famous review of Jenyns's *Free Inquiry into the Origin and Nature of Evil*. *Rasselas* is, among many other things, a kind of scholarly inquiry, and the fact that Johnson wrote it in a prose that approaches the language of scholarship rather than in the traditional patois of romance vividly distinguishes it from contemporary novels. His *Proposals for Printing the Dramatick Works of Shakespeare* (1756), although brief, is without doubt the first comprehensive statement about the difficulties of editing Shakespeare. While Johnson begins this piece with an allusion to the editorial techniques of classical scholarship,[14] his edition is as new to the editing of English texts as Politian's techniques were new to fifteenth-century editing of classical texts. That is, Johnson abandoned the tradition of variorum-style commentary already familiar in England with editions of Butler, Spenser and Milton, in favour of a great spareness of annotation and commentary that makes his edition accessible (and quoted) even in the late twentieth century. Before Politian, Niccolo Perotti had devoted 1,000 folio columns to annotating a single book of Martial's *Epigrams* in his aptly titled *Cornucopiae* (1489); before Johnson, Zachary Grey had almost obliterated *Hudibras* with excessive documentation (1744). Johnson undoubtedly learned something about the proper treatment of early English texts from Thomas Percy's *Reliques of Ancient English Poetry* (1765), for he assisted Percy in its preparation, in correcting the proof, and in writing the dedication.[15] During these years of editing, then, Johnson shows himself the mature scholar somewhat less concerned with ostentatious learning and documentation than he had been during the *Rambler* years. For example, his edition of Shakespeare reprints his commentary on *Macbeth* almost unchanged from the *Observations* of twenty-one years earlier, retaining all the obscure allusions that had suited his scholarly style in the mid 1740s, but he does not introduce anything remotely comparable for any of the other plays in 1765. Johnson's later scholarly style, then, is less encumbered with an *apparatus criticus* than his more youthful method.

In the last two decades of his life, Johnson's major scholarly contribution is the *Lives of the Poets*, although he continued to write prefaces and dedications for friends and to advise an ever-widening circle of acquaintances about scholarly matters. For this period, however, we have a record that is lacking for his earlier years, his scholarly table talk as collected principally by Boswell and Mrs. Thrale. Indeed, many of the conversations that these two memoirists record are similar to the *quaestiones quodlibeticae* of the medieval and Renaissance schools, in which the master scholar would hold a sort of scholarly press conference on virtually any topic with his students and colleagues. In this respect, Mrs. Thrale's *Anecdotes* and especially Boswell's *Life* resemble the famous collections of the sayings and brief comments of Renaissance scholars. There were so many of these anthologies—*Scaligerana*, *Poggiana*, *Parrhasiana*, and so on—that they were actually called *Ana*-books.[16]

Nor should I slight Johnson's major revision of the *Dictionary* during this period (4th edn., 1773), which took him several years to complete. When we consider that he probably began work on the effort that would later become the *Lives of the Poets* as early as 1775, it is clear that Johnson devoted much of his time during his last twenty years—when his biographers give us the impression of great literary leisure—to major scholarly projects.[17] Students of the *Lives*—or, to give them their original title, *Prefaces, biographical and critical, to the works of the English Poets*—have often commented on their miscellaneity and their eighteenth-century English antecedents.[18] The English collections of poets' lives that preceded Johnson's collection could scarcely be called scholarly, but Johnson had other predecessors, seldom noticed. These are similar collections of memoirs, mostly seventeenth- and early eighteenth-century, all Continental, that present the lives and accomplishments of scholars, physicians, scientists, philosophers, and others definable by profession as learned, in which the 'character' of the subject, a feature which Johnson introduced only in his longer *Lives*, is a usual ingredient. The fact that Johnson knew many of these works—as he certainly did—does not make his *Lives of the Poets* scholarship, but it does suggest that his last major work was similar to, if not consanguineous with, a genre of Continental scholarship that we would now be likely to forget.

In his account of Johnson's last month of life, Boswell writes, 'Still his love of literature did not fail.'[19] To this sentence he adds an extraordinary footnote, printing *in toto* a catalogue, which Johnson had given to Bennet Langton, of literary projects which he had 'formed schemes' of undertaking. The list, evidently a notebook that Johnson had kept for more than thirty years, is as strong a corroboration of Johnson's scholarly interests as we are likely to find. The works that Johnson proposed cover all the seven categories of eighteenth-century scholarship that I mentioned earlier. Here are editions of English authors, commentaries on the ancient classics, methodological works, historical compilations, anthologies, chronology, philology, theology. The one title that we are accustomed to single out from this list is the proposed 'History of the Revival of Learning in Europe', but the catalogue tells us a great deal about Johnson's life as a scholar, for what scholar worthy of the name has not proposed to himself or herself—or, better yet, to some patron, foundation, or publisher—projects that never got further than mere plans? What better evidence need I present of Johnson's lifelong dedication to scholarship?

4

What Johnson thought of the great scholars of the three centuries previous to his own, and how their writings and techniques may have influenced his own, I cannot say for certain, since he never offers an objective assessment of the contributions of any of them. He alludes to the great fifteenth-century scholar Politian, but without showing that he was aware of his epochal innovations in the nature of literary commentary or his insistence on the primacy of Greek literature over Latin.[20] Yet perhaps there is no coincidence that Johnson pioneered a notable spareness of commentary in his own time and that he was a better Graecicist than almost any of his literary contemporaries. He was easily familiar with the works of the three greatest scholars of the sixteenth century—Erasmus, the younger Scaliger and Lipsius—for he refers to all of them, but we cannot know for certain how thoroughly Johnson appreciated Erasmus's contributions to New Testament textual scholarship, Scaliger's ordering of chronology and knowledge of cultural history, or Lipsius's great Latinity and knowledge of Stoicism.[21] Yet, again, perhaps it is significant that Johnson projected scholarly works that followed the major contributions of all these men. In his catalogue of scholarly schemes, he proposes 'A Body of Chronology' that doubtless would have derived to some extent (as all such works after the early seventeenth century did) from the younger Scaliger's chronological labours, 'A Collection of Proverbs from various languages' that may remind us of the *Adagiae*, and 'A Comparison of Philosophical and Christian Morality' that surely would have encompassed Stoicism and would thus have been indebted to Lipsius. Johnson's interest in two of the greatest historians of the sixteenth century—Father Paolo Sarpi and Jacques de Thou (or Thuanus)—is also well known, for he had projected English translations of their works. He started a translation and edition of Sarpi's *History of the Council of Trent* in 1738, and his admiration for de Thou was so great that he spoke of translating the seven-volume folio edition of his *Historia sui temporis* on his deathbed in 1784.[22] Johnson admired Sarpi because of the great objectivity he had maintained in historical writing which he undertook despite the hostility of the Church, but it is difficult to see how he might have formed his own methods on Sarpi's.[23] And he must have admired de Thou because of the vast chronological sweep of his history and the many objective evaluations of French history, politics and leaders that it contained. But a reading of Sarpi or de Thou side by side with similar passages in Johnson's works does not reveal any striking consonance that I would call influence.

To find closer affinities between Johnson and important scholars it is preferable to turn to his own century. Here Johnson's acquaintance—both personal and through reputation—was very wide, and he refers at various times to almost every English scholar of any distinction. For Richard Bentley, for example, England's greatest classical scholar, whom he never met, Johnson shows great admiration, not so much for Bentley's editions of the classics as for the learning of his great critical study, *A Dissertation on the Epistles of Phalaris.* The *Dissertation* is a landmark in the history of evidentiary thought, showing for the first time how contemporary linguistic and cultural evidence could be used for historical proof. Johnson was certainly indebted to Bentley's evidentiary techniques in his annotation to Shakespeare, while even his miscellaneous comments on false information and the trustworthiness of witnesses sound like similar statements by Bentley.[24] 'Snatches of reading', he told Langton, 'will not make a Bentley or a Clarke',[25] and it would be fair to say that Johnson found the greatest learning of his age among the scholars of the first half of the century. His debt to Clarke is perhaps greatest in his sermons,[26] but Clarke's learning was not limited to theology any more than Bentley's had been confined to classical scholarship (Bentley had also been the first Boyle Lecturer in 1692–93). Clarke, like Bentley, was a prominent Boyle

Lecturer, yet he also wrote on the life of Milton, translated Newton's *Optics*, and produced a Latin translation and edition of the works of Homer.[27] It is clear that the general breadth of Clarke's learning attracted Johnson most, but he gave equal credit to the orderly and logical arrangement of his works. Johnson, incidentally, always criticized scholars who, despite their learning, expressed themselves poorly. His comment on Maittaire is typical: 'He seems to have been a puzzle-headed man, with a large share of scholarship, but with little geometry or logick in his head, without method, and possessed of little genius.'[28]

While Johnson's scholarly contemporaries undoubtedly had strong opinions about him, few of them have left any substantial evaluations. Only Richard Porson took a public position on a Johnsonian subject, but it is an ironical critique of Sir John Hawkins's *Life of Johnson* and is too peripheral to Johnson's scholarship to be of value. Perhaps the most substantial scholar of Johnson's time whose consideration of him is useful today is Samuel Parr, and even Parr's statements about Johnson are somewhat indirect. Parr's learning was far greater than his productivity—indeed, he wrote very little—so that, when Johnson's friends commissioned him to compose the inscription for the monument to Johnson in St. Paul's, Parr first spent several months reading thousands of epitaphs and inscriptions and then took more than four years to write his text (which is not long, just a dozen lines).[29] But Parr, unlike other scholars associated with Johnson, actually intended to write a biography of his learned friend, which he meditated for twenty years and then abandoned. Nothing remains of Parr's intention but a few pages of notes and a selection of books in the catalogue of his enormous library, but these hints are more than any other contemporary scholar has left us about Johnson. The biographer, Parr thought, was essentially a scholar:

> From the ordinary occurrences of life, as they influence the conduct of extraordinary men, the biographer collects such scattered rays as may be concentrated into one bright assemblage of truth upon the character which he has undertaken to delineate.[30]

The collecting of 'scattered rays' is a pleonasm for the type of scholarly investigation that Parr evidently loved most; it describes his years of work on Johnson's inscription. The shards of his unwritten biography, then, tell us something both of his own method and of the context in which he planned to present Johnson.

Parr planned a life of Johnson that would be 'the third most learned work that has ever yet appeared', third only to Bentley's *Dissertation on the Epistles of Phalaris* and a book on the Greek of the New Testament entitled *Funus linguae Hellenisticae* (1643), which Parr supposed to be the work of Salmasius.[31] These books are among the most profound scholarly proofs of the seventeenth century; Bentley's book is a study of literary authenticity, while the *Funus* settles a centuries-long argument on the Greek dialects of the New Testament. Salmasius and Bentley have something else in common: both were great controversialists, rather in the mold of the contentious Parr himself, famous specialists in the art of personal invective against colleagues and rivals. And Parr, after all, was the man who would not concede Johnson so much as a stamp in an argument! We sometimes overlook the abusive, castigating nature of late Renaissance scholarship today; perhaps only A. E. Housman, in our own century, has been really effective at scholarly abuse. No doubt Parr managed to transfer some of his own personal qualities to his subject, although there is some evidence that Johnson was frequently satirically abusive of the shortcomings of other scholars.

Over a period of years, then, from the early 1790s to 1812, Parr read and set aside in a special corner of his library books that he knew Johnson admired or that were relevant to the kind of life he planned.[32] There are about fifty of these works, and they tell us much about the unwritten story of Johnson as scholar. First, Parr meant to use the epistles of Renaissance scholars, miscellanies in which the learned dealt with a wide variety of scholarly topics. He mentions only the most famous of such works, those of the fifteenth-century Ciceronians Pietro Bembo and Poggio Bracciolini, of Politian and the Scaligers, of Isaac Casaubon, Jean LeClerc and Bishop Huet. Second, Parr was interested in books on scholarly methodology like Morhof's *Polyhistor*, Joannes Wowerus's *De Polymathia Tractatio* (1665), and Samuel Werenfels's *Dissertatio de Logomachiis Eruditorum* (1716). A third category of books consists of collections of scholarly lives and memoirs, all emanating from late Renaissance Germany and Scandinavia. Fourth, Parr put aside several collections of philological commentary, both biblical and classical. And fifth, he secluded a number of works that deal with famous scholarly controversies of Renaissance Europe. A close study of Parr's working collection for his life of Johnson shows that not a single one of the authors he cited was English, but that almost all, except for the fifteenth-century (and therefore pre-Reformation) Italians, were Protestants. Nearly all, too, were combatants in the scholarly wars of the Reformation and Counter-Reformation, men who often brought their polymathic learning to the defence of Protestantism and religious moderation. They were students of Christian origins, defenders of classical studies, and chroniclers of the scholarship that led to the development of late seventeenth-century neo-classicism in northern Europe and England.

5

Our first reaction to Parr's planned biography may well be that Johnson was not like this, that he is not a scholar in the tradition of Continental humanism. He is not, yet he is. Johnson, unlike most of the scholars with whom Parr tacitly compares him, did not lecture in a university (but, then, neither did Lipsius, who simply refused to do so), although he wrote lectures for others. He left no *Nachlass* for his disciples to continue to exploit, yet he had many more informal followers who nevertheless continued to imitate his manner and style. He collected no miscellaneous commentary on scholarly topics, yet Boswell, Mrs. Thrale, and many scholars from John Wilson Croker to George Birkbeck Hill to Aleyn Lyell Reade have meticulously gathered scholarly anecdotes and conversations about him which amount to nearly the same thing as the *opuscula* of the Renaissance scholars. Johnson did not engage in public disputes, yet he took part in many controversies—those involving Lauder, Macpherson and Chatterton come to mind—behind the scenes. He did not found a school, yet he advised scores of contemporaries on scholarly matters in such a way as to leave his stamp on their works—Percy, Burney, the young Bentham, Lort, Lysons, Jones, Reed, Steevens, Farmer, Oldys, Lloyd, Carter, Elstob (the last two women)—the list is very long.

Like all great productive scholars of the European Renaissance, Johnson enjoyed intimate relationships with publishers, many of whom he knew socially, and he avidly promoted his own works as well as those of others with them. His writing of prefaces and dedications to a great variety of works and his book reviewing are the scholarly chores that all of Parr's exemplars carried out, and that scholars ever since have engaged in for little money and with little complaint. And he produced a body of lexicography and scholarly commentary that, two centuries after his death, the works of the learned continue to cite, just as classical scholars still cite Bentley, Porson and Wolf, just as zoologists and botanists still cite Linnaeus and von Humboldt, just as mathematicians still cite Newton, the Bernouillis and Euler. Let me return, at last, to my beginning with *Rasselas* and provide, finally, one gloss. A scholar's business, Johnson has Imlac tell the Prince, is 'To talk in publick, to think in solitude, to read and hear, to inquire and answer inquiries' and he is 'neither known nor valued but by men like himself'. Now I think we can see how ironical Johnson is, through Imlac, in this speech, which Rasselas never has the chance to question. The scholar is, perhaps, all these things but, as Johnson's own scholarly life shows, he or she is much more besides.

NOTES

1. Boswell refers to the anecdote; see *Life*, Vol. 1, p. 59. Of course, we do not know what Johnson quoted.
2. For the list of Johnson's undergraduate library, see A. L. Reade, *Johnsonian Gleanings*, 11 vols. (privately printed, 1909–52), Vol. V, pp. 213–29.
3. *Catalogue Bibliothecae Harleianae*, 5 vols. (London, 1743–45), Vol. III, p. 150 (Lot 1963). Johnson's comment, typically, has nothing to do with Sigonio's *Historia de Regno Italorum Libri XV* (Bologna, 1574). Thomas Kaminski, 'Johnson and Oldys as Bibliographers: An Introduction to the Harleian Catalogue', *Philological Quarterly*, LX (1981), 439–53, mentions the difficulty of attribution of the annotations, but also notes that the

Catalogus demonstrates Johnson's 'considerable capabilities as a scholar' (p. 450). Johnson owned at least one of Sigonio's works; see Donald Greene, *Johnson's Library: An Annotated Guide* (Victoria, B. C.: English Literary Studies, 1975), p. 103.

4. *Life*, Vol. 4, p. 20.
5. *The Works of Samuel Johnson*, 9 vols. (Oxford, 1825), Vol. I, p. 215.
6. See *The Cambridge History of the Bible*, 3 vols. (Cambridge: Cambridge University Press, 1963–70), Vol. I, pp. 113–59, 284–308; Vol. II, pp. 27–53.
7. See S. Schoenbaum, *Shakespeare's Lives* (Oxford: Clarendon Press, 1970), pp. 221–33. For Parr's opinion of Bentley's *Dissertation*, see William Field, *Memoirs of the Life, Writings, and Opinions of the Rev. Samuel Parr, LL.D.*, 2 vols. (London, 1828), Vol. I, p. 164.
8. On Sholokhov, see the 'Obituary: Mikhail Sholokhov, Author of "The Quiet Don"', *The Times*, 22 February 1984, p. 16. The charge of plagiarism was made most recently in 1974 by Alexander Solzhenitsyn.
9. See G. A. Padley, *Grammatical Theory in Western Europe, 1500–1700: the Latin Tradition* (Cambridge: Cambridge University Press, 1976), pp. 154–209; and Murray Cohen, *Sensible Words: Linguistic Practice in England, 1640–1785* (Baltimore: Johns Hopkins University Press, 1977), pp. 1–77.
10. For a fine overview of scientific scholarship in the period, see G. S. Rousseau, 'Science Books and their Readers in the Eighteenth Century', in *Books and their Readers in Eighteenth-Century England*, ed. Isabel Rivers (Leicester: Leicester University Press, 1982), pp. 197–255.
11. Robert Anderson, *Life of Samuel Johnson, LL.D.*, 3rd edn. (Edinburgh, 1815), p. 491.
12. I refer to *Ramblers* 7, 11, 13, 14, 17, 24, 32 and 38. It would be easy to multiply this list many times.
13. On Johnson's use of Continental dictionaries, see Paul J. Korshin, 'Johnson and the Renaissance Dictionary', *Journal of the History of Ideas*, XXXV (1974), 300–12.
14. See *Works* (1825), Vol. V, p. 95: 'The business of him that republishes an ancient book, is, to correct what is corrupt, and to explain what is obscure.'
15. See Anderson, *Life*, p. 309, and cf. W. P. Courtney and David Nichol Smith, *A Bibliography of Samuel Johnson* (Oxford: Clarendon Press, 1915), p. 111.
16. For a discussion of this genre, see Paul J. Korshin, '*Ana*-Books and Intellectual Biography in the Eighteenth Century', *Studies in Eighteenth-Century Culture*, III (1973), 196–201.
17. On the possibility that Johnson started the *Lives* in 1775 (Boswell assigned 1777 as the year), see W. R. Keast, 'Samuel Johnson and Thomas Maurice', in *Eighteenth-Century Studies in Honor of Donald F. Hyde*, ed. W. H. Bond (New York: Grolier Club, 1970), pp. 63–79.
18. See, for example, Lawrence Lipking, *The Ordering of the Arts in Eighteenth-Century England* (Princeton: Princeton University Press, 1970), pp. 405–22.
19. *Life*, Vol. 4, p. 381; cf. pp. 381–83.

20. See Anthony Grafton, 'On the Scholarship of Politian and Its Context', *Journal of the Warburg and Courtauld Institutes*, XL (1977), 150–88. When he was 25, Johnson issued proposals for an edition of Politian's *Poemata*; he must have been aware of his scholarship as well.
21. See Rudolf Pfeiffer, *History of Classical Scholarship, 1300–1850* (Oxford: Clarendon Press, 1976), pp. 71–81, 124–26; Anthony Grafton, *Joseph Scaliger: A Study in the History of Classical Scholarship. I. Textual Criticism and Exegesis* (Oxford: Clarendon Press, 1983), pp. 227–29. Johnson refers to Lipsius as 'the great master of Stoicism'.
22. On Sarpi's popularity in England, see Frances A. Yates, 'Paolo Sarpi's *History of the Council of Trent*', *Journal of the Warburg and Courtauld Institutes*, VII (1944), 123–43. Only three paragraphs of Johnson's unfinished translation of Sarpi survive.
23. See Johnson's 'Life' of Sarpi in *Works* (1825), Vol. VI, p. 268.
24. For Johnson's comment on false information, see his review of Joseph Warton's *Essay on the Writings and Genius of Mr. Pope*, Vol. I, in *Works* (1825), Vol. VI, pp. 41–42.
25. See Boswell, *Life*, Vol. 4, p. 21.
26. On Johnson's debt to Clarke's theology, see James Gray, *Johnson's Sermons: A Study* (Oxford: Clarendon Press, 1972), pp. 65–92.
27. For a general view of Clarke's scholarship, see J. P. Ferguson, *Dr. Samuel Clarke: An Eighteenth-Century Heretic* (Kineton: Roundwood Press, 1976), passim. This overlooked book is the only modern biography of Clarke.
28. See Boswell, *Life*, Vol. 4, p. 2.
29. See Warren Derry, *Dr. Parr: A Portrait of the Whig Dr. Johnson* (Oxford: Clarendon Press, 1966), pp. 169–87.
30. *Aphorisms, Opinions, and Reflections of the Late Dr. Parr* (London, 1826), p. 14.
31. See Field, *Memoirs of Parr*, Vol. I, pp. 164–65. The *Funus linguae Hellenisticae*, long ascribed to Salmasius, we now know to be the work of an anonymous scholar; see Pfeiffer, *History of Classical Scholarship, 1300–1850*, p. 123.
32. For the full list, see *Bibliotheca Parriana: A Catalogue of the Library of the Late Reverend and Learned Samuel Parr, LL.D.* (London, 1827), pp. 706–708.

4

Johnson on 'The Rise of the Novel'

by MARK KINKEAD-WEEKES

My title, I fear, must seem pretentious, for what strikes one first about Johnson's criticism of 'the novel' is that there should be so very little. As against the wealth of the *Lives of the Poets*, and the view of drama both there and in the great Preface and Notes on Shakespeare, there is left to us: one characteristically generalizing *Rambler* essay (No. 4); a number of remarks praising Richardson and damning Fielding, which bothered Boswell by their self-evident one-sidedness; and a few comments about *Robinson Crusoe, Gulliver's Travels* and *Tristram Shandy*, the latter two of which show little comprehension and less sympathy. There is a letter to Smollett asking help to rescue Johnson's black servant from the Navy; and a glimpse of Johnson polishing the Latin for the Smollett monument at Loch Lomond; but on the novels there is nothing at all. This seems meagre indeed—yet the slender remnant is out of all proportion illuminating, not so much of the novelists as of the nature and quality of Johnson's own sensibility; as though the uncharted subject and the unguarded spontaneity of judgement laid bare, more clearly than usual, the sources of the more collected and pondered criticisms of poetry and drama.

Reasons for the dearth are not hard to find. What we now call 'the novel' was so new in 1750 that the Rambler does not know how to name it—he suggests 'familiar history'—though he is clear what defines its opposition to 'romance': that it exhibits 'life in its true state, diversified only by accidents that daily happen in the world, and influenced by passions and qualities which are really to be found in conversing with mankind'. The word 'novel', defined by the Dictionary as 'a small tale, generally of love', would clearly not, then, do for *Tom Jones* or *Clarissa*, whose authors indeed always used the term contemptuously for what their works were not. It would be many years before the term became current in its modern sense. Moreover, though 'the novel' might have seemed in 1750 to be 'rising' sufficiently, because of Richardson and Fielding, to devote an essay to it, between the '50s and the '80s there was so little of major note by others—apart, perhaps, from *Humphry Clinker*; what Johnson thought the transient oddity of *Tristram Shandy*; and his delight in *Evelina*—that it would have been as easy to conclude that, having 'risen' so extraordinarily, the novel had fallen no less fast. Johnson was never offered any occasion or inducement to write on the novelists, and without such prompting, both the indolence for which he always castigated himself, and his sense of the very limited importance of prose fiction, would ensure that it occupied little of his critical attention. He thought of prose fictions as largely directed towards 'the young, the ignorant, and the idle, to whom they serve as lectures of conduct, and introductions into life'.[1] Hawkins says he 'could at any time be talked into a disapprobation of all fictitious relations, of which he would frequently say they took no hold of the mind'.[2]

If, then, fictions are

> the entertainment of minds unfurnished with ideas, and therefore, easily susceptible of impressions; not fixed by principles, and therefore easily following the current of fancy; not informed by experience, and consequently open to every false suggestion and partial account,

it is clear why Johnson's general essay in *Rambler* 4 should attack romance, and justify familiar histories only on condition that they dealt realistically with ordinary life, and moreover, in a morally improving way. For

> when an adventurer is levelled with the rest of the world, and acts in such scenes of the universal drama, as may be the lot of

> any other man; young spectators fix their eyes upon him with closer attention, and hope by observing his behaviour and success to regulate their own practices, when they shall be engaged in the like part.
>
> For this reason these familiar histories may perhaps be made of greater use than the solemnities of professed morality, and convey the knowledge of vice and virtue with more efficacy than axioms and definitions. But if the power of example is so great, as to take possession of the memory by a kind of violence, and produce effects almost without the intervention of the will, care ought to be taken that, when the choice is unrestrained, the best examples only should be exhibited; and that which is likely to operate so strongly, should not be mischievous or uncertain in its effects.

It follows that realism in itself is not nearly enough; for if a fiction merely reflects the world 'without discrimination', why should we bother with the mirror rather than turning to the world direct? No, writers must select carefully what they show, in order to instruct; must not mingle good and bad qualities in their characters in such a way as to make us 'lose the abhorrence of their faults'; must always distinguish clearly between virtue and vice; and ought indeed not only to make vice disgusting, but to show, if always within probability, 'the highest and purest that humanity can reach.'[3]

One could predict from this that Johnson would praise Richardson's *Clarissa* and be somewhat critical of *Tom Jones* for making Tom's failings too attractive; but what is surprising is the extremism of his views, and the vehemence of their expression. The comparisons in Boswell's *Life* begin fairly judiciously:

> Sir . . . there is all the difference in the world between characters of nature and characters of manners; and *there* is the difference between the characters of Fielding and those of Richardson. Characters of manners are very entertaining; but they are to be understood, by a more superficial observer, than characters of nature, where a man must dive into the recesses of the human heart.

Boswell, who thought Johnson overestimated Richardson and had an unreasonable prejudice against Fielding, goes on:

> In comparing those two writers, he used this expression: 'that there was as great a difference between them as between a man who knew how a watch was made, and a man who could tell the hour by looking on the dial-plate'[4]

and the distinction has become derogatory. On a later occasion Johnson called Fielding a 'blockhead' and a 'barren rascal'; and when Boswell tried to defend him as drawing 'very natural pictures of human life', Johnson slapped him down.

> Why, Sir, it is of very low life. Richardson used to say, that had he not known who Fielding was, he should have believed he was an ostler. Sir, there is more knowledge of the heart in one letter of Richardson's than in all 'Tom Jones'. I, indeed, never read 'Joseph Andrews'.

On Thomas Erskine's objecting that Richardson was 'tedious', Johnson replied

> Why, Sir, if you were to read Richardson for the story, your impatience would be so much fretted that you would hang yourself. But you must read him for the sentiment [the moral opinion or felt thought], and consider the story as only giving occasion to the sentiment.[5]

In a headnote to *Rambler* 97 which he invited Richardson to contribute—one of only three to receive that honour—he described him as an author 'who has enlarged the knowledge of human nature, and taught the passions to move at the command of virtue'. To Mrs. Thrale he said that 'Richardson had picked the kernel of life . . . while Fielding was contented with the husk'[6]; and he told Miss Reynolds that *Clarissa* 'was the first book in the world for the knowledge it displays of the human heart'—though she says he never spoke of Richardson himself 'with any degree of cordiality'.[7] (Indeed evidence abounds that he saw Richardson's failings as a human being very clearly.) The height of praise was perhaps Mrs. Thrale's report of how 'Johnson used to say that he believed no combination could be found and few sentiments that might not be traced up to Homer, Shakespeare and Richardson.'[8] The opposite extreme of vehemence came in his outburst to Hannah More, the only time (she says) she ever made him angry, when she confessed to having enjoyed *Tom Jones*.

> I am shocked to hear you quote from so vicious a book. I am sorry to hear you have read it: a confession which no modest lady should ever make. I scarcely know a more corrupt work. . . . He went so far as to refuse to Fielding the great talents which are ascribed to him, and broke out into a noble panegyric on his competitor, Richardson; who, he said was as superior to him in talents as in virtue; and whom he pronounced to be the greatest genius that had shed its lustre on this path of literature.[9]

Making all allowance for conversational over-emphasis, exuberance or arguing for victory, the consistency, vehemence and extremism of the comparative judgement makes it challenging, especially to those who cannot believe (as I cannot) that it is at all necessary to denigrate the one writer in order to do justice to the very different vision of the other. The judgement would seem as excessively one-eyed, as unbalanced, as Thackeray's onslaught on Richardson in Fielding's favour, and as the bluff writing-down of Richardson that was commonplace thirty years ago. Yet what is even more challenging and interesting is the apparent inconsistency with Johnson's own earlier position in *Rambler* 4. All the ways in which Fielding would seem to fit the requirements of that earlier essay, and of Johnson's taste and opinion elsewhere—indeed fit rather better in some respects than Richardson—seem to have gone for naught because of the apparent failure to make immorality sufficiently unattractive. Even more significantly, the whole ground of value seems to have changed: from action, behaviour, struggle (setting a good example) to psychology, from 'manners' to 'the heart'. So radical-seeming a change of emphasis needs looking into.

As an earlier writer on this subject, R. E. Moore,[10] complained, surely Johnson *should* have liked Fielding better?—according to clear positions he took up in *Rambler* 4 and elsewhere. Both Fielding and Richardson attacked the older romance-fiction as Johnson did, and espoused realism, and for the same reasons. When, however, the *Rambler* says of the new fiction, 'This kind of writing may be termed not improperly the comedy of romance, and is to be conducted nearly by the rules of comic poetry', this may have some bearing on the Richardson of *Pamela*, but fits far better the comic epic in prose that Fielding outlined in his Preface to *Joseph Andrews* than the manifestly tragic structure of *Clarissa*. Indeed, if Johnson had read *Joseph Andrews*, he might have been annoyed at the mockery of those who believed in the exemplary power of books, but he would certainly have been struck, also, by the clear affinity between Fielding and Cervantes, for whom he had the greatest respect. (He carried on the attack on Romance, himself, by helping Charlotte Lennox with the final conversion of Arabella in *The Female Quixote*.[11]) When, moreover, the *Rambler* talks of the qualities necessary to write the new fiction, as opposed to the mere closet-fancy of the Romance, and speaks of the need not merely for learning, but also for 'general converse, and accurate observation of the living world', there is the closest affinity with Fielding's requirements for authorship in the Preface to Book 9 of *Tom Jones*, which also finishes, as the *Rambler* doesn't actually do, with the demand that above all the author must have a good heart. Johnson valued learning highly, and travelling through worlds of men and manners is a key theme in his own fiction, especially in *Rasselas*[11]; but while the epigraph to *Tom Jones* is Horace's description of Odysseus the traveller, who (like Imlac) 'saw the customs of many men', Samuel Richardson, through no fault of his own, both lacked learning and had led a far more socially and geographically confined life than his rival. Indeed I suspect that any student of eighteenth-century fiction, coming absolutely fresh to *Rambler* 4, would be as likely for at least the first three-quarters of the essay to assume that Johnson had Fielding in mind, as Richardson, if not more so.

Fielding's work also seems better attuned to other well-known Johnsonian positions, especially his constant insistence on the generality of truth. I think particularly of those two classic instances: the paragraphs praising Shakespeare which begin 'Nothing can please many, and please long, but just representations of general nature', and end 'In the writings of other poets a character is too often an individual; in those of Shakespeare it is commonly a species'[12]; and that famous insistence of Imlac that

> The business of a poet is to examine, not the individual but the species; to remark general properties and large appearances. . . .

> He is to exhibit in his portraits of nature such prominent and striking features, as recal the original to every mind; and must neglect the minuter discriminations, which one may have remarked and another have neglected, for those characteristicks which are alike obvious to vigilance and carelessness.[13]

Now this as clearly points to Fielding as it points away from Richardson. Fielding specifically aimed at just the typicality of character Johnson seems to have had in mind, as his remarks on the lawyer and Mrs. Tow-wouse make clear: 'I declare here once for all, I describe not men, but manners; not an individual, but a species.'[14] Whereas Richardson not only takes us deep into the unique, subjective individuality of his characters, but explores them to the point at which each individual, *in extremis*, uniquely determines her or his being. And no writer before Henry James was more anxious than Richardson to number the streaks of the tulip, or concern himself with the minutest discrimination of character and conduct—that vocabulary of 'delicacy', and 'punctilio', that meticulous attention to circumstance—while upbraiding his readers for carelessness and lack of vigilance.

Again, Johnson's robust common-sense always recognized that a book had to give pleasure if it were to do good. He clearly enjoyed *Clarissa* ('though the story is long, every letter is short'), but his reservation about the lethal effect of reading Richardson for the story was confirmed, tactfully, to the author himself, in the course of asking for an index to the 'sentiment': 'Clarissa is not a performance to be read with eagerness, and put away for ever.'[15] Yet we know he could not put *Amelia* down, but read it through in one sitting-up in bed,[16] a point to which I shall return. We also have a lucky piece of evidence to show how Johnson must have enjoyed even Fielding's 'low' comedy when delighting in the 'fine varnish of low politeness' of the Holborn beau in *Evelina*: ' "Oh Mr. Smith, Mr. Smith is the man!" cried he, laughing violently. "Harry Fielding never drew so good a character!" '[17] Fielding moreover was an 'authorial' writer, in whose fiction, as Mary Lascelles says of *Rasselas*, the characters are intended to express not 'the diversity of several views' but 'the complexity inherent in one'.[18] In the dependence of his writing on his own personality and views, as well as in the basic tendency to moral fable, Fielding is far closer to Johnson than either is to Richardson the dramatist, who created by banishing 'the author' and allowing his characters to create themselves and 'write' the book, as though by a real correspondence.

If nevertheless, in spite of all these affinities, Johnson consistently and vehemently felt what he did about *Tom Jones*, there is no use bewailing the fact, or trying to suggest as R. E. Moore does, that somehow it was not really so, but that Johnson was misled by his view of Fielding's own low character, and by Richardson's malice, and by Fielding's flippancy of tone in *Tom Jones*. None of these is at all convincing. Dr. Burney, in a note to the third edition of Boswell's *Life*, does indeed show us how Fielding may have been regarded by the Johnson circle, and suggests that Johnson's severity may have been owing not to any 'viciousness' in Fielding's style, but to a combination of his own loose life and the profligacy of his heroes.[19] But Johnson was manifestly capable of separating the writing he admired and valued from the authorial character he did not, as in the *Lives* of Milton, Pope and Gray, to go no further. He did so with Richardson, whose vanity he saw very clearly; and he did so with Fielding, over *Amelia*. His judgements are his own, and in this case obviously deeply felt. Though facetiousness might have irritated him, it could not have produced the language he used. We have to search much deeper for the reason why an art which was as morally didactic in intention and as Augustan in culture as his own should have affected him so adversely; and why on the other hand he should have been moved so deeply by an art very unlike his own, and indeed in many ways not Augustan at all, but pointing a long way into the future—in its exploration of inward consciousness and madness, particularly, a century and a half before its time.

The difference between the standpoint of the *Rambler* essay in 1750, and that of the critical judgements of Richardson and Fielding in 1768 and 1772, has everything to do, I think, with Johnson's immersion in Shakespeare in the interim, before the Edition of 1765. Nichol Smith argued,[20] many years ago, that there was a shift within the Edition itself, between the great Preface, 'a summation of critical opinion' looking backwards over a long tradition, and the Notes, which look forward to a new kind of character-criticism, to Morgann, to Coleridge, to Bradley. Now what the Notes show that Johnson valued in Shakespeare's characterization corresponds very closely to what he praised in Richardson. He dismisses Warburton's description of Polonius as making him 'a character only of manners', and again and again refers to Shakespeare's people as characters of 'nature' or, like Polonius, of nature and manners mixed.[21] The distinction is the same as between Richardson and Fielding; the praise is of that psychological mastery 'where a man must dive into the recesses of the human heart'.[22] If Thomas Edwards, too, had called Richardson 'Master of the Heart . . . next to Shakespear', and David Garrick thought of *Clarissa* as 'Of *Nature* born, by *Shakespeare* got',[23] this pointed not only to the essentially dramatic nature of Richardson's new way of writing, but especially to a new 'Shakespearean' sense of the inward complexity of characterization.

The author of the *Life of Savage* had not been unresponsive to the ambivalences, the strange individual depths of the human character; but re-immersion in Shakespeare clearly sharpened his sense of complexity in character and consciousness, as notes like those on Hal and John, and especially Falstaff and Polonius show. So the emphasis now falls, not so much on realistic *behaviour*, as in the *Rambler* essay, as on psychological 'knowledge of the heart'. Before, he had condemned authors who 'for the sake of following nature . . . mingle good and bad qualities in their principal personages' and 'instead of helping to settle their boundaries, mix them with so much art, that no common mind is able to disunite them'. Vice 'should always disgust', hence must never be so united with 'graces of gaiety' or 'supported by either parts or spirit' as to 'reconcile it to the mind' (*Rambler* 4). Now in the Notes he can delight in the complexity of character and consciousness: from characters like John who 'hide themselves from their own detection in ambiguities and subterfuges' or like Hal show 'a great mind offering excuses to itself, and palliating those follies which it can neither justify nor forsake'; to the fusion of wisdom and dotage in Polonius, or again of heroism and trifling in Hal; and above all to unimitated, unimitable Falstaff, how shall I describe thee? Thou compound of sense and vice; of sense which may be admired but not esteemed, of vice which may be despised, but hardly detested. Falstaff is a character loaded with faults, and with those faults which naturally produce contempt. . . . Yet the man thus corrupt, thus despicable, makes himself necessary . . . by the most pleasing of all qualities, perpetual gaiety, by an unfailing power of exciting laughter.[24]

Moreover nothing is more arresting in these Notes than the evidence of how powerfully Johnson responded, in imagination and feeling, to Shakespeare's tragic creations. He may have enjoyed the comedies more and thought them better done, but who ever responded to tragedy more powerfully than the man who wrote of the murder scene in *Othello*: 'I am glad that I have ended my revisal of this dreadful scene. It is not to be endured'? Or 'I was many years ago so shocked by Cordelia's death, that I know not whether I ever endured to read again the last scenes of the play till I undertook to revise them as an editor'? This capacity for involvement, however, made Shakespeare all the more censurable when he seemed to write 'without any moral purpose'. Of Hamlet's soliloquy over the kneeling Claudius he writes, 'This speech, in which Hamlet, represented as a virtuous character, is not content with taking blood for blood, but contrives damnation for the man that he would punish, is too horrible to be read or to be uttered.'[25]

It is not to be wondered at, then, that he should praise a novelist who offered him 'Shakespearean' mastery of the heart's complexity; who called deeply on the passions and the characterizing imagination; *but who moved both passion and imagination consistently in the cause of virtue*, as he felt Shakespeare failed, or at least neglected to do. The note on Falstaff needs a moral excuse at the end, that his turpitude 'is not so offensive but that it may be borne for his mirth'.[26] But there can be full-hearted praise for the character of Lovelace, though he is both immensely attractive and evil, because there is a steady process of moral discrimination which focuses the vice and finally shows it unmistakeably.

It was in the power of Richardson alone to teach us at once esteem and detestation; to make virtuous resentment overpower

> all the benevolence which wit, elegance, and courage naturally excite, and to lose at last the hero in the villain.[27]

And although *Clarissa* does not give the pleasure of poetic justice which, 'if other excellencies are equal', Johnson thinks a reader would 'rise better pleased' with[28]; there is a more specifically Christian view of 'the triumph of persecuted virtue' through death than in *Lear*. Johnson's immersion in and admiration of Shakespeare is precisely consonant with his admiration of Richardson; and it is hardly surprising that he was so fervent a supporter of the 'Shakespearean' novelist.

Perhaps we can now, also, imagine ourselves more sensitively into the mind which reacted so violently against *Tom Jones*, yet admired *Amelia*. For we are now in a better position to see how fiction, though only a limited good and only on certain conditions, may by the same token become, in Johnson's view, a dangerous evil. We have to discern in him a power of imaginative involvement, and a depth of feeling, not only much greater, but also more *uncontrollable* than our thick-skinned age can easily imagine. We have to reckon with a marked shift of sensibility, dividing our responsiveness very sharply from his. Nobody now responds to Desdemona or Cordelia, or to Hamlet, as he did. I do not find in my colleagues, my students, or myself 'that hunger of imagination which preys incessantly upon life'[29]—and which may make imaginative experiences literally unendurable; for I believe Johnson means exactly what he says. Lady Bradshaigh described how, after finishing *Clarissa*, 'My spirits are seized, my sleep is disturbed; waking in the night, I burst into a passion of crying; so I did at breakfast this morning, and just now again.'[30] But Johnson was 'more strongly and more violently affected by the force of words . . . than any other man in the world I believe' and could never repeat the *Dies Irae* 'without bursting into a flood of tears'. He also 'burst into a passion of tears' reading his own portrait of the scholar,[31] and other examples abound. To such a sensibility the power of literature to affect, and even change, the mind and the heart was bound to seem more extensive and more dangerous than we would think.

Hence the extraordinary language—as soon as one really

looks at it—about the *power* of example in the *Rambler* essay. For 'if the power of example is *so great, as to take possession of the memory by a kind of violence, and produce effects almost without the intervention of the will*'—like hypnotism or witchcraft—'care ought to be taken that, when the choice is unrestrained, the best examples only should be exhibited; and that which is likely to operate so strongly, should not be mischievous or uncertain in its effects.' How, to a susceptibility and sensitivity to 'example' so much greater than ours, would the experience of *Tom Jones* come across? The title-page's proclamation that the novel begins from bastardy; the persistent sexual incontinence that the 'author' regularly condones; the duel; the flirting with incest; the becoming a gigolo (all in a hero consistently presented as charmingly good-hearted)—we may begin to imagine how these would affect the Johnson whom we now see to have been implicit in the critical language. There is, moreover, in Sophia's rebellious running away from home a deliberate *reversal* of Clarissa, no less ostentatiously challenging to the Richardsonian view Johnson invited into the *Rambler*. Without inner complexity or conflict in the characters, the emphasis fell for him on manners, and the manners seemed licentious. We ought—without of course necessarily agreeing—to be able at least to imagine the shock and anger with which Johnson heard a modest woman confess her pleasure in such a book, whose power over imagination and feeling he genuinely felt was corrupting, in that it glamorized vice and misdoing, and could *obviously* take 'possession' of young and female readers by a kind of violence and against their moral will. Moreover, Johnson would have found the central moral idea of the innate goodness of some human hearts profoundly untruthful and the optimism facile. Nothing is more characteristic of him than his explosion at a foolish lady who claimed to be '*really* happy'.[32] To his sombre view of the precariousness of health and reason, the fragility of virtue, the power of sin, the evil and darkness of the world, the core of optimism in *Tom Jones* must have seemed that of a simpleton, a 'blockhead'. On the other hand, a work which could give him 'harmless pleasure' deserved

> the highest praise. Pleasure is a word of dubious import; pleasure is in general dangerous, and pernicious to virtue; to be able

> therefore to furnish pleasure that is harmless, pleasure pure and unalloyed, is as great a power as man can possess.[33]

(Richardson, like Shakespeare, offered the pleasures of both comedy and tragedy, the full range of pleasures and responses in the cause of virtue.) Yet that the response to *Tom Jones* is not an insensibility but rather a sensitivity—we might feel an over-sensitivity—the response to *Amelia* proves. For as soon as there is a Fielding novel with a virtuous suffering heroine, a hero whose profligacy is not extenuated, and a Christian point of view within the pages, making articulate its moral discrimination, the pleasure is *there*, and Johnson reads on in bed until he has read it through, and praises with real affection.

Yet there remains, of course, something radically imperceptive about his response to *Tom Jones*, and it is to be found also in his response to *Gulliver's Travels* and *Tristram Shandy*.[34] What distorts Johnson's view is not simply a moral but a technical matter, a failure to understand Fielding's *form*. Johnson himself was an ironist of a kind: a sardonic measurer of the gap between appearance and reality, expectation and experience, pretension and truth. But of what Empson called 'double irony', the subversive technique of the 'unreliable author' so crucial to Swift and Fielding at their best, he clearly had no idea. He undoubtedly identified Gulliver with Swift and the 'author' of *Tom Jones* with Fielding; he was unable to see how the real moral vision of both depended on an unreliable author teasing and challenging the reader, forcing him to discover and test moral vision through the presentation of false or at least inadequate alternatives. It needs careful reading to show how different Fielding's view of the Molly Seagrim episode, or the goings-on at Upton, or the apparent 'moral' that the good-heart only needs to learn worldly prudence for everything to be fine, is from the pseudo-author's; but in that difference (I think) lies the whole moral discrimination of the book and the true sense of the value of Tom and his 'Sophia' (which Cicero was so careful to distinguish from Prudentia).[35] What Johnson wanted, and what Fielding never provided in *Tom Jones* but did in *Amelia*, was a firm and reliable moral critique within the fiction—yet Fielding's least ironic is also his least lively book. But only two centuries of hindsight into the craft of fictions allows us to see technically better than Johnson did. When the 'novel' was so new and extraordinary, and when moreover it was not one but several quite different new ways of writing, it is hardly surprising either that Richardson and Fielding (having quite different modes of vision) should be unable to read each other, or that Johnson should fail to see one of them clear. It is even less surprising that he should fail to detect, behind the apparently zany oddity and innuendo of *Tristram Shandy*, Sterne's penetrating comic Essay on Human Misunderstanding.

However, the strength and consistency of Johnson's responses, once one comes to understand them, seem admirable not only when they are at their strongest on Richardson, but also when they seem most mistaken on Fielding. The sensibility and sensitivity so much greater than one's own, the demands on fiction, are such as to challenge us to examine our responses more closely and produce criticism more discriminating than much that has passed for praise of *Tom Jones*, if we seek to show that Johnson was wrong. Moreover, what I find finally most valuable is the revelation of how complex Johnson's sensibility actually was, and how it only comes into deep-focus at the point where apparent contradictions meet in a unity that holds both. In his criticism, as well as in his poetry, true generality is reached *through* particularity: the praise of Shakespeare as poet of nature backed by the detailed perceptions of the Notes; the minute observation that there is always something Clarissa prefers to truth,[36] showing what he meant by 'virtue not angelical, nor above probability, for what we cannot credit we shall never imitate'.[37] The earlier and later Johnson may differ in emphasis but there is deeper consistency beneath. We ought to see not so much a contrast between complex individual and general species as an insistence that an individual truly and complexly imagined by a master of the heart *is* a revelation of species. The power of imagination, and the depth of feeling, are inseparable from the fear of their corruptibility. With the melancholy sense of the darkness of human life goes the robust commitment to it, each defining and limiting the other. Similarly the sense of the limitation of fiction and its dangerousness is also the condition of the sense of its value, and of the demand that it should meet the highest standards.

NOTES

1. *Rambler* 4 (1750), Yale, Vol. 3, p. 21.
2. Sir John Hawkins, *The Life of Samuel Johnson*, ed. Bertram H. Davis (London: Jonathan Cape, 1962), 96–7.
3. *Rambler* 4, Yale, Vol. 3, pp. 21–4.
4. *Life*, Vol. 2, pp. 48–9 (Spring 1768).
5. *Life*, Vol. 2, pp. 173–75 (6 April 1772).
6. Yale, Vol. 4, p. 153; *Johnsonian Miscellanies*, ed. George Birkbeck Hill (Oxford: Clarendon, 1897), Vol. 1, p. 282. (Hereafter referred to as *Miscellanies*.)
7. *Miscellanies*, Vol. 1, p. 251.
8. Mrs. Piozzi annotating *Life*, Vol. 4, p. 236 in her copy of the 1816 edition, *Life*, Vol. 4, p. 524.
9. *Miscellanies*, Vol. 2, p. 190.
10. Robert Etheridge Moore, 'Dr. Johnson on Fielding and Richardson', *P.M.L.A.*, 66 (1951), 162–81.
11. See Carey McIntosh, *The Choice of Life: Samuel Johnson and the World of Fiction* (New Haven: Yale, 1973) Chap. 6; to whom I also owe the observation about how the novel might have seemed to be 'falling'. On the theme of the Quest see Chap. 2.
12. Yale, Vol. 7, pp. 61–2.
13. *Rasselas*, Chap. 10.
14. *Joseph Andrews*, Book 3, Chap. 1.
15. *Letters*, Vol. 1, pp. 35–6.
16. *Life*, Vol. 3, p. 43.
17. *Diary and Letters of Madame D'Arblay*, ed. A. Dobson (London, 1904), Vol. 1, pp. 71–2.
18. Mary Lascelles, '*Rasselas* Reconsidered', *Essays and Studies* n.s. IV (1951), 45.
19. *Boswell*, Vol. 2, 495: 'Johnson's severity against Fielding did not arise from any viciousness in his style, but from his loose life, and the profligacy of almost all his male characters. Who would venture to read one of his novels aloud to modest women? His novels are *male* amusements, and very amusing they certainly are.—Fielding's conversation was coarse, and so tinctured with the rank weeds of *the Garden*, that it would now be thought only fit for a brothel.'
20. D. Nichol Smith, *Shakespeare in the Eighteenth Century* (Oxford, 1928), pp. 61–91, esp. 78–9.
21. Yale, Vol. 8, p. 974.
22. *Life*, Vol. 2, p. 49.
23. A. D. McKillop, *Samuel Richardson* (Chapel Hill, N.C., 1936 repr. 1960), p. 163. Edwards in a letter of January 1748/9; Garrick in a poem inscribed on the flyleaf of *Clarissa*, 20 April 1751.
24. Ibid., Vol. 7, pp. 425, 458; 8, p. 974; 7, p. 523.
25. Ibid., Vol. 8, pp. 1045, 704; Vol. 7, p. 71 (Preface); Vol. 8, p. 990.
26. Ibid., Vol. 7, p. 523.

27. *Life of Rowe*, comparing Lovelace with Lothario in *The Fair Penitent* (*Lives*, Vol. 2, p. 67).
28. Yale, Vol. 8, p. 704.
29. *Rasselas* Chap. 32.
30. *The Correspondence of Samuel Richardson*, ed. A. L. Barbauld (London, 1804), Vol. 2, p. 242, 'Mrs. Belfour' to Richardson, 11 January, 1748/9.
31. *Miscellanies*, Vol. 1, pp. 284, 280; *Life*, Vol. 4, pp. 165 note 4, 186; *Miscellanies*, Vol. 1, pp. 6, 279.
32. *Miscellanies*, Vol. I, p. 335.
33. *Life*, Vol. 3, p. 388 (24 April 1779).
34. 'He that had formed those images [of the Yahoos] had nothing filthy to learn' (*Life of Swift*: *Lives*, Vol. 3, p. 63); 'Nothing odd will do long. "Tristram Shandy" did not last' (*Life*, Vol. 5, p. 449 (20 March 1776)).
35. I have tried to argue this case in 'Out of the thicket in *Tom Jones*', *The British Journal for Eighteenth Century Studies* (Spring 1980), 1–19.
36. *Miscellanies*, Vol. 1, p. 297. I cavilled at this in *Samuel Richardson: Dramatic Novelist* (London: Methuen, 1973), p. 168, 'because the verb is too active. No character in fiction tries harder to be true.' Nevertheless the perception that something, in her, *does* continually blind her to the truth she seeks, is a very sharp one; salutarily and instantly disposing of much nonsense about her being supposed to be perfect, including Richardson's own clumsy defences.
37. *Rambler* 4, Yale, Vol. 3, p. 24.

5

The Fall of Orgilio: Samuel Johnson as Parliamentary Reporter

by ROBERT GIDDINGS

1

Only a month separates the first publication of Johnson's *London*, which appeared on 12 May 1738, and the reports of the debates in Parliament, to which Johnson so notably contributed, which began to appear in the *Gentleman's Magazine* in June the same year. The figure of Sir Robert Walpole, and his impact on British social, economic and political experience, is a marked feature of both poem and debates. Yet there appears to be a strange tension between the character of Walpole which dominates *London* and the Walpole figure we find in the *Debates in the Senate of Magna Lilliputia*.[1]

London is described by its author as an 'Imitation'. This was a new genre, used to brilliantly ironic effect by Pope.[2] Johnson said of the imitation in his *Life of Pope*: 'This mode . . . in which the ancients are familiarised by adapting their sentiments to modern topicks . . is a kind of middle composition between translation and original design, which pleases when the thoughts are unexpectedly applicable and the parallels lucky.'[3] Pope's imitations of Horace were very much in vogue, and Johnson resolved to imitate Juvenal in contemporary terms. The *Third Satire* of Juvenal is his model, in which the protagonist is appalled by the corruption he sees around him and resolves to leave Rome. In *London* the protagonist, Thales, is shocked by the squalid materialism and political jobbery of the metropolis, and tries to get away from it all by going to Wales. The core of the poem is in Thales's speech to a friend as he embarks at Greenwich.

Thales feels that he has been treated with indifference by Sir Robert Walpole, and that the civilizing mission of poetry and the arts is being swamped by trade, commerce and materialism. Walpole is perhaps caricatured in the figure of Orgilio, the proud and pompous statesman, who maintains himself and his faction in power by a complex system of bribery, pocket boroughs, manipulating public opinion and a well oiled political machine which involves lies, pensions, vote-buying and various other 'public Crimes'. Those who go along with the system enjoy the benefit: 'Who shares *Orgilio*'s Crimes, his Fortunes shares.' *London* is a very hard-hitting satire, and its contemporary relevance is unmistakable. Johnson does everything except name Sir Robert Walpole; even the newspaper he financed to orchestrate public opinion, the *Gazetteer*, is mentioned by name.[4]

Johnson's most sustained treatment of Sir Robert Walpole is to be found in the *Debates*, although there are two other political satires of this period—*Marmor Norfolciense* and *A Compleat Vindication of the Licensers of the Stage*.[5] Some of his comments about Walpole made in later life have been preserved. These are of great interest in the light of his treatment of Walpole at the great crisis of his career, which the young Johnson portrayed for readers of Edward Cave's *Gentleman's Magazine*. Both the political satires show Johnson as the spokesman of patriot, Tory, anti-Walpolean views. The debates cover the period of the collapse of confidence in Walpole as Britain was pushed into war with Spain and Walpole was hounded from office. But it would be true to say that the portrayal of Sir Robert in the *Debates* is not altogether unfavourable.

The comments of the mature Johnson on Walpole are also interesting. Boswell records very little evidence of Johnson's views of Walpole, but we have other sources. Sir John Hawkins (1719–89), the lawyer and magistrate, who knew Johnson well, and whose biography of Johnson was published in 1787, four years before Boswell's *Life*, records that Johnson had a high opinion of Walpole:

> Of Sir Robert Walpole, notwithstanding that he had written against him in the early part of his life, he had a high opinion: he said of him, that he was a fine fellow, and that his very enemies deemed him so before his death: he honoured his memory for having kept his country in peace many years, as also for the goodness and placibility of his temper.[6]

George Birkbeck Hill has preserved this comment of Johnson's on Walpole: 'He was the best minister this country ever had, as if he would have let him he would have kept the country in perpetual peace.'[7] Is it possible to reconcile these seeming contradictions? It is worth recalling that Johnson publicly affirmed the importance of getting at the truth about politics at the very time he was writing the *Debates*. In January 1739 he wrote:

> Political Truth is undoubtedly of very great Importance, and they who honestly endeavour after it, are doubtless engaged in a laudable Pursuit. Nor do the Writers on this Subject ever more deserve the Thanks of their Country, than when they enter upon Examination of the Conduct of their Governors, whether Kings, Senates, or Ministers. . . .[8]

2

The *Debates* are of outstanding interest in Johnson's output. They are fascinating evidence of his political thinking, and impressive examples of the political journalist's art at a very early stage of its development. A careful reading of the *Debates* will make inevitable a severe overhaul of the oft repeated assertion of Johnson's unqualified Toryism. Further, the *Debates* reveal themselves as an important staging post in our progress towards parliamentary democracy.

The relationship between the centres of political power and the means of communication which exist within society is invariably tense and complex. It is in the nature of things that this should be so, and indeed it continues to be so.[9] On the one hand the ruler cannot exist unless he or she is seen to rule over us. This implies that rulers must encourage communication of some sort. To enable them to exist as a political fact, they must be seen. On the other hand, if free communication of ideas and information is openly allowed, those ideas will include criticism which may be more than a ruler can stomach. The ideal state of affairs for rulers is 'news' without criticism or analysis. This is very difficult to bring about, as most societies have discovered. The social experiences which immediately preceded Johnson's appearance as a political journalist are important here. The early Stuart kings had relied on censorship, operated through the court of the Star Chamber. This was abolished during the English revolution. Oliver Cromwell then replaced censorship with licensing, which lasted until 1695. This meant that only publishers likely to favour the status quo were allowed to print and publish.[10] After the Licensing Act lapsed in 1695 Britain enjoyed what was probably the freest press in Europe. Then in 1712 came the Stamp Act, which meant that all publications paid a duty levied by the government. This made publication expensive. Not one penny paper survived. This was one method of attempting to prevent murmuring against the state. It succeeded to some extent, but unintentionally produced a splendid crop of political satires. Political debate, like water, has a habit of finding its own level.[11] An acute interest in political debate, commercial and colonial obsessions, and the development of print technology and transport would have made the early development of our newspaper industry possible, but in fact it was a difficult birth and of sickly growth—thanks very considerably to government restrictions. It was only as the result of the work of a few mavericks such as Abel Boyer,[12] who began to publish a yearly register of political and other occurrences between 1703 and 1713, and began the monthly publication of the *Political State of Great Britain* in 1711, that the trade was opened up at all. Boyer's journal continued to publish accounts after his death, until 1737.

Even though the electorate was still a very small section of the public, the battle for public opinion was clearly being waged as early as the 1720s. Stamp Duty and Paper Tax were not sufficient to control public opinion. After a somewhat patchy start to his political career[13] Robert Walpole unquestionably came to the fore after the sensational collapse of the South Sea Scheme. He was perceived as the saviour of the nation and his alleged grasp of economic and fiscal affairs became part of Whig mythology. By 1721 he was First Lord of the Treasury and Chancellor of the Exchequer. He was really personally responsible for the government of the country, and under him there soon occurred a transfer of power to the Commons, in which house he was able to manage a Whig majority. His major political rival Bolingbroke, a pardoned Tory Jacobite, was not allowed to resume his seat in the Lords, and direct political opposition was thus precluded him. But there was still the press.

Among the group of Tory wits which surrounded Bolingbroke was one Nicholas Amhurst. In 1720 Amhurst began to edit the *Craftsman*, which was to be for ten years a sharp and scathing voice raised against Walpole and his system: 'corruption is a poison', the *Craftsman* opined, 'which will soon spread itself through all ranks and orders of men; especially when it begins at the fountainhead.' During the election of 1727 Bolingbroke wrote in Amhurst's paper an account of Robert Walpole as a bluff villain:

> with a Smile, or rather a Sneer, sitting on his Face and an arch Malignity in his eye. . . . They no sooner saw him, but they all turned their Faces . . . and fell prostrate before him. He trod on their Backs . . . and marched directly up to the Throne. He opened his Purse of Gold which he took out in great Handfuls and scattered amongst the Assembly. While the greater Part were engaged in scrambling these Pieces he seized . . . without the least Fear, upon the sacred Parchment itself. He rumpled it unduly and crammed it in his Pocket. Some of the People began to murmur. He threw more Gold, and they were pacified. . . .[14]

Walpole was so enraged at this portrait of him that he had Amhurst arrested, though proceedings failed.[15] In the face of opposition such as this, administrations had no recourse but to prosecute the printers and publishers for seditious libel, or buy their silence, or subsidize rival publications to refute them.[16] It was rumoured that Walpole spent some £50,000 from Treasury funds in buying the support of the press, and the Duke of Newcastle spent £4,000 on pensions for journalists. A note in Pope's *Dunciad* has this comment on one such newspaper, the *Daily Gazeteer*:

> Into this, as a common sink, was received all the trash, which had been before dispersed in several Journals, and circulated at

> the public expence of the nation. The authors were the same obscure men; though sometimes relieved by occasional essays from Statesmen, Courtiers, Bishops, Deans, and Doctors. The meaner sort were rewarded with Money; others with Places or Benefices, from an hundred to a thousand a year.

The note goes on to estimate that between 1731 and 1741 'not a Pension at Court, nor Preferment in the Church or Universities, of any Consideration, was bestowed on any man distinguished for his Learning separately from Party-merit, or Pamphlet-writing.'[17]

In 1731 the *Gentleman's Magazine* began to publish parliamentary reports, and this was followed later the same year by the *London Magazine*. Initially both publications relied heavily on Boyer's *Political State of Great Britain*, but gradually they began to print their own versions of parliamentary debates. They were obviously successful in appealing to the appetites of their readership, and they managed to avoid being legally taken to task by feigning only to publish during the parliamentary recess. This was a loophole in the law, which was closed by a resolution passed in the Commons on 13 April 1738. In order to escape the consequences of defiance they had no alternative but to pretend that the debates they recorded were fictions. The *London Magazine* purported to carry the accounts of the debates of a non-existent club. The *Gentleman's Magazine* carried the accounts of the *Debates in the Senate of Magna Lilliputia*. Being a Lilliputian Correspondent was the first well paid job that Samuel Johnson had.[18]

3

It was an accident of history that Johnson arrived on the scene as an ambitious young writer, willing and ready to bend his skills to political journalism, at the final stages of the career of Sir Robert Walpole. Johnson was to write in his *Preface to Shakespeare* some years later that Elizabethan tragedy was not 'a poem of more general dignity or elevation than comedy; it required only a calamitous conclusion, with which the common criticism of that age was satisfied, whatever lighter pleasure it afforded in its progress.'[19] As a young writer he appeared on the scene opportunely to observe and portray the spectacular and calamitous fall from office of the presiding political genius whose personality undoubtedly dominated the first half of the eighteenth century. The fail of Orgilio was nigh when Edward Cave employed the young Johnson in the offices of the *Gentleman's Magazine* in St. John's Gate.

Walpole's career had not been a glittering or untarnished success, but it had been—until the late 1730s—apparently unstoppable. The deaths of Stanhope in 1721 and Sunderland in 1722, and the despatch of Carteret to Ireland in 1724, removed his most serious rivals.[20] He bought favour in the Commons and exercised sole influence over George I.[21] One obvious measure of his success was the frequency of his decoration. He was made a Knight Bachelor in 1725, a Knight of the Garter in 1726 (the first Commoner Blue Ribbon since 1660),[22] and in 1723 his eldest son had been made a peer. The *Craftsman* described parliament as 'a Polyglott with 500 Mouths and as many Tongues . . . his Mane and his Tail were tied up with *red Ribbons* at vast expence; but he was usually led by the Nose with the *blue one*.'[23] By manipulating the matter of the royal allowances and influencing George II through his wife, Queen Caroline of Ansbach, while others mistakenly sought favour through the new king's mistress, the future Countess of Suffolk,[24] Robert Walpole ensured the survival of his political influence after the sudden death of George I in 1727. As he himself commented: 'I have the right sow by the ear.'

The basic principles of his policies were simple—peace abroad and prosperity at home. These required his maintaining the alliance with France, encouraging colonial trade by removing restrictions 1730–35, and aiding the landowning class (his main support) by adjusting the taxes paid on land, while raising revenues from alternative sources. His Excise Bill (1733), Gin Act (1736), Playhouse Act (1737) and unpopular foreign policy made him enemies within his own party (led by William Pulteney, later Earl of Bath) and at court. But he managed to steer a safe course through these stormy waters, at least until the crisis with Spain in 1737. Even George II had to admit his courage: 'He is a brave fellow. He had more spirit than any man I ever knew.'[25]

But there were serious signs of Walpole's growing unpopularity. His attempts to restrict smuggling and regulate trade were interpreted as assaults on British liberties, and there were riots in Edinburgh and London. The city interests in London were disaffected towards him. His attempts to prevent satiric stage attacks on his policies were resented. He lost the support of Frederick Prince of Wales by opposing the increase to his allowances. The death of his great protectress Queen Caroline of Ansbach in November 1737 was a serious blow. Frederick controlled boroughs in the county of Cornwall, and he attracted the support of Pitt and the Greville family.[26] It was the war with Spain which brought Robert Walpole's career to catastrophe. Johnson's account of these final scenes is more moving than his unsuccessful attempt at tragedy, *Irene.*

4

Public attention now turned to Britain's relations with Spain. The claim was made that English traders to the West Indies were roughly handled by Spanish officials searching for contraband. It was claimed that one Robert Jenkins, master mariner, had his ear cut off by a coastguard. The question raised was whether the Spanish had the right to search our vessels. Sir Robert Walpole's seemed to be the sole voice for peace. The Lords passed resolutions on 2 May 1738 against the Spanish right to search, but Walpole managed to exclude this resolution from the Commons. The clamour for war with Spain continued during the autumn, while Walpole exerted all the diplomatic muscle he could through his minister at Madrid, Sir Benjamin Keene.[27] Keene was able to negotiate a convention with Spain. While this was achieved, Walpole managed to get parliament prorogued, and it did not assemble again until 1 February 1739. The convention provided for a settlement of disputes within eight months, which would be negotiated between specially appointed plenipotentiaries. Walpole feared that war with Spain would precipitate a French invasion and a Jacobite rebellion. One of our major markets—Spanish America—could only be maintained by force. It was known that much of our trading there was illegal. English settlers were beginning to make their claim to Honduras by cutting logwood on the coast, and our colonization of Georgia brought us into conflict with the Spanish in

Florida.[28] These attempts at peace with which Walpole hoped to paper over the cracks were described by William Pitt as 'an insecure, unsatisfactory, dishonourable convention'. The popular cry of the day was 'No search!' Although Walpole spoke well in the Commons in defence of his policies, the address of approval was only carried by a majority of twenty-eight on 8 March 1739. Some of his enemies combined to form a group, the Patriots, led by Sir William Wyndham,[29] who resolved to secede from the Commons the next day.

Walpole's answer was to push through measures which would gain him support from the commercial interests, granting to molasses and sugar the same principle of free export which applied to rice, and removing duties from Irish wool and woollen yarn and preventing their being exported to anywhere but Great Britain. By these means he hoped to have the powerful of the land behind him when the time came to ratify the Convention in May 1739.

Walpole knew that the British demand for the rejection of the right claimed by the Spanish to search British vessels for contraband would be the core of the discussion. It was. Two of his colleagues—the Duke of Newcastle and the Earl of Hardwicke—both spoke on behalf of the nation in taking a high-handed tone with the Spanish.[30] George II was of the war party. Against his better judgement Walpole instructed Keene to demand the surrender of the right to search. The Spanish refused. On 19 October 1739 war was declared amid popular acclaim. 'They now ring the bells,' he said, 'they will soon ring their hands.' His career in public office now reached its climax.

The catastrophe was worthy the pen of a tragedian. Samuel Johnson rose to the task. His handling of these final moments of Walpole's career is very interesting. The most obvious quality to be noticed in Johnson's account of the debates which brought Walpole's public life to an end is the position of sympathy in which he is placed. Reading the *Debates* as a drama one would be bound to describe Sir Rub Walelop, as he appears in the Senate of Lilliput, as the tragic hero. In giving Walpole such a good press Johnson was in part yielding to his own instincts as an author, and shaping political material which had come into his hands with the almost unconscious skill of the true artist. But he was also guided by political motives. The fact is that Walpole's career was terminated by a faction of his own party. To paint this group as the goodies in a dramatic version of events would not serve the ends of Johnson's Toryism. I further believe that the curmudgeon in Johnson drove him to give Walpole a fair hearing in the face of all the opposition stacked against him.

Walpole was a sick man. Bad health had dogged him all his days. In the summer of 1710 he had suddenly been taken ill, and his life had been feared.[31] He recovered. On 3 May 1715 he was again taken seriously ill for a month. In the spring of 1716 his life was again despaired of and he convalesced in Chelsea. He wrote to his brother Horatio on 11 May, 'I gathered strength daily . . . from the lowest and weakest condition that ever poor mortal was alive in.' In April 1927 he further showed signs of considerable physical weakness. In June of this year, when living in daily fear of his dismissal by George II, he received a visit from Arthur Onslow,[32] who found him in a very weak condition. Walpole burst into tears and declared: 'he would never leave the court if he could have any office there, and would be content even with the comptroller's staff.'[33] Now, at the very crisis of his career, he was suffering from two terrible ailments—gout and the stone. Alexander Pope wrote at this time: 'And all agree, Sir Robert cannot live.'[34] He could have resigned. In fact he twice attempted to, but George II begged him 'not to desert him in his greatest difficulties'.[35] It is hard to deny him the status of a political tragic hero. His policies had collapsed around him. He had no recourse but to stay in office, broken in health, because he could not resign, and compelled to wage a war he had done his best to avoid. Additionally he was burdened by the sure knowledge that there would be considerable pressure to have him impeached, as he had been the sole advocate for peace. He knew that Newcastle, the greatest borough-monger of them all, was already working against him behind the scenes, and that the Duke of Argyll, his chief advisor in Scotland, had gone over to the opposition.[36] Even the elements, true to the manner of poetic drama, turned against him. From 1715 until 1740 Britain had enjoyed abundant harvests, with only two minor exceptions in 1727 and 1728. But the winter of 1739–40 was a long and cruel one, with severe frost and resulting distress. Bread prices rose, there were public riots, and Sir Robert Walpole got the blame for this as well.[37]

Tory opposition to him was weakened by the divisions which existed between Bolingbroke and Pulteney, rivals for the leadership after the death of Wyndham in 1740. The war was not going well and Britain faced the storm on the continent alone.[38] A scapegoat was clearly called for. The process of Walpole's toppling was put in motion in the House of Lords on 13 February 1741 when Lord Carteret introduced a motion to address the king requesting Walpole's dismissal, and Samuel Sandys, M.P. for Worcester, introduced the same motion in the Commons.[39]

On 25 April 1741 George II's second parliament was dissolved, and the new parliament assembled on 1 December. Walpole's majority had gone. The Pelhams and Hardwicke, his former cronies, came to terms with the opposition Whigs, with the proviso that Sir Robert Walpole was not to be persecuted. On 9 January 1742 he was made Earl of Orford. Two days later he resigned his offices.

Johnson's account of these proceedings achieves dramatic grandeur; it is among the finest things he composed. He was writing within severe restrictions. He was recreating events he had not personally witnessed, handling issues of considerable complexity and attempting dramatic verisimilitude.[40] His version of the debate in the Lords of 13 February 1741 appeared in July and August 1741. He reports eleven of the speeches on the main motion for removing Walpole, and the course of the debate is well balanced. Carteret appears in the Lilliputian version as Hurgo Quadrert and his speech covers twelve pages. His argument is a mixture of national pride as Britain (Lilliput) faces the combined might of France and Spain (Blefuscu and Iberia) and outrage at the folly of the nation's commercial policy:

> Nor has our Trade . . . been only contracted by the Piracies of *Iberia*, but has been suffered to languish and decline at Home, either by criminal Negligence, or by their compliance for *Blefuscu*, which has given rise to other Calamities. The State of our Woollen Manufactures is well known, and those whose Indolence or Love of Pleasure keep them Strangers to the other

Misfortunes of their Country, must yet have been acquainted with this, by the daily Accounts of Riots and Insurrections, raised by those who having been employed in that Manufacture, can provide for their Families by no other Business, and are made desperate by the Want of Bread.[41]

The motion was opposed by the Duke of Newcastle, supported by Hardwicke, Cholmondeley, the Bishop of Salisbury and Hervey.[42] In part it might be Johnson's sense of the dramatic which prompted him to portray the attempted support of Walpole in the way that he did, but it is certainly effective. He seems to be true to character. Newcastle's speech is rather heavily elaborated, and Lord Hervey's is passionate, almost shrill—as Hurgo Heryef he concludes:

To condemn a Man unheard is an open and flagrant Violation of the first Law of Justice, but it is still a wider Deviation from it to punish a Man unaccused; no Crime has been charged upon this Gentleman proportioned to the Penalty proposed by the Motion, and the Charge that has been produc'd is destitute of Proof.

Let us therefore . . . reverence the great Laws of Reason and Justice, let us preserve our high Character and Prerogative of Judges, without descending to the low Province of Accusers and Executioners, let us so far regard our Reputation, our Liberty, and our Posterity, as to reject this motion.[43]

The debate lasted eleven hours. When put to the vote the motion was defeated 108 to 59.

The debate in the House of Commons (Clinabs) on the same day did not appear in *The Gentleman's Magazine* until eighteen months after the report of the debate in the Hurgos[44]: that is to say, a full two years after the events it recounts. It may be that Edward Cave considered the speeches too robust, violent and painful, and that it was not wise to print them while Sir Robert Walpole was still in office. Certainly there was much cut and thrust and plenteous blood was drawn.

Samuel Sandys, introducing the motion, gave a fiery speech which referred to the 'Corrupters of the Country', 'the Enemies of Commerce', 'the Deserters of their Allies' and 'the Corrupter and his Associates, the Lacqueys of his Train'. This was simple and brutal, but we sense a vastly higher level of mentality in the finely honed rhetoric of William Pitt (Ptit):

> The minister who neglects any just Opportunity of promoting the Power or increasing the Wealth of his Country is to be considered as an Enemy to his fellow Subjects; but what Censure is to be passed upon him who betrays that Army to a Defeat, by which Victory might be obtained; impoverishes the Nation whose Affairs he is intrusted to transact by those Expeditions which might enrich it, who levies Armies only to be exposed to Pestilence, and compels them to perish in sight of their Enemies without molesting them?
>
> It cannot surely be denied that such conduct may justly produce a Censure more severe than that which is intended by this Motion, and that he who has doomed Thousands to the Grave, who has co-operated with foreign Powers against his Country, who has protected its Enemies and dishonoured its Arms, should be deprived not only of his Honours but of his Life; that he should be at least stripped of those Riches which he has amassed during a long Series of prosperous Wickedness, and not barely be hindered from making new Acquisitions, and increasing his Wealth by multiplying his Crimes.[45]

The presentation of Sir Robert Walpole's final speech reveals Johnson's genius as a writer of political journalism which, in his hands, becomes the stuff of high drama. It is important to stress that this moment is actually constructed by Johnson. If we compare it with other respectable historical sources, we see immediately that the creative writer in Johnson has taken over entirely. The account given in William Coxe's *Life of Sir Robert Walpole* (1798) is dignified if not indignant, prolix, and packed with an almost paranoid detail.[46] Walpole, really the accused in a trial, is now the focus of attention. What will he say in his own defence? In Johnson's version he begins by requesting to know the whole accusation before he addresses himself to his defence. This is a fine stroke, as it prepares us finally for his great moment, and brings the whole matter into sharp relief. William Pulteney (Pulnub) summarizes the case against him.[47] Walpole then answers:

> The Gentlemen who have already spoken in my Favour have indeed freed me from the Necessity of wearying the House with a long Defence, since their Knowledge and Abilities are so great that I can hope to add Nothing to their Arguments, and their Zeal and their Friendship are so ardent, that I shall speak with less Warmth in my own Cause. . . .

He goes on to say that if they suffer the terrors of a dream in which the army is annually established by his authority, in which the disposal of all posts and honours is his alone, and in which he uses this power only to the destruction of liberty and of the nation's commerce, then compassion would compel us to awaken them from these painful delusions, so that by opening their eyes they would clearly see that

> the Prerogative has made no such Incroachments, that every Supply is granted by the Senate, and every Question debated with the utmost Freedom, as before that fateful Period in which they were seized with this political Delirium that so long harrassed them with the Loss of Trade, the Approach of Slavery, the Power of the Crown, and the Influence of the Minister.

The irony is masterly, coming as it does after his use of the defence offered by his supporters. Beneath the seeming breadth and generosity of his utterance there is the reduction of his enemies' case to the level of dream and delusion. Beneath calm surface eloquence lurks the monster of contempt.

The final thrusts come when he replies to Pulnub's charges of personal corruption, which he apparently fails to understand. How could he be accused of rapacity? or avarice? or excessive demands upon His Majesty's liberality?

> Since, except the Places which I am known to possess, I have obtained no Grant from the Crown, or fewer at least than perhaps any Man who has been supposed to have enjoyed the Confidence of his Sovereign. All that has been given me is a little House at a small Distance from this City, worth about Seven Hundred Pounds, which I obtained that I might enjoy the Quiet of Retirement without remitting my Attendance on my Office.

He then gives his attention to the order on his shoulder, for which he had so often been attacked, which, he says, he had almost forgotten to mention:

> But this surely cannot be mentioned as a Proof of Avarice; though it may be looked on with Envy and Indignation in another Place, can it be supposed to raise any Resentment in this House, where Many must be pleased to see those Honours which their Ancestors have worn restored again to the Commons.[48]

He then awaits the verdict of the House with a calm arrogance worthy of Coriolanus:

> Having now, Sir, with due Submission offered my Defence, I shall wait the Decision of the House without any other Solicitude than for the Honour of their Counsels, which cannot but be impaired if Passion should precipitate, or Interest pervert them. For my Part, that Innocence which has supported me against the Clamour of the Opposition will establish my Happiness in Obscurity, nor shall I lose by the Censure which is now threatened any other Pleasure than that of serving my Country.[49]

When the motion was put to the vote, Walpole was saved. He had a majority of 290 to 106 votes. William Shippen[50] and thirty-four Jacobite Tory M.P.s walked out of the House, and several Tories took the lead offered by Edward Harley[51] and voted for Walpole.

It was the election of midsummer 1741 which destroyed Walpole. Whig support in Scotland was whittled away, and the influence exerted by the Prince of Wales over boroughs in Cornwall gave Whig seats to Lord Falmouth and Thomas Pitt of Boconnoc. Walpole now saw the end of his political career was inevitable. His son Horace Walpole has left a description of him at this time, sitting 'without speaking, and with his eyes fixed for an hour together'. But he still hoped against hope. He believed that a promised increase in income of £50,000 a year to the Prince of Wales might remove the Prince's support for the opposition, and that the Tories might be unable to form a government. Although conscious that his support in the Commons was diminishing, he defended his war policy against the attacks of Pulteney: 'He exceeded himself; he particularly entered into foreign affairs, and convinced even his enemies that he was thoroughly master of them. He actually dissected Mr. Pulteney.'[52] It was finally his family who persuaded him to resign.[53] On 9 February 1742 he was created Earl of Orford, and on the 11th he resigned. He was awarded a pension of £4,000 a year. George II wept.

5

It is a deeply enjoyable irony that Walpole's very attempts to restrict satiric attacks on his policies and limit discussion of his activities should have resulted in his being immortalized in the majestic prose of one of the giants of our literature. Johnson's achievement as a political journalist is indeed a worthy one. By putting these accounts of parliamentary debates in circulation—however craftily disguised and dramatically written up they may be—Johnson contributed generously and characteristically to the further development of our nation's political consciousness. And this achievement must place him in company which would certainly have surprised him, for he therefore belongs with John Wilkes, William Cobbett, William Hazlitt and the other ornaments of our radical tradition. Henry Flood, M.P. for Winchester, who knew Johnson, once declared that he would not have made a very good parliamentarian, as, 'having been long used to sententious brevity and the short flights of conversation, [he] might have failed in that continued and expanded kind of argument, which is requisite in stating complicated matters in publick speaking.'[54] But Johnson made his own invaluable contribution to that much wider and more significant continuous and expanded kind of argument. Albert Camus asked: 'What is a rebel? A man who says no.' Throughout Mark Twain's discourse with the world there is an implied 'Oh yeah?' Samuel Johnson's contribution was the civilized 'yes but'. It is a just and fitting coincidence that Cobbett inhabited the rooms in Bolt Court once used by Samuel Johnson.[55]

NOTES

1. See Walter Jackson Bate, *Samuel Johnson* (London: Chatto and Windus, 1978), pp. 175ff.
2. See Maynard Mack, 'Wit and Poetry and Pope: Some Observations on his Imagery' in *Eighteenth-Century English Literature: Modern Essays in Criticism*, ed. James L. Clifford (London: Oxford University Press, 1959), pp. 33–4.
3. *Lives*, Vol. 3, p. 176.

4. See Yale, Vol. 6, pp. 47–52; for Orgilio as Walpole, see J. P. Hardy, *Reinterpretations: Essays on Poems by Milton, Pope, and Johnson* (London: Routledge and Kegan Paul, 1971), pp. 113ff.
5. See Yale, Vol. 10.
6. Sir John Hawkins, *Life of Samuel Johnson* (London, 1787), p. 514.
7. *Johnsonian Miscellanies*, ed. G. B. Hill (Oxford: Clarendon, 1897), Vol. 2, p. 309. The comment was made by William Seward (1747–99), man of letters, a friend of Johnson.
8. Johnson in *The Gentleman's Magazine*, January 1739, p. 3.
9. 'We must confront the highly centralised, and secretive, power that still characterizes our society under a government that is centralising every day' (Tony Benn in the *Guardian*, 3 October 1983). See Stuart Gerry Brown, 'Dr. Johnson and the Old Order', *Marxist Quarterly*, 1, October–December 1937, pp. 418–30, reprinted in *Samuel Johnson: A Collection of Critical Essays*, ed. Donald J. Greene (Englewood Cliffs, New Jersey: Prentice Hall, 1965), pp. 158–71.
10. See Christopher Hill, *Reformation to Industrial Revolution* (Harmondsworth: Penguin, 1971), pp. 197ff.; Samuel Rawson, *The Constitutional Documents of the Puritan Revolution 1625–1660* (Oxford: Clarendon, 1906), pp. 374ff.; F. S. Siebert, *Freedom of the Press in England 1476–1776* (Urbana, University of Illinois Press, 1952), pp. 346–52.
11. John Arbuthnot, *The John Bull Pamphlets* (1712); Jonathan Swift, *The Drapier's Letters* (1724), and *Gulliver's Travels* (1726); John Gay, *The Beggar's Opera* (1728); Alexander Pope, *The Dunciad*, Books I–III (1728); John Gay, *Polly* (1729); Jonathan Swift, *A Modest Proposal* (1729). Book IV of *The Dunciad* dates from 1742. These works establish a tradition of social and political satirical debate which we tend to think of as characteristic of the eighteenth century, and the tradition continues in the pamphleteering of John Wilkes, *The Letters of Junius*, (1769–71), and Smollett's *Adventures of an Atom* (1769).
12. Abel Boyer (1667–1729) came to England from Upper Languedoc in 1689 and was employed as French tutor to William, Duke of Gloucester. He developed a flourishing printing and publishing trade in London.
13. Walpole had been supported early in his career by Sarah, Duchess of Marlborough, and was recognized leader of the Whigs by 1703. By 1711 he was leader of the House of Commons, but was damaged by the fall of Marlborough. He was imprisoned in 1712 on charges of venality in the Navy accounts. His support of the Hanoverian succession and his leading the prosecution of Oxford, Bolingbroke, Stafford and Ormonde in 1715 for intrigue with the Stuarts again established his political authority. The Jacobite rising of 1715 confirmed his status. He was driven from office by the manipulations of Stanhope and Sunderland in 1717 and for a time joined forces with the Tory opposition.
14. Quoted in S. E. Ayling, *The Georgian Century 1714–1837* (London: Harrap, 1966), p. 118.
15. For accounts of the struggles between Walpole, ministerial control and the press, see L. Hanson, *The Government and the Press* (Oxford: Clarendon,

1936), and I. R. Christie, *Myth and Reality: The British Newspaper in the Later Georgian Age* (London: Macmillan, 1970).

16. See Dorothy Marshall, *Eighteenth-Century England* (London: Longmans, 1982), pp. 67–8 and C. B. Really, 'The London Journal', *Bulletin of the University of Kansas Humanistic Studies*, Vol. 5, No. 3 (1935), 10ff.
17. *The Dunciad*, ed. James Sutherland (London: Methuen, 1943, repr. 1965), pp. 311–12. This is a comment on Book II, line 314. See also J. B. Owen, *The Rise of the Pelhams* (London: Methuen, 1957), Ch. 1.
18. J. P. Hardy, *Samuel Johnson: A Critical Study* (London: Routledge and Kegan Paul, 1979), pp. 34–6, 41ff.; W. J. Bate, *Samuel Johnson*, pp. 162–71; John Wain, *Samuel Johnson* (London: Macmillan, 1980), pp. 79–82; James L. Clifford, *The Young Samuel Johnson* (London: Heinemann, 1959), p. 148; Boswell, *Life*, Vol. 1, p. 115ff.
19. 1765: Yale, Vol. 7, p. 68.
20. Dorothy Marshall, op. cit., p. 130.
21. J. B. Owen, op. cit., pp. 55–7; Lewis Namier, *The Structure of Politics at the Accession of George III* (London: Macmillan, 1960, pp. 28ff.; J. H. Plumb, *Sir Robert Walpole: The Making of a Statesman* (London: Cressett Press, 1956), pp. 353ff.
22. In modern times Sir Winston Churchill and Sir Anthony Eden have been similarly honoured.
23. *The Craftsman*, 22 July 1727.
24. Henrietta Howard (1681–1767), bedchamber woman to Caroline when she was Princess of Wales. A celebrated beauty, she was the original of Pope's Chloe. See Alan Bold and Robert Giddings, *True Characters* (London: Longmans, 1984), p. 55. For Walpole's survival after George I's death, see Lord Hervey, *Some Materials Towards Memoirs of the Reign of King George II*, ed. Romney Sedgwick (London: Eyre and Spottiswoode, 1931), Vol. 1, p. 22ff.).
25. For a brief summary of these early years of Walpole's administration see Keith Feiling, *A History of England* (London: Macmillan 1969), pp. 654–59. This period saw the vast influx of wealth to this country as the result of his economic policies. See Robert Giddings, 'Smollett and the West Indian Connexion' in *Smollett: Author of the First Distinction*, ed. Alan Bold (London: Vision Press, 1982), pp. 55–8.
26. For an interesting discussion of the influence exerted by Frederick, see Betty Kemp, 'Frederick Prince of Wales' in *The Silver Renaissance*, ed. A. Natan (London: Macmillan, 1961), pp. 38ff.
27. Keene (1697–1757) was a skilled diplomatist. An agent for the South Sea Company in Spain, Consul at Madrid in 1724, and our Ambassador there in 1727–39 and (after the Spanish war) 1748–57. He died in Madrid.
28. Feiling, op. cit., pp. 658–59; Gerald Graham, *A Concise History of the British Empire* (London: Thames and Hudson, 1972), pp. 62–7.
29. Wyndham (1687–1740), 3rd Baronet, Tory M.P. for Somerset. A staunch Jacobite, he was implicated in the Jacobite rebellion of 1715: a firm supporter of Bolingbroke.
30. Thomas Pelham-Holles (1693–1768), first Duke of Newcastle. A Whig and initially a supporter of Walpole, and his Secretary of State. He

became Premier in 1754 but retired two years later. Philip Yorke (1690–1764), first Duke of Hardwicke, was Lord Chancellor from 1737, later holding office under Newcastle. Remembered for presiding over the trial of the rebel Lords in 1745, and promoting the laws which forbade the wearing of tartan.

31. His clerk, James Taylor, wrote to Walpole's brother, Horatio (16 June 1710) that he was suffering from 'collero morbus'.
32. Arthur Onslow (1691–1768): Whig M.P. for Guildford and later for Surrey 1728–61, Speaker of the House of Commons. Onslow left interesting accounts of contemporary politics and politicians. See the *Onslow MSS* in *Historical Manuscripts of the House of Commons* 1895, 14th *Report, Appendix, Part ix.*
33. *Onslow MSS*, p. 517.
34. '1740. A Poem' in *Imitations of Horace*, ed. John Butt (London: Methuen, 1939, repr. 1969), p. 334.
35. William Coxe, *Memoirs of the Life and Administration of Sir Robert Walpole, Earl of Orford* (London, 1798), 1, 625.
36. Archibald Campbell (1682–1761): 3rd Duke of Argyll, Keeper of the Privy Seal 1725 and of the Great Seal 1734–61. He later advised the raising of Highland regiments in 1746, after the second Jacobite rebellion. His defection was a serious blow to Walpole's political machinery.
37. See Thomas Tooke, *A History of Prices* (London, 1838), p. 43, and *The Gentleman's Magazine*, IX (January 1739), 7–10.
38. Our victory in Porto Bello in 1739 was eclipsed by the failure of the expeditions in the Main and Cuba in 1741. The catastrophic campaign at Cartagena, portrayed by Smollett in *Roderick Random* (1748), brought great suffering. Smollett served on H.M.S. *Chichester* (see Robert Giddings, *The Tradition of Smollett* (London: Methuen, 1967), pp. 87–91). The death of the Emperor Charles VI at the end of 1740 brought the union of France and Spain with the aims of Frederick II of Prussia to partition Hapsburg lands and place the Elector of Bavaria on the imperial throne (see Johnson's memoirs of Frederick, *Gentleman's Magazine*, 1756). The French occupation of Prague and an additional French army in the Rhineland caused George II to conclude a treaty of neutrality between France and Hanover without consulting Walpole. The alliance with France had been a cornerstone of Walpole's European policy.
39. Sandys (1695–1770) had long opposed Robert Walpole, from the moment of the Excise Bill onwards. He was a member of the Committee of Enquiry into Walpole's conduct in 1742. He was created Baron Sandys in 1743. John Carteret (1690–1763), later first Earl Granville, was the son of Baron Carteret and a long standing rival of Walpole. He had been Secretary of State in Walpole's administration, 1721–24. Carteret was a favourite of George I as a result of his speaking fluent German and supporting pro-Hanoverian policies. Walpole got rid of him by sending him to Ireland as Lord Lieutenant, 1724–30. Although he attempted to prosecute Swift after the publication of the *Drapier's Letters*, the two became warm friends, and intrigued against Walpole in and out of Parliament. Carteret's motion was seconded by Bertie Willoughby

(1692–1760), 3rd Earl of Abingdon, and supported by John Campbell (1678–1743), 2nd Duke of Argyll, Henry Howard (1694–1758), 4th Earl of Carlisle, George Montagu Dunk (1716–71), 2nd Earl of Halifax, and John Russell (1710–71), 4th Duke of Bedford.

40. Sir John Hawkins (1719–89), author and student of politics, who knew Johnson well through connections in *The Gentleman's Magazine*, asserted that the style of each speaker was accurately represented. Later critics, such as George Birkbeck Hill (1835–1903), claimed that Johnson's reports displayed an ignorance of debating. See Donald J. Greene, *The Politics of Samuel Johnson* (New Haven: Yale, 1960), pp. 114ff.; Medford Evans, *Johnson's Debates in Parliament*, dissertation, Yale University, 1933; Benjamin B. Hoover, *Samuel Johnson's Parliamentary Reporting* (Berkeley and Los Angeles: University of California Press, 1953); John Butt's review article on Hoover, *R.E.S.*, n. s., VIII (Oct. 1956), 433–35; F. V. Bernard, 'Johnson and the Authorship of the Four Debates', *P.M.L.A.*, LXXXII (1967), 408–19; Donald J. Greene, 'Some Notes on Johnson and *The Gentleman's Magazine*', *P.M.L.A.*, LXXIV (1979), 75–84. The *Debates* which Johnson wrote for *The Gentleman's Magazine* were reprinted several times, almost immediately after they first appeared in Cave's magazine—by John Torbuck (1739–42), Ebeneezer Timberland (1743), and William Sandby (1744). They appeared in *Cobbett's Parliamentary History of England from the Norman Conquest to the Year 1803*, ed. John Wright, Vols. XI and XII, printed by T. C. Hansard in 1812.
41. *The Gentleman's Magazine*, XI (July 1741), 347.
42. See note 30, above. George Cholmondeley (1703–70), 3rd Earl of Cholmondeley, Thomas Sherlock (1678–1761), Bishop of Salisbury, and John Hervey (1696–1743), Baron Hervey of Ickworth, a friend of Lady Mary Wortley Montagu. He was several times attacked by Pope, who immortalized him as Lord Fanny, and Sporus in his *Epistle to Dr. Arbuthnot*. Hervey's *Memoirs of the Reign of George II*, an invaluable sourcebook of the period, were edited by J. W. Croker in 1848: see also notes 24 and 47.
43. *The Gentleman's Magazine*, XI (August 1741), 416.
44. *The Gentleman's Magazine*, XIII (March 1743).
45. Ibid., p. 133.
46. Cf. Coxe, op. cit., I. 657–69, and Hoover, op. cit., pp. 96–103. Coxe seems to have worked from the account in the *London Magazine*, as well as from private authentic sources.
47. Pulteney (1684–1764) was elected Whig M.P. for Heydon in 1705. Believing that Robert Walpole was deliberately keeping him from the high office he felt he deserved, he developed into one of Walpole's most severe critics, and considerably aided Bolingbroke in *The Craftsman*. He was a leading light in the anti-Walpolean group, the Patriots. He was M.P. for Middlesex, 1734–42. A forceful advocate of the war with Spain. In 1731 he fought a duel with Lord Hervey. He was a truly fearsome orator: Walpole once said, 'I fear Pulteney's tongue more than another man's sword.'

48. He refers here to the Order of the Garter. 'Another Place' is a House of Commons term of the House of Lords. See note 22 above.
49. *The Gentleman's Magazine*, XIII (April 1743), 180–83.
50. Shippen (1673–1743): M.P. for Bramber 1707–13 and Newton 1714–43. He declared the motion was a scheme for maintaining the Whigs in power by turning out one minister only to have him replaced by another Whig.
51. Edward Harley (1699–1755), nephew of Robert Harley (1661–1724), first Earl of Oxford (who had been impeached by Walpole in 1717 for his intrigue with James Stuart, the Old Pretender), became Earl of Oxford on the death of the first Earl's son Edward in 1741. His example was followed, according to Nugent, 'by the country gentlemen to a man' (*Memoirs of Robert Earl Nugent* (London, 1898), p. 94).
52. Horace Walpole to Horace Mann, 19 Oct. 1741 (*Correspondence*, ed. W. S. Lewis *et al.* (New Haven: Yale University Press, 1937–82), Vol. 17, p. 171); Coxe, op. cit., Vol. 3, p. 588.
53. Horatio Walpole (Sir Robert's brother), *Memoirs of Horatio, Lord Walpole* (London, 1820), Vol. 1, p. 123.
54. Quoted in Boswell's *Life*, Vol. 2, p. 139.
55. Daniel Green, *Great Cobbett: The Noblest Agitator* (London: Hodder and Stoughton, 1983), p. 442.

6

The Political Character of Samuel Johnson

by HOWARD ERSKINE-HILL

1

Johnson is as firmly Tory in his general reputation as Milton is republican and revolutionary. In *The Politics of Samuel Johnson*, however, Donald Greene enters a protest against this picture. Johnson became the hero of Boswell's 'great work of art'; worse still he is caught up in the 'even larger' myth of the 'Tory'.[1] As a result our idea of Johnson is oversimplified and vulgarized. Greene's insistence on the need to be critical of Boswell as a source, to see Johnson's politics in the first place in terms of his own time, and to look behind political labels to the more complex and not necessarily consistent realities of a powerful individual mind, certainly put the study of Johnson's politics on the right track. His presentation nevertheless poses some problems. To be wary of Boswell is one thing; to brush him aside another. Further, to see Johnson in terms of his time is to rely on the accounts of the eighteenth century which the historians are still giving. The picture has significantly changed since the publication of Greene's views.[2] I propose to reconsider Johnson in this light. Some consistency of political principle in Johnson may be thought to emerge from an account which includes Johnson himself, the Boswellian record and the most recent views of some historians.

To start with historians. They may be divided for the sake of simplicity into three successive schools. The old Whig Interpretation, viewing the eighteenth century retrospectively and ideologically, presented a period in which Lockeian thought swiftly became dominant and led not only to the failure of George III's attempts to 'be a king' but to the American War of Independence and the American Constitution. In this view the eighteenth century led inexorably to the nineteenth-century reform bills and to the eventual establishment of parliamentary democracy on a universal franchise. Were that view still accepted—and it is not altogether so easy to abandon as historians have argued—then Johnson would at first sight appear as a figure of intransigently reactionary opinion. Such a picture would not only be based on Boswell, but on the most important of Johnson's political tracts, *Taxation No Tyranny* (1775). The Whig Interpretation, challenged in precept by Sir Herbert Butterfield in 1931, but in practice by Sir Lewis Namier two years earlier, gave way to the Namierite view.[3] Namier turned away from both retrospective and ideological explanation. In his analysis later eighteenth-century politics were largely explicable in terms of the material interests of groups and individuals; neither 'party' nor 'theory' were of key significance. The great merit of Namier's method was its readiness to descend from generalization to particular cases, and under his inspiration the *History of Parliament* in the form of multiple biography of the members of the Commons was begun. It is the Namierite view of the eighteenth century, as inflected in J. B. Owen's *The Rise of the Pelhams* (1965), which has been most fully assimilated by Donald Greene.[4] Johnson can in this way be made to seem a great individualist in an age of political individualism, though it would have to be conceded that Johnson was an individualist in ideas rather than in family or group interests.

It is not yet clear what name should be given to the picture yielded by the most recent phase of historical interpretation. While there is disagreement among post-Namier scholars, several recent historians have been making three primary points, each of relevance to an understanding of eighteenth-century writers. First, the new view abandons the search for a single model of eighteenth-century politics to recognize three different political systems, the first extending from 1688 to

1715, the second from 1715 to 1760, the third (the original Namier phase) from 1760 to the administrations of the younger Pitt and after. Secondly, it reinstates the importance of party and ideology in the first two periods, but not as the sole determinants of political change. Recognition that the Namierite model will not fit the evidence of the earlier eighteenth century has not prevented Namierite method from reaping a harvest of new information about both principles and material interests of the politicians of that time. In particular the multiple biography of *The History of Parliament: The House of Commons, 1715–1754*, ed. Romney Sedgwick (1970), is the firm foundation of the new historiography of the period. And among the insights gained from that great enterprise is the third point made by a number of recent historians: a serious reassessment of Jacobitism between 1689 and 1753 which, on the evidence of material interests, of diplomatic records, British and continental, and of political ideology and religion, is thus brought back from the margins of our picture of eighteenth-century politics to the centre of events.

If we think of the century or so after 1688 in the way proposed above we shall see, first, a period of vigorous party activity with a mixed pattern of 'Whig' and 'Tory' administrations holding office under the exceptionally decisive monarchies of William and Mary, William, and Anne. (It need not be much stressed that the Whigs and Tories of this time do not correspond to twentieth-century two-party systems.) Secondly, we see a period in which the dynastic question (originally sustained in the first period by the wars with France) assumes greater importance than ever as it becomes clear that the Hanoverians will give office only to Whigs. The proscription of the Tories from office between 1715 and 1760 produced a period when the court of the ruling dynasty kept one party in office, while the party out of office, from material as well as ideological considerations, looked for a restoration of the exiled dynasty, to be accomplished peacefully as had happened in 1660. Each party thus had its candidate for the throne, and the Tories, though not wholly Jacobite, were in a large measure either committed Jacobites, or penetrated by Jacobite sympathy, or opportunistically inclined towards a restoration.

Thirdly, we see a period in which, George III having ended the proscription of the Tories from office, all the material attractions of Jacobitism, and all but the most high-flying ideological attractions, melted away. Foreign support for the cause was exhausted. Jacobitism ceased to be dangerous politics and people began to talk about it more freely. Most soon forgot about it. The demise of serious Jacobitism removed one salient difference between Whig and Tory, while under a more obviously English and 'patriot' king the parties of the earlier decades of the century dissolved into the looser and less ideological groupings of the Namierite era.

Johnson's adult life is divided between the second and third periods here distinguished. The Johnson of *London*, *The Vanity of Human Wishes*, the parliamentary debates written for the *Gentleman's Magazine*, the *Dictionary* and the 'Introduction to the *Political State*' is on one side of the political divide; the Johnson of *Taxation No Tyranny*, of *The Lives of the Poets*, and above all Boswell's Johnson is on the other. It is to Boswell's Johnson that I shall now turn, since (in Greene's argument) it is through the instrumentality of Boswell that we find Johnson entangled not only in a great work of art but in the myth of the 'Tory'.

2

The *Life of Johnson*, though short on the long pre-Boswellian period, is copious in its treatment of Johnson's later years. It is not a book with a political programme but holds a variety of political opinion, expressed on different occasions and in different ways. In particular it is important to distinguish between deliberate published or written statements by Johnson, which Boswell may quote, and the provocatively or quietly intimate conversational statements through the presentation of which Boswell makes Johnson so successful a central figure in the work. From a source that can sometimes seem inexhaustible, I have attempted to make a balanced selection, attending to both tone and content of what is said.

First of all, Boswell recognized the political watershed of 1760. Commenting on the criticism Johnson incurred by defending the government in his pamphlet *The False Alarm*

(1770), Boswell refers to 'the change of system which the British court had undergone upon the accession of his present Majesty' (2. 112).[5] It is significant that this remark follows directly on from a quotation from *The False Alarm*:

> . . . the Tories, who being long accustomed to signalise their principles by opposition to the Court, do not yet consider, that they have at last a King who knows not the name of party, and wishes to be the common father of all his people.

Boswell here follows a Johnsonian lead, on record in an independent published work by Johnson. Each writer recognizes three salient features of eighteenth-century Toryism: the ideal of the paternal, non-partisan monarch; the repudiation of party in the *ideal* government; and, in practice, the long history of Tory opposition to court and administration during the earlier part of the century. These had all been key points in Bolingbroke's Tory teaching, whatever Johnson's judgement of Bolingbroke's religious views.

Boswell, of course, alludes to Johnson's *Dictionary* definition of 'Tory' ('One who adheres to the ancient constitution of the state, and the apostolical hierarchy of the church of England; opposed to a *whig*') and of 'Whig' ('The name of a faction') (1. 294); and it must be remembered that Boswell's phrase at this point, 'his own opinions, and even prejudices', applies not just to these but all Johnson's more provocative *Dictionary* definitions. Boswell's agreement with the definition of 'Tory' is later made clear (3. 175). These definitions conform with eighteenth-century Tory opinion; they are not peculiar but partisan. Prompted, perhaps, by recognition of this, Boswell later (1781) pressed Johnson for a more reasoned account which he then wrote down:

> A wise Tory and a wise Whig, I believe, will agree. Their principles are the same, though their modes of thinking are different. A high Tory makes government unintelligible : it is lost in the clouds. A violent Whig makes it impracticable: he is for allowing so much liberty to every man, that there is not power enough to govern any man. The prejudice of the Tory is for establishment; the prejudice of the Whig is for innovation. A Tory does not wish to give more real power to the Government; but that the Government should have more reverence. Then

> they differ as to the Church. The Tory is not for giving more legal power to the Clergy, but wishes they should have a considerable influence, founded on the opinion of mankind; the Whig is for limiting them and watching with a narrow jealousy.

This statement impressed Boswell by its candour and expression (4. 117–18). By candour he certainly meant its reconciliatory tone. Turning its back on all the memorably provocative sallies against vile Whigs, Whigism as a negation of all principle, the Devil as the first Whig (2. 170; 1. 431; 3. 326) etc., it supports, in a piece of perceptive analysis, the apparently paradoxical Tory aspiration towards the non-partisan. It is significant that Johnson's combative definitions were published before 1760 while his more reconciliatory distinctions were given Boswell to take down as late as 1781, when the 1714–60 Whig/Tory system was a thing of the past. In all these instances we have seen Boswell following Johnson with approval (though possibly in different degrees) and with no slanting or distortion. Unless it is contended that the above passage is an untrue record of what Johnson said in May 1781 (which Greene does not claim), then there is so far no reason to doubt the historical veracity of Boswell's 'work of art'. If further corroboration from the pages of Boswell may be allowed, the memoir of Johnson by the Rev. William Maxwell, included in the *Life* under the year 1770, draws the same portrait of the shrewd eighteenth-century Tory, living through two radically different political periods.

A further feature of Boswell's presentation is that series of remarks in which Johnson displays a marked concern with Jacobitism. Greene is here even more suspicious of Boswell, for surviving evidence has enabled him to catch him, once at least, turning Boswellian surmise into Johnsonian statement.[6] It is, however, worth considering the chief Jacobite references in the *Life* and noting the manner of their presentation. Boswell may be thought to work up with some care to his first remarkable anecdote concerning King George and King James. Under the year 1739, for example, he tells of Johnson's violent hostility to George II as an 'unrelenting and barbarous' king (1. 147). It is clear that this episode really belongs to 1753 since its occasion is the execution of the Jacobite Dr. Archibald

Cameron. Under 1746 he writes of its being well known that Johnson 'had a tenderness' for the unfortunate House of Stuart, but calls the 1745 Rebellion 'a rash attempt' and says that Johnson's literary career was only suspended in 1745–46 because he was working on the *Dictionary* (1. 176). This paragraph is soon followed by Boswell's own reminiscence of Johnson repeating 'with great energy' the verses on the execution of the Jacobite lords which had been printed in the *Gentlemen's Magazine* in April 1747 (1. 180). These verses, of unknown authorship, pity Kilmarnock, praise Balmerino, both pity and praise Radcliffe ('Steady in what he still mistook for truth'), and condemn Lovat. They have some features in common with the poem on the same subject by John Byrom, who was sufficiently Jacobite to kiss the hand of the Prince when the Highland Army came through Manchester. But Byrom's poem, unlike the one Johnson used to recite, comes close to endorsing 'the Cause/Of injur'd Monarchs and of ancient Laws'.[7]

These moments prepare the reader for the 'unrestrained frankness' of the occasion when Johnson tells Boswell that, although he has accepted a pension from George III,

> I am the same man. . . . I retain the same principles. It is true, that I cannot now curse (smiling) the House of Hanover; nor would it be decent of me to drink King James's health in the wine that King George gives me money to pay for. But, Sir, I think that the pleasure of cursing the House of Hanover, and drinking King James's health, are amply overbalanced by three hundred pounds a year. (1. 429)

It is not on the face of it a Jacobite moment; what strikes one is surely the release into a marvellous comic freedom in which it is possible to put King James and King George in the scales and let £300 settle the value. This now seems happily reduced to a matter of decency though 'the same principles' must mean a reverence for government and a preference for monarchy. Johnson's words well express a moment when many Tories felt, for the first time in nearly fifty years, that there was no need to look to the restoration of the *de jure* line. Yet immediately Boswell, far from playing the Jacobite reference up, plays it down. Johnson has seemed to admit to cursing

Hanover and pledging King James; but Boswell moves in to speak of 'an affectation of more Jacobitism than he really had' (1. 429). Yet Boswell does not dismiss the topic; there is some balance within Johnson's opinion and feeling that he wants to get right. He next tells us how Johnson (before his pension) declared 'that if holding up his right hand would have secured victory at Culloden to Prince Charles's army, he was not sure he would have held it up' (1. 430). This was a remarkable admission. Ostensibly adduced to play down Jacobitism, this reported doubt brings Johnson to the very brink of treason in any Hanoverian view. We are next told Johnson's opinion that it was become 'impossible' for James II 'to reign any longer in this country'. (This remark does not necessarily defend his deposition. It is a political observation on what will, not on what should happen, on a par with his later statement that 'if a sovereign oppresses his people to a great degree, they will rise and cut off his head': 2. 170.) Few Jacobites, whether Roman Catholic or not, by this time defended the measures of James II between 1685 and 1688. A good case of one who did not but who risked his life in the cause was Lord George Murray, the Prince's General.[8] Boswell concludes the second paragraph of his present discussion by stating that Johnson 'no doubt had an early attachment to the House of Stuart; but his zeal cooled as his reason strengthened' (1. 430).

But he has not done yet. A third paragraph is devoted to Johnson's 'pleasantry and ingenuity in talking Jacobitism', and there follows the beautiful example of Johnson's avuncular provocation, at old Mr. Langton's—' "My dear [to Mrs. Langton's niece], I hope you are a Jacobite . . ." '—with its lovely logical demonstration of the underlying religious principles of this political creed (1. 430–31). This anecdote too might seem to convey all the air of pleasure in a new freedom of political speech, and though Boswell is at pains to assign such talk to 'earlier periods' (1. 430), there is again some reason to suppose that he is ignoring chronology in conformity with his claim of an early Jacobitism that has cooled.[9]

The next salient Jacobite reference in the *Life* is Johnson's 'violent Argument' with his friend Taylor which Boswell, who was there, assigns to 18 September 1777. As usual Boswell adds some playing-down remarks ('the spirit of contradiction'—

3. 155), but nevertheless presents us with the clash between Whig and Tory on what people then thought of the House of Stuart. To Taylor's claim that they thought of it with 'abhorrence' Johnson declared:

> Sir, the state of the country is this: the people knowing it to be agreed on all hands that this King has not the hereditary right to the crown, and there being no hope that he who has it can be restored, have grown cold and indifferent on the subject of loyalty, and to have no warm attachment to any King. They would not, therefore, risk any thing to restore the exiled family. They would not give twenty shillings a piece to bring it about. But, if a mere vote could do it, there would be twenty to one; at least, there would be a very great majority of voices for it. For, Sir, you are to consider, that all those who think a King has a right to his crown, as a man has to his estate, which is the just opinion, would be for restoring the King who certainly has the hereditary right, could he be trusted with it; in which there would be no danger now, when laws and every thing else are so much advanced: and every King will govern by the laws. (3. 156)

This carefully moderated explanation, which does not *sound* like one side of a 'violent argument', gives the heart of the case for the exiled Stuarts: the enshrinement of hereditary right in the law of the land. Among the terms of the Tory lords for accepting office in 1744 had been that there should be a free parliament (i.e. one uninfluenced by patronage of the administration) which they supposed would result in a restoration, as the free convention parliament had done in 1660. This is more serious Jacobitism than the *Life* has yet disclosed in Johnson; we have now heard him put the central Tory/Jacobite case.

In the sequence of Boswell's narrative the above argument is rapidly followed up by a moral and emotional affirmation. The very next day, and in the chaise of the Whig Taylor, as Boswell and Johnson approached Derby, Boswell observed 'that we were this day to stop just where the Highland army did in 1745'. 'Johnson: "It was a noble attempt".' The peculiar interest of these conversational records is immediately underlined by the subsequent discussion as to whether a history by Boswell of the events of 1745 could be published in his lifetime. To Johnson's suggestion that it might be published abroad (as much subversive political literature had been published, or pretended to have been published), Boswell proposed the ideal of a disinterested account which might be published in Britain. The suggested title is studiedly neutral: ' "History of the Civil War in Great-Britain in 1745 and 1746" ' (3. 162). Boswell is trying to educate his reader out of prejudice. His strategy is to insinuate certain ideas and emotions into the reader's mind, at first seeking to avoid danger or offence by playing them down, later by holding up the ideal of a completely impartial presentation. This explains, I suggest, why so often the hard core of Boswell's material is slightly at odds, either in time or tone, with his presentation.

The last notable Jacobite reference in the *Life* belongs to Johnson's latest years. It links with his explanation to his Whig friend Taylor, and is occasioned by the lack of reverence for the Hanoverian government in spring 1783:

> He talked great regret and indignation of the factious opposition to Government at this time, and imputed it, in a great measure, to the Revolution. 'Sir, (said he, in a low voice, having come nearer to me, while his old prejudices seemed to be fermenting in his mind,) this Hanoverian family is *isolée* here. They have no friends. Now the Stuarts had friends who stuck by them so late as 1745. When the right of the King is not reverenced, there will not be reverence for those appointed by the King.' (4. 164–65)

It is another eloquent moment. Consistent with Johnson's argument with Taylor and with his definitions of Whig and Tory, these remarks are dramatically effective because they are a *confidence*; the 'low voice' and the drawing nearer help us to see an old man uttering his innermost convictions to an intimate friend. Despite the usual gesture of dissociation ('old prejudices'), Boswell's handling of this moment, the last stage of what has been a theme in the *Life*, makes the reader feel how far he has come from those two wonderful moments of talking for victory with which the subject of Jacobitism was introduced. If Boswell is to be trusted, it is now less easy to see Johnson's political inclination as having been modified by £300 a year.

Of less dramatic interest but of real significance is all the discussion on Non-Juring scattered through the *Life*. The following is the most important instance:

> Talking of the family of Stuart, he said, 'It should seem that the family at present on the throne has now established as good a right as the former family, by the long consent of the people; and that to disturb this right might be considered as culpable. At the same time I own, that it is a very difficult question, when considered with respect to the house of Stuart. To oblige people to take oaths as to the disputed right, is wrong. I know not whether I could take them: but I do not blame those who do.' So conscientious and delicate was he upon this subject, which has occasioned so much clamour against him. (2. 220)

This is significant on two counts. It concedes the principle of the habituation of *de facto* monarchs into legitimacy. This argument can be traced back to Jean Bodin's *Six Livres de la République* (1576) and had long been a feature of royalist thought. The difficulty lies in knowing at what stage those with reverence for Government can take an oath of allegiance to the powers that be. Johnson says that when the right is still disputed those powers should not impose oaths. And, in the light of the difficulty which he has acknowledged, he quite plainly implies that he himself has been so far (April 1773) a Non-Juror, in that he has either refused or managed to evade the Oaths. The Oaths should have been tendered to all in 1745–46. This is an important moment; there is no question here of colouring, of playing up or down. If Boswell is telling the truth, Johnson was a Jacobite-inclined non-juring Tory, at least until 1773. If he is not telling the truth, then little in the *Life* can be trusted unless specifically confirmed by reliable non-Boswellian evidence.

To sum up Boswell's political portrait of Johnson in the *Life*. Where 'Whig' and 'Tory' (but not 'Jacobite') are used, Boswell presents Johnson as a Tory along the lines of Johnson's own independent statements of what a Tory was. This generally conforms with the notion of an eighteenth-century Tory propounded by the most recent historical study, and does not, of course, conform with Greene's outline of what 'Tory' has come to mean in our time.[10] It may be conceded that Boswell often refers to Johnson as a more extreme Tory than he shows him to have been when he comes to set down Johnson's actual views.

Turning to the question of Jacobitism, we should note what was the establishment view. The Hanoverian tracts at the time of the Rebellion made much of the menace of Popery, Arbitrary Power and threat to property. Such sentiments were expressed by the Whig Akenside, of whom Johnson said that he 'retained an unnecessary and outrageous zeal for what he called and thought liberty', and who described the defeat of Prince Charles as follows:

> The tyrant from our shore,
> Like a forbidden demon, fled;
> And to eternal exile bore
> Pontific rage and vassal dread.[11]

The remarks Boswell attributes to Johnson are nothing like this. If we turn to the opposite political extreme from Akenside, to the Jacobite Byrom, nothing in his four volumes of letters and journals (though set down in his own, not entirely private, shorthand) matches Johnson's remarks—though it may be significant that Byrom was an old man by 1760 and died in 1763. No other writer of the eighteenth century, major or minor, is so far as I know on record as having made such remarks. Taken as a series and at face value they surely express Jacobite sympathy. But while the expression of such sympathy in print would have been political dynamite in earlier reigns, these are *conversations*, introduced into print long afterwards; and sympathy stops short of being commitment. Furthermore, numerous references in the *Life* show Johnson feeling a not uncritical loyalty as well as gratitude to King George III. On the issue of Jacobitism, Boswell portrays Johnson drawn two ways, in thought as in feeling. Only when he has Johnson imply that he has not taken the Oaths does he show Johnson in a clear formal position, that of the Non-Juror.

To the charge that Boswell was a sentimental Scottish Jacobite who projected his own feelings onto Johnson it can certainly be replied that Boswell everywhere makes clear his loyalty to the House of Hanover, while yet being deeply moved by the events of 1745; that 'ill-advised, but brave attempt' moved him to tears, and he could admit that 'The very Highland names, or the sound of a bagpipe, will stir my blood . . .' (5. 140; 2nd edn.). This may be what is meant by sentimental Jacobitism. His representation of Johnson as sympathetic to Jacobitism, on the other hand, has proved a more complex matter. It is hard to claim that he exaggerates Johnson's views when he constantly tries to play them down. It seems more probable that he is attempting, on a small scale, what his 'History of the Civil War in Great-Britain in 1745 and 1746' would have had to do on a large scale: to lead the reader out of partisan prejudice of either kind, so that Jacobite argument and feeling might, with Whig argument and feeling, be appreciated as features in the character of many good and great men. And here we may note that while a Johnson with Jacobite sympathy looked eccentric and archaic against the background drawn by both Whig and Namierite historians, the most recent historians, arguing for a wider prevalence of Jacobitism within the Tory outlook, enable us to see in Boswell's Johnson a more representative figure. Boswell can thus be acquitted of presenting us with the improbable. The charge of minor exaggeration his text itself seems to deny. If Boswell *has* artistically falsified the truth, he has done so by major exaggeration—even invention. But this charge can, of course, be neither confirmed nor denied from the pages of Boswell himself.

3

We must therefore pursue our investigation into the pre-Boswellian period of Johnson's career, before their meeting in 1763. At once we are struck by the narrower range of evidence. With minor exceptions there is no record of Johnson's earlier conversation to compare with what we find in Boswell. The comparison of a work published by Johnson with a conversation presented by Boswell and published only after Johnson's death is not a comparison of like with like. Johnson would not have been unusual in finding that publication involved a measure of discretion. A relevant example of this from the later period is seen from a comparison of Johnson's *Journey to the Western Islands* (1775) with his letters to Mrs. Thrale from the Hebrides. The latter show an interest in Jacobitism not revealed in the *Journey*, which Johnson may have expected

George III to read, and which the King did read.[12] There is, however, evidence, both literary and biographical, from the pre-Boswellian period which endorses Boswell's portrait.

The first piece of evidence is Johnson's *Marmor Norfolciense* (1739). The pretended excavation, translation and interpretation of a monkish prophecy concerning Britain, it is a convincing example of Scriblerian irony. Yet unlike *The Memoirs of Martinus Scriblerus* and even *A Tale of a Tub*, it encloses, at the heart of its enjoyable ironic pedantry, matter deep and dangerous. 'Then o'er the world shall Discord stretch her wings', runs the translation,

> Kings change their laws, and kingdoms change their
> kings . . .
> Nor shall the lyon, wont of old to reign
> Despotic o'er the desolated plain,
> Henceforth th' inviolable bloom invade,
> Or dare to murmur in the flow'ry glade;
> His tortur'd sons shall die before his face,
> While he lies melting in a lewd embrace;
> And, yet more strange! his veins a horse shall drain,
> Nor shall the passive coward once complain. (Yale, 10. 25)

The lion of England loses his old power; the lion of kingship cannot protect his subjects. It debauches itself in lust; a horse drains its blood. The befogged commentator notes that a lion is 'one of the supporters of the arms of England' but asks 'in what place can the English be said to be trampled or tortur'd. . . . Is not the very name of England treated by foreigners in a manner never known before?' He notes that

> a horse is born in the arms of H———. But how then does the horse suck the lyon's blood? Money is the blood of the body politic. ———But my zeal for the present happy establishment will not suffer me to pursue a train of thought that leads to such shocking conclusions. The idea is detestable, and such as, it ought to be hoped, can enter into the mind of none but a virulent Republican, or bloody Jacobite. (Pp. 40–2)

As Greene notes, the white horse of Saxony, part of the arms of the Electors of Hanover, was introduced into the royal arms of Britain from the accession of George I.

What is remarkable about this work is the way Johnson

keeps comedy and sedition going at the same time. For its thrust (though emerging from a parade of allegory and indirection) is specifically pointed and extreme. Greene's comment that 'Politically, *Marmor* is not very interesting; its targets are the commonplaces of opposition propaganda . . . (except that Johnson goes further . . . in insulting the King, and indeed kings in general)' (Yale, 10. 21) outdoes Boswell in the art of playing down. In making the common charge that government and court sacrificed the interests of England to those of Hanover, Johnson handles it in such a way that he not only reflects on George II specifically, and on kings generally, but, much more dangerous, on the Hanoverian succession precisely: the horse. This is Jacobite sedition. Sir John Hawkins, far from a Jacobite himself, perceived its drift clearly. 'The principles it contained were such as the Jacobites of the time openly avowed.'[13] A little contemporary comparison shows that *Marmor* is more virulent than the political poems of the Jacobite John Byrom, more obvious than the political attack of the Jacobite David Morgan's *The Country Bard* (1739–41),[14] and altogether more offensive to the Hanoverian Succession than those remarks in the *Works* of the Duke of Buckingham which caused Pope and his publisher to be taken up and questioned in 1723.[15] Indeed it implies the sentiments which, when plainly stated, had caused the publisher William Anderton to be executed for high treason in 1693—admittedly a more turbulent time than the 1730s. No attempt was evidently made to arrest the author of *Marmor Norfolciense*; but the rumour that a warrant had been issued and Johnson gone into hiding, first printed in Hawkins's *Life*, shows that the nature of the tract was well enough understood in its time.

A further piece of evidence tending to endorse Boswell is the letter to the Earl of Bute of 31 July 1762 recommending Johnson for a pension. We now know that this anonymous letter was from Richard Farmer, of Emmanuel College, and written in the hand of Edward Blakeway of Magdalene College, Cambridge.[16] This letter was known to Boswell only in 1793, having been sent to him by the then Earl of Bute in response to the publication of the *Life*. It thus constitutes evidence independent of Boswell. Its significance lies in the objections Farmer foresees to the securing of a government pension for Johnson, and the arguments he uses to overcome them.

> If it be objected that his political principles render him an unfit object of His Majesty's favour, I would only say that he is to be more pitied on this account, and that it may sometimes happen that our opinions however erroneous are not always in our own power.

What political principles could these be? Farmer cannot just have meant that Johnson was a Tory, since by summer 1762 it was clear to all that the long proscription of the Tories from office and favour had ended. He cannot have meant that Johnson was too much a Whig to deserve a pension. Farmer's implication is pretty obvious, but he did not need to spell it out—indeed there was a way by which he could be more precise and yet render Johnson more fit for favour. 'I am told', Farmer goes on, 'that his political principles make him incapable of being in any place of trust, by incapacitating him from qualifying himself for any such office—but a pension My Lord requires no such performances . . .'.[17] This phrasing could not be more explicit. These were the words applied to those who would not or could not take the Oaths. What Farmer is telling Bute is that Johnson is a Non-Juror. Now Farmer, though not yet acquainted with Johnson, was one of a group including Thomas Percy who knew him well and were in an excellent position to deny any false reports that Johnson was in some way disaffected towards the Hanoverian establishment. They would know too if, at the accession of the new King, Johnson had felt able to take the Oaths. Such a change would have greatly increased the chances of his being granted a pension. No such denials or announcements were made by Farmer. He admitted Johnson's 'political principles', but argued that the pension had already been earned by services to English letters and should be conferred with no implied obligation on Johnson's part to serve further administrations with his pen.

Johnson (in the words of Hawkins) 'had very little claim to the favour of any of the descendants of the House of Hanover' (Hawkins, *Life*, p. 168). It is well known that his acceptance of a pension from the King drew the attack of political and literary enemies, especially when, in 1770 and after, he had published pamphlets in support of Lord North's administration. These attacks may not (from their point of view) have been utterly groundless. As Greene and Clifford have shown in their admirable discussions of the pension episode, it is not clear that the pension actually *was* granted on literary grounds alone. We do not know whether it was Farmer's letter which secured the pension for Johnson; and if it did contribute to that decision, we do not know how fully its high-minded reasoning was shared by all the people involved.[18] The Farmer letter, undiscussed by Greene, is first-class evidence only on Johnson's political position prior to 1760. And what Farmer sought to admit and extenuate, Charles Churchill in his anti-Bute satire *The Ghost* (1762–63) makes brutally clear:

> POMPOSO; *Fame* around should tell
> How he a slave to int'rest fell. . . .
> How to all Principles untrue,
> Nor fix'd to *old* Friends nor to *New*,
> He damns the *Pension* which he takes
> And loves the STUART he forsakes. (III. 797–8, 817–20)[19]

Much of *The Ghost* is devoted to anti-Jacobite attack and there is no doubt that 'STUART' in Churchill's lines has the double allusion to both the surname of Bute's family and to the exiled royal line.

Against *Marmor Norfolciense*, the Farmer letter, and the record of Hawkins and Churchill, there is some evidence of a contrary trend. Robert Giddings reads the parliamentary debates as evidence of Johnson's sympathy with Sir Robert Walpole in the last days of his power (see above, pp. 94–5); but this was true of several parliamentary Jacobites. Commenting on James II in 'An Introduction to the Political State of Great Britain' (1756), Johnson wrote of 'the necessity of self-preservation' which 'had impelled the subjects of James to drive him from the throne . . .'. 'If a Jacobite is one who thinks James II should have retained the English throne,' Greene says, 'this uncompromising statement may be taken as evidence against the theory that SJ had "Jacobite tendencies" ' (Yale, 10. 142). We may add the anecdote of the British radical

Thomas Cooper, who remembered hearing Johnson reject 'the *jure divino* of kings', defend the right of the people to establish the government 'they may think most conducive to their interest and happiness' while at the same time affirming his own belief in monarchy (Yale, 10. xxx). It may be thought that neither of these latter pieces of evidence is intrinsically strong; in 'The Political State' for the new *Literary Magazine* Johnson may have found it prudent to conform in print with the orthodoxy of the establishment, while the Cooper anecdote was doubtless what Cooper wanted to hear, or have heard. Nevertheless Maxwell apparently recorded that Johnson 'no less respected the constitutional liberties of the people' than 'the legal and salutary prerogatives of the crown' (2. 117) while Hawkins, who saw in him a Tory with strong Jacobite prejudice, also supposed him to hold that resistance to tyranny and oppression could be lawful (Hawkins, *Life*, pp. 223–24). Many readers may settle for the common-sense view that Johnson was simply inconsistent, and that we must accept the majority opinion on his political character. But it may be worth suggesting that a belief in the legal right of the exiled Stuart line is not inconsistent with the view that it might be justifiable to resist the 'impossible' measures of a particular Stuart king. To support the hereditary (but not indefeasibly hereditary) monarchy was now an orthodox Tory position. We now know how many of the political nation were driven towards Jacobitism, not by divine right theory but material interests, and as a reaction from what they saw as Hanoverian corruption and oppression. Johnson may be thought to have shared this position.

On balance the political character of Johnson before Boswell can be seen to bear out the Boswellian portrait. Here again, but on non-Boswellian evidence, is the Non-Juror. Here again is the eighteenth-century Tory with strong Jacobite inclinations. And, just as Boswell presents both Johnson and himself as holding that a *de facto* monarchy can become legal through time and the eventual failing of the *de jure* challenge, thus rejecting indefeasible hereditary right of kings by divine commission, so there is non-Boswellian evidence that Johnson thought subjects might, in the last resort, be justified in resisting oppression by their governors.

4

Johnson is valued as a poet as well as a talker and writer of political tracts. Of his three famous poems, *London* (1738) is certainly political, the poem *On the Death of Dr. Robert Levet* (1782) is certainly not, but about *The Vanity of Human Wishes* (1749) opinion may be more divided. I shall look briefly at *London* and *Vanity* in the light of the political character set forth above.

Both the Tory Boswell and the Whiggish Hawkins found *London* a poem of bitter Tory attack on the Britain of Walpole and George II. Each of them, looking back from the late eighteenth century, saw it as part of a vanished political era which it was the task of the biographer to recall. For Hawkins 'the topics of this spirited poem' were drawn from the weekly journalism of 'a malevolent faction' 'professing themselves to be Whigs' and particularly from *The Craftsman*, 'now deservedly forgotten' (*Life*, p. 34). An unvarnished Whig view! Boswell, comprehensive and magnanimous, noted that

> The nation was then in that ferment against the court and the ministry, which some years after ended in the downfall of Sir Robert Walpole. . . . as a whig administration ruled with what force it could, a tory opposition had all the animation and all the eloquence of resistance to power, aided by the common topicks of patriotism, liberty and independence! Accordingly, we find in Johnson's *London* the most spirited invectives against tyranny and oppression. . . .

He proceeds in generous retrospect to defend the achievement of Walpole and claim (correctly) that Johnson himself came to acknowledge his merit (I. 129–31). We are again reminded of the great political divide at 1760, which had shown, what the 1730s and 1740s could not know, that the worst fears of the Tories were not to be fulfilled, fears from which exile had sometimes seemed the only way out.

London is a poem about departure and exile, a *sermo* of farewell. The body of the poem is the grieved but unrelenting condemnation uttered by the fictional Thales, his own imminent departure from the capital lending dramatic force to his judgement. His bidding farewell, prominent from the start, is brought to a climax by the double departure at the end: the King in his latest return to Hanover, Thales to 'internal exile' in Wales.

> Scarce can our Fields, such Crowds at *Tyburn* die,
> With Hemp the Gallows and the Fleet supply.
> Propose your Schemes, ye Senatorian Band,
> Whose *Ways and Means* support the sinking Land;
> Lest Ropes be wanting in the tempting Spring,
> To rig another Convoy for the K––ng. (ll. 242–47)[20]

The innuendo in the last line is a more cryptic expression of what Johnson was to say in *Marmor Norfolciense*. Not only did the Tories complain about George II's voyages to Germany to see his Hanoverian mistresses; they alleged that he drained wealth from Britain to Hanover, just as they had accused William III of draining wealth from England to Holland. The charge was an intrinsically anti-Hanoverian attack, which Hawkins, for one, had no trouble in recognizing: 'that in his visits to his native country, the king drained this of its wealth' (Hawkins, *Life*, p. 35). With the help of Boswell we can also see in this passage Johnson's view of George II as 'unrelenting and barbarous', a king of executions. As, in the corresponding part of Juvenal's Third Satire, so much iron is used for chains there is none left for ploughshares or tools, so Johnson, with a memorable mingling of anger and contempt, binds together the royal convoys and the executions at Tyburn with one rigging, the emblem of modern slavery: hemp.

If we are alert to the small print of Jacobite innuendo, we shall find in the poem a further consonant allusion to departure. Thales will, the poem tells us at the beginning, 'fix'd on Cambria's solitary Shore,/ Give to St. David one *true Briton* more' (ll. 7–8). The *True Briton* had been the journal created by the newly Jacobite Duke of Wharton in 1723–24 to defend the Jacobite leader Bishop Atterbury in his trial at the House of Lords.[21] The proceedings ended with Atterbury's departure into exile, whither Wharton was soon to follow for the final, unstable but openly Jacobite phase of his extraordinary career. The idea of Jacobite exile, therefore, lurks within the printing of Johnson's lines, and it is only necessary to recall that the pseudonymous author of *Marmor Norfolciense* was to be 'Probus Britanicus' to clinch the point.

Between the composition of *London* and *The Vanity of Human Wishes* there occurred two sensational events in the history of Britain. In 1742 Walpole fell after the longest period in power of any first minister or favourite. Three years later, as one result of a major realignment of the European powers, and after a formidable French invasion threat in support of the Jacobite claim, Prince Charles, with no military support, landed in the Highlands, gathered a small army, took Edinburgh, routed the Hanoverian troops at the Battle of Prestonpans, and seemed master of Scotland. To those who shared the pessimistic Tory/Jacobite diagnosis of the condition of Britain, expressed among other works in *London*, these two events held out startling hope for a national regeneration. The fall of a corrupt favourite, and a military bid to set the government of the land on a new footing, each seemed a way to purge the nation of a prevailing apathy and corruption. Indeed the two events were politically closely linked: the civilian and martial sides of the same new coin. By the later 1740s, as is well known, the new coin had in the eyes of discontent bought no improvement, only deeper cynicism, and the bitterness of military defeat and reprisal.

During this period the Tenth Satire of Juvenal was apt for Johnson's purpose in ways both general and specific. In general it enabled him to set forth 'the miseries that await empire, grandeur, wealth, and power, and the disappointments that frustrate the hopes of ambition, learning, eloquence and beauty' (Hawkins, *Life*, p. 87). But specifically it suited his need because the sequence of this *sermo* offered him, first, the portrait of the fall of a corrupt minister, and second, a narrative of the defeat and death of a meteoric martial hero. Juvenal thus gave Johnson the opportunity to reflect upon the fall of favourites and the challenge of arms, in the order in which these had recently been experienced by Britain.

Johnson's evident aim at comprehensiveness and generality, it may seem, has led commentators on this poem to ignore some specific political allusions. It is not right to think that generality precludes the specific; indeed it seems probable that the two are felt most powerfully when they are seen in relation—when, as can sometimes be done, specific example is superimposed on comprehensive view. It is highly probable that in the Britain of 1748 the opening of Johnson's third paragraph was meant to be specific as well as general:

> Let Hist'ry tell where rival Kings command,
> And dubious Title shakes the madded Land,
> When Statutes glean the Refuse of the Sword,
> How much more safe the Vassal than the Lord,
> Low skulks the Hind beneath the Rage of Pow'r
> And leaves the wealthy Traytor in the *Tow'r*. . . .
> Untouch'd his Cottage, and his Slumbers sound,
> Tho' Confiscation's Vulturs hover round. (ll. 29–36)

This is an exact portrait of Britain in the Rebellion and after. That such was Johnson's intention is also shown by his original choice of the word 'bonny' rather than 'wealthy' in l. 34 of the first edition. That was another coded reference (like that to the King's convoys at the end of *London*) and would have specified those Scottish Jacobite lords, after the Rebellion imprisoned in the Tower and then beheaded, whose death Johnson was later to commemorate by the recitation of other verses (l. 180). With this revision Johnson drew back from this particular specification. But as a point in his political biography, there is no doubt whom he had chiefly in mind.

As explicit, speaking as specifically to contemporary England, is the paragraph of the poem which immediately precedes the portrait of Wolsey:

> But will not *Britain* hear the last Appeal,
> Sign her Foes Doom, or guard her Fav'rites Zeal;
> Through Freedom's Sons no more Remonstrance rings,
> Degrading Nobles and controlling Kings;
> Our supple Tribes repress their Patriot Throats,
> And ask no Questions but the Price of Votes;
> With Weekly Libels and Septennial Ale,
> Their Wish is full to riot and to rail. (ll. 91–8)

These lines strike a note of parliamentary liberty, traditionally threatened by mighty favourites, and lament the decline of patriotism into corruption. The Act for Septennial parliaments (1716) was particularly associated with the coming of the Hanoverians and the Walpole era. The repeal of this Act had been one of the Tory conditions on which Gower reneged in 1742; nearly forty years later a mellower Johnson would still allude to it as 'that contempt of national right with which . . . by the instigation of Whiggism, the Commons, chosen by the people for three years, chose themselves for seven'.[22] All this ushers in the 'full-blown Dignity' of Wolsey,

> Law in his Voice, and Fortune in his Hand:
> To him the Church, the Realm, their Pow'rs consign,
> Thro' him the Rays of regal Bounty shine,
> Turn'd by his Nod the Stream of Honour flows,
> His Smile alone Security bestows. . . . (ll. 99–104)

To recall a great favourite like this Johnson's reader did not have to think back to Wolsey. To know that Wolsey here parallels Juvenal's Sejanus, is to recall a succession of three over-mighty ministers at least. No reader of *London* and other opposition poetry of the 1730s can doubt that the portrait of Wolsey also suggests a portrait of Walpole. Had not the three been linked in Tory polemic? As Pope himself had put it the same year as *London* came out: '*Sejanus*, *Wolsey*, hurt not honest *FLEURY*,/ But well may put some Statesmen in a fury' (*Epilogue to the Satires*, I. 51–2). Johnson so shapes his strategy with the particular and general, the near and the far, that 'Septennial Ale', Walpole and Wolsey assume the outline of the perennial Sejanus.

Such figures dominate the Tory nightmare of the 1730s and 1740s—the nightmare of corruption. Theirs was a 'Conquest unresisted' (l. 107); they grew great out of satisfied 'slavery' and perpetuated it. The fall of Walpole in 1742 only revealed the suppleness of the Patriot Tribes (l. 95) while George II continued to debar the principled Tories from government. Only great moral and perhaps physical courage could resist this decay. Bolingbroke had called for a renewal of the original Machiavellian *virtù*, while the Tories, perhaps for this among other reasons, had become a war rather than a peace party by the late 1730s. Into this scene of apparent inertia and decay, and after the abandonment of the major French/Jacobite invasion attempt of 1744, entered Prince Charles with his small Highland army, its chiefs 'unsullied' by a 'corrupt age', as a contemporary Jacobite poet put it,[23] and with nothing sustaining it but its rash folly (as it seemed to some) or its courage and *virtù* (as it seemed to others). In the eyes of 'the present happy establishment' it did not seem a trifling threat,

> when late we view'd
> Our fields in civil blood imbru'd?
> When fortune crown'd the barbarous host,
> And half the astonish'd isle was lost . . .

as Akenside was to put it in his Ode XVIII, Bk. I, in 1747 (*Poems*, p. 304). In Tories of Jacobite sympathy hope surged as conflicting reports came in:

> . . . great talk of the Pretender coming. . . . news is come that the rebels have beat Sir John Cope. . . . Carlisle is surrendered to the rebels. . . . a letter from Penrith says the rebels are but 7,000 men but other accounts say they are 25,000 or 30,000. . . . the P. and the main body of them came, I cannot guess how many. . . . about four o'clock the King [James III] was proclaimed, the mob shouted very cleverly. . . . an officer called on us to go and see the Prince . . . and a noble sight it is. . . .

Thus John Byrom's daughter recorded the experience from Manchester (her whole account, which has realism and humour as well as enthusiasm, is worth reading).[24] What Johnson thought of these events at the time we can only conjecture from his political character before and after. It is Hawkins, first acquainted with Johnson between 1739 and 1749, who tells of the difficulty of being a member of a club with him in the aftermath of the Jacobite defeat:

> It required . . . some degree of compliance with his political prejudices: the greater number of our company were Whigs . . . and we all saw the prudence of avoiding to call the then late adventurer in Scotland, or his adherents, by those names which others hesitated not to give them, or to bring to remembrance what had passed, a few years before, on Tower Hill. (*Life*, p. 106)

Did Johnson think at the time, as later, that the Rebellion was 'a noble attempt?' Did he, in *The Vanity of Human Wishes*, seek to express something of the experience of seeing martial valour in defeat, as he expressed the experience of seeing a mighty favourite fall? At this point in my discussion of the poem I claim only to suggest an answer.

Poetry of opposition had long been accustomed to deal in

cryptic or double allusion. Dryden in his poem 'To Congreve', ll. 45–8, spoke of Edward II and III when he wished to speak also of James II and III; in writing of William the Conqueror, in *Windsor Forest*, Pope seems also to have alluded to William III. '*Sejanus, Wolsey*' referred also to Walpole. Johnson needed a figure, *not* to supply him with a disguised portrait of Prince Charles, but whose career could convey the emotion of 1745–46 to a Jacobite sympathizer, and recall, where possible, some features of that episode of meteoric but transient conquest. Charles XII of Sweden was his answer because this monarch had long been a Tory and a Jacobite hero. A brave and resourceful military leader, a Protestant, a king inveterately opposed to the interests of Hanover, Charles XII was believed to have backed the Jacobite conspiracy of 1716–17.[25] '*Swedish Charles*' could remind of '*Scottish Charles*'.[26] That Scottish Charles, back in exile in France after his defeat at Culloden, reminded of Swedish Charles is a matter of record. On his arrest after the Treaty of Aix la Chapelle,

> Some people compare his Conduct on this Point with that of Charles XII. King of Sweden at *Bender*, and imagine that, had he been attacked in his own House, he would have defended himself as well as that Prince did.

A separate comparison of Prince Charles's situation with that of Charles XII at Bender had reached John Byrom at Manchester soon after 10 December 1748 (N.S.).[27] This, at all events, is the phase of the lost leader which comes through strongly in Johnson's poem:

> The vanquish'd Hero leaves his broken Bands,
> And shews his Miseries in distant Lands;
> Condemn'd a needy Supplicant to wait
> While Ladies interpose, and Slaves debate. (ll. 211–14)

In the case of Wolsey, Sejanus in the Juvenalian original already suggested Walpole; it was a cant term for him. '*Swedish Charles*' and Hannibal were not, I believe, cant terms, but Hannibal had, for obvious reasons perhaps, also been already associated with the Jacobite threat. Defoe was the probable author of *Hannibal at the Gates: or, the Progress of Jacobitism. With the present danger of the Pretender* (1712).[28] There was a revised second edition in 1714, which answered *Hannibal Not at our*

Gates, Or, An Enquiry into the Grounds of our present Fear of Popery and the Pretender. Hannibal represented, in these eyes, an alien power and religion. After 1715 and 1745 he had in common with the two Pretenders that he came from the south but invaded from the north. After 1745 the fact that Prince Charles turned back from Derby when many believed he had London at his mercy may have prompted comparisons with Hannibal's withdrawal from the gates of Rome and eventual retreat by sea. In 'Verses pasted on the Gates of M. Puissieux', appended to *A Satyr: In French and English* . . . (Paris, 1749), Prince Charles was called a Hannibal in a wholly laudatory sense. Protesting at the Prince's arrest in Paris after the Treaty of Aix-la-Chappelle, the poem hails him as '*A Hannibal*, the Glory of Mankind!/ Fair *Albion*'s Prince! who were Desert obey'd,/ Of Earth's vast Empire would be Emp'ror made' (pp. 6–7).[29] This particular publication, though too late to have influenced Johnson, may derive from a source which did, and is certainly suggestive in terms of the present argument. Johnson's later reflections on Hannibal and Charles XII are also suggestive: in *Rambler* 127 that Hannibal had not known how to use the victory he gained; in *Adventurer* 102 that it was a moot point whether he lost Italy 'by his own negligence or the corruption of his countrymen'; in *Adventurer* 99 on political projectors who aim at vast achievements with small means: Columbus, Alexander the Great, Charles XII and his adversary Czar Peter among others. If they fail their attempts are deemed rash; if they succeed they are great.

My suggestion is that the portrait of '*Swedish Charles*' expresses part of Johnson's experience of 1745 and after, not that the poem holds a complete parallel (the beginning and end of the portrait obviously do not fit Prince Charles, though the end may be thought to have been plausibly prophetic in the late 1740s). The suggestion may thus be considered primarily biographical. My *argument*, on the other hand, is that *The Vanity of Human Wishes* is not a poem of generality in the sense that it excludes recent historical particulars, but that it is 'comprehensive' in assimilating them to famous examples from the past. All this leads up to the Christian stoicism of the conclusion. A great part of the vanity of human wishes is the tragedy of political hope.

5

The complete political character of Johnson naturally includes not only the later political tracts but *The Lives of the Poets*. The former, and especially the important and successful *Taxation No Tyranny*, are fully discussed by Greene. The latter offer a full picture of the literary profession in the political and social circumstances of the eighteenth and later seventeenth centuries. Far from being political only on occasion (on Milton, Waller, Butler and Akenside, it has been suggested), the *Lives* are penetrated with a political understanding dominated by the opposing terms of 'Whig' and 'Tory'. 'Court' and 'Country' are rarely used. The lives of Addison, Swift, Prior and Savage are especially striking in this way, while those of Fenton and Yalden show a nice sense of what were the obligations and dangers of being a Non-Juror. Johnson's disinterested and independent judgement is not less because he writes in the political terms of his time. That he recognized the involvement of the *Lives* in eighteenth-century political history, and that he had not shrunk from openly taking a side, is shown by his letter to Mrs. Thrale on 10 March 1779, where he says of the *Lives*: 'If the King is a Whig, he will not like them; but is any King a Whig?'

In the present essay I hope to have shown Johnson's eighteenth-century Toryism as it evolved and modified across the divide of 1760, defended Boswell as a generally accurate recorder of this trajectory, reinstated the issue of Jacobite sympathy as of central Johnsonian concern, and offered the political reading of his two imitations of Juvenal which their historical and biographical contexts seem to demand.

NOTES

1. Donald J. Greene, *The Politics of Samuel Johnson* (New Haven: Yale University Press, 1960; Kennikat Press reissue, 1973), p. 231. His views are further developed in Yale, Vol. 10. The former work is hereafter referred to as *Politics*.
2. By the assimilation of Romney Sedgwick (ed.), *The House of Commons, 1715–54*, 2 vols. (London: H.M. Stationery Office, 1970); and the

publication, among other works, of Geoffrey Holmes, *The Trial of Dr. Sacheverell* (London: Duckworth, 1973); J. P. Kenyon, *Revolution Principles : The Politics of Party*, 1689–1720 (Cambridge, 1977); Eveline Cruickshanks, *Political Untouchables: The Tories and the '45* (London, 1979); Eveline Cruickshanks (ed.), *Ideology and Conspiracy: Aspects of Jacobitism*, 1680–1759 (Edinburgh: John Donald, 1982). I am particularly indebted to J. C. D. Clark, 'A General Theory of Party, Opposition and Government, 1688–1832', *Historical Journal*, 23, No. 2 (1980); and I am grateful to Dr. Clark for his advice, though he does not necessarily concur with the views I express.

3. Lewis Namier, *The Structure of Politics at the Accession of George III*, 2 vols. (London: 1929; Macmillan, 2nd edn., 1956), and *England in the Age of the American Revolution* (London, 1930; Macmillan, 2nd edn., 1961); Herbert Butterfield, *The Whig Interpretation of History* (London, 1931: Penguin, 1973).
4. See his account of the Staffordshire magnates in *Politics*, pp. 34–44: ideology is played down, material interests played up. He considers Jacobitism largely ideological. But politicians are more rather than less Jacobite if their material interests prompt them in that direction.
5. References to Boswell's *Life* are hereafter given in the text, by volume and page no. only.
6. The point in question concerns Johnson's motive in wanting to equate 'Renegade' and 'Gower' in the *Dictionary* (*Politics*, pp. 15–16). Gower had been the leader of a powerful body of Tories pressing for office in the early 1740s. In December 1744 he achieved major office by sacrifice of the principles and terms for which the group had been holding out. Other members of this group included the six Tory magnates who in Spring 1743 had formally requested French help for a Stuart restoration. Gower had not been an active Jacobite since the early 1730s, though the Jacobite Tories may have assumed he was still one of them. Gower also had an earlier episode to live down, for in 1715 he seems to have set out to join the Lancashire Jacobites at Preston, but quickly returned home on the news of their defeat. (See Cruickshanks, *Political Untouchables*, pp. 7, 12, 36–78.) Whether Johnson thought Gower a renegade because he sold out on the Tory parliamentary conditions in 1744, or because he was then seen to have abandoned a long-waning Jacobite commitment, can probably never be known. He was possibly thinking of Gower's whole career.
7. 'The Contrast Between Two Executed Lords', ll. 25–6: *Byrom, Poems*, ed. A. W. Ward (Manchester, 1894), Vol. 2, p. 322.
8. See Katherine Tomasson, *The Jacobite General* (Edinburgh and London: Blackwood, 1958) pp. 39–40.
9. Certainly this episode is unlikely to have been before 'About' 1757, when old Mr. Langton offered him a benefice (Vol. 1, p. 320). It gave offence to Langton; we next hear of a visit early in 1764 (Vol. 1, 476) when and after which Langton is convinced Johnson is a Roman Catholic. The episode is likely to have fallen between these two dates, perhaps in 1758 when there is evidence of contact with the 'Mr Langtons' (Vol. 1, 336).
10. *Politics*, p. 232.

11. *Lives*, Vol. 3, p. 411; 'Ode xii, Bk. I' in Akenside, *Poems* (London, 1772), p. 274.
12. *Letters*, Vol. 1, pp. 367, 423.
13. *The Life of Samuel Johnson*, ed. and abridged by Bertram H. Davies (New York, 1961), p. 41. Hereafter referred to in the text as Hawkins, *Life*.
14. On Morgan, see Cruickshanks, *Political Untouchables*, pp. 91, 99, 101, 105, and Howard Erskine-Hill, 'Literature and the Jacobite Cause' in *Ideology and Conspiracy*, ed. Cruickshanks, pp. 56–7.
15. Howard Erskine-Hill, 'Under which Caesar? Pope in the Journal of Mrs. Charles Caesar, 1724–41', *R.E.S.*, n.s. XXXIII (1982), 438–39.
16. Bertram H. Davies, 'The Anonymous Letter Proposing Johnson's Pension', Johnson Society (of Lichfield), *Transactions* (Lichfield, 1981), pp. 35–9.
17. *The Correspondence and Other Papers of James Boswell Relating to the Making of the Life of Johnson*, ed. Marshall Waingrow (New York and Toronto, 1969), pp. 512–15. J. L. Clifford thought Farmer the probable author of the letter. In the same connection he speaks of Johnson's 'known anti-Hanoverian position' (*Dictionary Johnson: Samuel Johnson's Middle Years* (London, 1979), pp. 263–65, 269).
18. Greene, *Politics*, pp. 189–91; Clifford, *Dictionary Johnson*, pp. 263–65; Bertram H. Davis, 'The Anonymous Letter', *loc. cit.*, p. 39.
19. *Poetical Works*, ed. Douglas Grant (Oxford: Clarendon Press, 1956), pp. 126–27.
20. Quotations are from Samuel Johnson, *The Complete English Poems*, ed. J. D. Fleeman (Harmondsworth: Penguin, 1971).
21. The allusion of Johnson's restored italics to *The True Briton* is suggested by Fleeman (p. 197), but not the significance of the allusion within the poem as a whole. See also Erskine-Hill, 'Under Which Caesar?' (note 15 above), pp. 438, 441, and 'Pope: The Political Poet in his Time', *Eighteenth-Century Studies*, XV (1981–82), 123–48.
22. Life of Addison: *Lives*, Vol. 2, p. 114.
23. Erskine-Hill, 'Literature and the Jacobite Cause', *Ideology and Conspiracy*, p. 58.
24. *The Private Journal and Literary Remains of John Byrom*, ed. Richard Parkinson, 2 vols. in 4 parts (Manchester: Chetham Society, 1854–57), II, 2, pp. 385–93.
25. See *The House of Commons, 1715–54*, I, 513–14 ('Charles Caesar'); Cruickshanks, *Political Untouchables*, pp. 7–8; F. P. Lock, *The Politics of Gulliver's Travels* (Oxford: Oxford University Press, 1980), pp. 56–65, and *Swift's Tory Politics* (London: Duckworth, 1983), pp. 25, 126, 131, 173; and Cruickshanks, intro., *Charles XII of Sweden* (Brisbane: Lock's Press, 1983). One may add that *A Short View of the Conduct of the King of Sweden* (London, 1716), p. 4 and end, had defended him from attack by those who also attacked indefeasible hereditary right. Having described his defeat at Pultava and eventual return to Sweden, it promised a second part concerning the relation of Charles XII to 'our own Nation'. This must refer to the 'Swedish' Plot on behalf of the Jacobites, of 1716–17. Johnson, of course, was working on a tragedy on Charles XII in June 1742. Six

years later there appeared a catchpenny theatrical entertainment entitled *The Northern Heroes; or, The Bloody Contest Between Charles the Twelfth, King of Sweden, and Peter the Great* . . . (London, 1748) which dramatized Charles's invasion of Russia and defeat at Pultava. It is strongly pro-Czar. But Charles is portrayed, not without some admiration, as a rash and 'wild Romantic Hero'. At one point he appears before his adversary the Czar accompanied by his allies and a 'Piper' (p. 16).

26. The phrase was to be used of Prince Charles by Churchill in *The Ghost*, III. 665 (*Poetical Works*, p. 123).
27. *An Authentick Account of the Prince from his Arrival in Paris to Aix-la-Chapelle*, 3rd edn. (London, 1749), p. 34; Byrom, *Journal and Remains*, II, 2, pp. 466–67.
28. I am grateful to F. P. Lock for bringing this to my attention.
29. British Library pressmark: C.131.f.16. The poem is S46 in D. F. Foxon (ed.), *English Verse 1701–50* (Cambridge; Cambridge University Press, 1975), where the B.L. pressmark is given as 840.k.4/5 Foxon is surely right to suspect that the place of publication was really London.

7

The Essayist, 'Our Present State', and 'The Passions'

by J. S. CUNNINGHAM

Reading the periodical essays published by Johnson during the decade which separates *The Vanity of Human Wishes* and *Rasselas*, we come repeatedly upon pronouncements about 'our present state'. Here are some characteristic examples (numbered for ease of reference):

> (1) It is the condition of our present state to see more than we can attain. (*Rambler* 14, Yale, Vol. 3, p. 76)

> (2) It seems to be the condition of our present state, that pain should be more fixed and permanent than pleasure. (*Rambler* 78, Vol. 4, p. 45)

> (3) A perpetual conflict with natural desires seems to be the lot of our present state. (*Rambler* 111, Vol. 4, pp. 227–28)

> (4) It is necessary to that perfection of which our present state is capable, that the mind and body should both be kept in action. (*Rambler* 85, Vol. 4, p. 184)

> (5) All the attainments possible in our present state are evidently inadequate to our capacities of enjoyment. (*Rambler* 103, Vol. 4, p. 184)

> (6) It is decreed by providence, that nothing truly valuable shall be obtained in our present state, but with difficulty and danger. (*Rambler* 40, Vol. 3, p. 220)

(7) Of the happiness and misery of our present state, part arises from our sensations, and part from our opinions; part is distributed by nature, and part is in a great measure apportioned by ourselves. (*Rambler* 186, Vol. 5, p. 211)

(8) It has been remarked, perhaps, by every writer, who has left behind him observations upon life, that no man is pleased with his present state, which proves equally unsatisfactory, says Horace, whether fallen upon by chance or chosen with deliberation; we are always disgusted with some circumstance or other of our situation, and imagine the condition of others more abundant in blessings, or less exposed to calamities. (*Rambler* 63, Vol. 3, pp. 334–35)

(9) Envy, curiosity, and a sense of the imperfection of our present state, inclines us to estimate the advantages which are in the possession of others above their real value. (*Rambler* 180, Vol. 5, p. 182)

(10) Our present state admits only of a kind of negative security; we must conclude ourselves safe when we see no danger, or none inadequate to our powers of opposition. (*Rambler* 126, Vol. 4, p. 308)

(11) The writers who have undertaken the task of reconciling mankind to their present state, and relieving the discontent produced by the various distribution of terrestrial advantages, frequently remind us that we judge too hastily of good and evil, that we view only the superficies of life, and determine of the whole by a very small part. (*Rambler* 128, Vol. 4, p. 316)

(12) There is, indeed, no topic on which it is more superfluous to accumulate authorities, nor any assertion of which our own eyes will more easily discover, or our sensations more frequently impress the truth, than, that misery is the lot of man, that our present state is a state of danger and infelicity. (*Adventurer* 120, Yale, Vol. 2, p. 466)

In these assertions, the key phrase—'our present state'—chiefly refers not to our immediate and changing circumstances, but to the essential nature of temporal human life. What is the terrestrial condition of humanity? The question is met with firm and lucid generality. Earthly life is infelicitous.

We cannot live up to our ideals of virtue. The world will not answer fully to our high expectations of it. Such insistences are, of course, familiar to readers of Johnson. But we find that the degree of happiness or misery in our mortal condition is variously estimated, and that the grounds on which we estimate it, though sometimes so firm (quotation no. 12), are sometimes said to be untrustworthy. Questions arise about what we know about life and how we know it, and these questions may be brought into focus by considering Johnson's use of the phrase 'our present state'.

In the sense of our essential temporal condition, the phrase carries a contrast, more often implied than explicit, with 'another state', our ultimate 'future state', that 'invisible state' or 'better state' which we hope to enjoy in eternity (*Rambler* 54, Yale, Vol. 3, p. 292; No. 78, Vol. 4, p. 49; No. 7, Vol. 3, p. 39; *Adventurer* 120, Vol. 2, p. 470). Johnson usually, but not invariably, means this by 'futurity'. On this closing prospect the attention of the virtuous dying man is fixed, as he passes mildly away (*Rambler* 54, Vol. 3, p. 292); towards it, earthly affliction itself helps to direct our thoughts (*Adventurer* 120, Vol. 2, p. 470); and it is there that we shall join 'those whose probation is past, and whose happiness or misery shall endure for ever' (*Rambler* 78, Vol. 4, p. 50). Accordingly, one homiletic purpose of Johnson in the *Sermons* is to 'direct our desires to a better state' (Yale, Vol. 14, p. 166), and to deplore any loss of that perspective, a loss incurred when we become subjugated to 'the vanity of all that terminates in the present state' (Vol. 14, p. 270). We should judge, and conduct, our probationary life in the light of eternity; and our experience on earth not only makes us yearn for Heaven, but instructs us, as we learn to know our innate desires, what eternal felicity will be like. This connection between the nature of man and the nature of Heaven is in itself a highly significant kind of knowledge. Besides providing one theological argument for the existence of a 'future state', it has major implications for Johnson's account of desire or 'the passions'.

Closer reading of Johnson's moral observations requires of the modern reader that he attempt to give true meaning and weight to such words as 'happiness', 'pain', 'pleasure', 'enjoyment', 'security', 'good', and 'evil'. There is, Johnson declares, an irreparable discrepancy between our ideals of virtue—'what we see' speculatively—and the limited, fragile attainments which we find to be possible (quotation no. 1). Delighted gratification is intrinsically less durable than the keen awareness of its absence (no. 2). The fullest gratification possible in this life falls short of that entire fulfilment which our nature could, without offending, aspire to attain (no. 5). Although such constraints and oppressions are seen as providentially imposed, Johnson's emphasis falls on our inferring them from experience as it occurs. We know man's essential 'present state' from *within* the world of vicissitude. Thus, inference and generalization link 'our present state', as we live and observe it from day to day, with our conception of the generic state of humanity. Experience furnishes us, upon mature reflection, with a chastened wisdom concerning mortal life as a whole; the empirical modulates into the conceptual. Johnson is even prepared to assert that the daily evidence in support of one particular general view of life is so strong as to make that view irrefutable (no. 12).

But 'the present state' can also mean our condition in the immediate present, as individuals embroiled in experience. This usage is very clearly in play at two moments in *Rasselas*:

> 'Sir', said he, 'if you had seen the miseries of the world, you would know how to value your present state.' (Ch. 3)

> 'Of the present state, whatever it be, we feel, and are forced to confess, the misery, yet, when the same state is again at a distance, imagination paints it as desirable.' (Ch. 22)

There are many points at which the immediate experience of living might obstruct our judgement of life. Happiness and misery have diverse sources, and are variously chosen and imposed; and we encounter them with the aid of various faculties (no. 7). Given our continual dissatisfaction with life as it happens, we misjudge and overvalue the circumstances of others (nos. 8, 9). We necessarily judge life on incomplete evidence, and we judge impetuously and shallowly (nos. 10, 11). Johnson carefully identifies the deficiencies in our appraisal of life: bad and good impulses alike, envy and curiosity, introduce distortions. Most interestingly, the 'sense of the imperfection of our present state', as this is registered through our immediate circumstances, distorts our perception of the lives of others (no. 9). These distortions are so common and so resistant to correction, that we might well propose the difficulty of judging mortal life correctly as itself a defining characteristic of mortal life. Our state in the present persistently obscures the 'present state' of humanity. Equally, 'our present state' in its particular sense is the true source and test of our understanding of the condition of temporal life.

One text which could well have influenced Johnson's use of the phrase is William Law's *A Serious Call to a Devout and Holy Life* (1728). Law emphasizes the probationary nature of our earthly existence. We can achieve real felicity only 'by improving our talents, by so holily and piously using the *powers* and *faculties* of *men* in this present state, that we may be happy and glorious in the *powers* and *faculties* of *angels* in the world to come' (p. 186). Turning to the adjacent question of human judgement, Law declares that the promise of a future state provides the only dependable criterion for assessing the moral worth of men's actions:

> Now since our eternal state, is as certainly ours, as our present state; since we are as certainly to live for ever, as we now live at all; it is plain, that we cannot judge of the value of any particular time, as to us, but by comparing it to that eternal duration for which we are created. (p. 226)

This leads Law to exhort us to adapt our prayers to 'the difference of our *state*'. We should vary our prayers 'as our present state more especially requires' (p. 249), and this means responding to 'our *external state* or condition' as well as to 'the *present state* of our heart' (p. 250). For Law as for Johnson, 'our present state' can signify both the essential nature of human life and our condition in the present moment. But Law's insistent appeals to Nature and Reason as wholly dependable, indeed self-evident arbiters of holy living seem simplistic by comparison with Johnson's account of the processes of moral judgement and choice.

Johnson's essays are particularly eloquent and cogent concerning the many obstacles that confront our search for a steady and capacious understanding of our lives. There is, for example, the brevity of life itself; the elusiveness of the immediate experiential present; the pressure of calamity, sickness, malice, and disappointment; the intractable complexity of the evidence borne in upon our consciousness; the impossibility of knowing more than a little of all there is to be known; the relativism of each individual's awareness and judgement; the appetitive delinquency of our emotions and other faculties (hope, desire, imagination—the agents of 'wishing'); the continuous changing, often unregarded or barely perceptible, both within ourselves and in the world around us; the limitations imposed in its very nature on the scope and resilience of the human mind. The attempt to comprehend our mortal condition encounters many impediments which are not merely incidental to a particular life, but enduring features of human nature and the world of time. Comprehension is, therefore, to be won from a confrontation with intrinsically difficult materials. The inquirer is himself, of course, an example of the object of his inquiry. The difficulties which confront him, both from within and from without, establish themselves as material findings in the attempt to describe 'our present state'.

The range of difficulties is matched by the responsible opportunism of Johnson's vigilant prudence. 'Life is short' is a truism, but we do not *think* it as we say it—everyone repeats it, but 'no ideas are annexed to the words' (*Rambler* 71, Yale, Vol. 4, p. 7). 'The present is in perpetual motion, leaves us as soon as it arrives, ceases to be present before its presence is well perceived, and is only known to have existed by the effects which it leaves behind': it is, Johnson responds, the discipline of memory that places us 'in the class of moral agents' (*Rambler* 41, Vol. 3, pp. 223–24). We are beset by 'casualties' and dangers, our future uncertain; the present therefore, surprisingly, is 'the only time which we can call our own', in the sense that we are required to be diligently virtuous *now* (*Rambler* 29, Vol. 3, p. 162). The world continually fails to provide 'objects adequate to the mind of man': this is theologically significant, as 'a strong proof of the superior and celestial nature of the soul of man' (*Rambler* 41, Vol. 3, pp. 221–22). Seeking to decide in what occupation to spend our lives, we find 'the complication is so intricate, the motives and objections so numerous . . .' that we may spend much of our lives in making 'inquiries which can never be resolved'; provided that the choice does not offend Christian ethics, 'he who chuses earliest chuses best' (*Rambler* 19, Vol. 3, pp. 109–10). Gratifying appetites, we increase the demands which they make upon us, and may ultimately 'sink into the gulphs of insatiability'; but it is clear that most of what we crave is superfluous, because 'all real need is very soon supplied' (*Rambler* 38, Vol. 3, p. 208). 'The state of the world is continually changing'; this should deter us from entertaining not only unreasonable hope, but also needless fear, as 'the stream of time' may carry away what threatens us (*Rambler* 29, Vol. 3, p. 161). 'We very often differ from ourselves'[1]; we should therefore practise 'moderation and forbearance' towards those who, at any given moment, are in conflict with us (*Adventurer* 107, Vol. 2, pp. 442–45). Men are very ready to remark 'the fallibility of man's reason, and the narrowness of his knowledge'; but they tacitly exclude themselves from this judgement, as they are 'desirous of being thought exempt from faults in their own conduct, and from error in their opinions' (*Rambler* 31, Vol. 3, p. 167). Johnson does, eminently, test general observations and precepts against experience, requiring of the 'speculatist' that he take account of the living world; but although we see more than we can attain, and this is a condition of earthly life, we must nevertheless propose 'the idea of perfection' in order to maintain energetic moral involvement in that life itself (*Rambler* 14, Vol. 3, pp. 75–6). The world of lived experience is complex, but the complicated human being, often confused about himself, can find many grounds of reassurance and of moral action in face of his 'present state'. He can ask himself whether he really *means* the observations he habitually utters; he can emphasize, it seems, either the present or the past as the firm sphere of virtuous conduct; he can circumvent irresolvable perplexity or irrational dread, renounce self-indulgence, and turn the known fluctuations of selfhood to good account in the exercise of charity towards others.

The moralist's encounter with the twin themes of happiness and knowledge exhibits, in such moments as these, various kinds and layers of knowing. We are required really to bring home to ourselves what we think we mean; the clear description of obstacles to clear and steady understanding of life can emerge as itself a substantial accession of knowledge; and one's choice of response to a difficult and painful reading of life is itself guided by the knowledge of principle and by practical good sense. There is a continual interplay between negative and positive, and between large generality and minute particularity. The themes of knowledge and happiness are interwoven in the course of this activity, which is itself an explicit moral imperative; it is 'necessary to that perfection of which our present state is capable' (quotation no. 4). We seek to know what happiness is, how far temporal life may be happy, and how far we may depend on this assessment of life. As readers, we have to make our way between 'misery is the lot of man' (*Rambler* 45, Vol. 3, p. 244) and 'every state of life has its felicity' (*Adventurer* 107, Vol. 2, p. 444). On the one hand, it may be said that 'Life is not the object of science' (ibid., p. 445); on the other, Johnson will sometimes dwell on the firmness and scope of our knowledge of human nature: 'We are all prompted by the same motives, all deceived by the same fallacies, all animated by hope, obstructed by danger, entangled by desire, and seduced by pleasure' (*Rambler* 60, Vol. 3, p. 320).

Johnson begins one *Rambler* essay by observing, not simply that 'no man is pleased with his present state' (quotation no. 8), but that this observation is itself a commonplace. He does not challenge its validity, but rather seeks to detach it from the context of detraction in which it is generally to be found. It is a reasonable human discontent, so long as it is not allowed to predominate in the heart, because we all know that we ourselves are happier at some times than at others. But its basis in our assessment of the *external* evidence is fragile, because 'we cannot judge of the condition of others' (*Rambler* 63, Vol. 3, p. 335). Johnson explores various grounds of error and uncertainty. Lack of self-knowledge—seeing that our misery may be produced by 'our own passions and appetites'—leads us to seek causes and remedies outside ourselves. Our knowledge cannot sufficiently combine scope and precision; irrationality supplies what understanding and experience do not; and quests for an increase of happiness derive, not unreasonably or culpably, from our appraisal of our present state:

> To take a view at once distinct and comprehensive of human life, with all its intricacies of combination, and varieties of connexion, is beyond the power of mortal intelligences. Of the state with which practice has not acquainted us, we snatch a glimpse, we discern a point, and regulate the rest by passion, and by fancy. In this enquiry every favourite prejudice, every innate desire, is busy to deceive us. We are unhappy, at least less happy than our nature seems to admit; we naturally desire the melioration of our lot; what we desire, we very reasonably seek, and what we seek we are naturally eager to believe that we have found. (Ibid., Vol. 3, p. 336)

There is here a fine balance between unavoidable limitation and resistible error, between desire as a reasonable motive and desire as an agent of deception. And the relatively capacious understanding of human life which is achieved by some, is itself likely to cause them to misconceive possibilities of fulfilment:

> Irresolution and mutability are often the faults of men, whose views are wide, and whose imagination is vigorous and excursive, because they cannot confine their thoughts within their own boundaries of action, but are continually ranging over all the scenes of human existence, and consequently, are often apt to conceive that they fall upon new regions of pleasure, and start new possibilities of happiness. (Ibid., Vol. 3, p. 337)

At the same time, 'fluctuation of will' is a thoroughly normal consequence of our balancing of considerations, given the restrictions imposed on knowledge: 'The good and ill of different modes of life are sometimes so equally opposed, that perhaps no man ever yet made his choice between them upon a full conviction, and adequate knowledge' (Ibid., Vol. 3, pp. 337–38). We conclude that 'men may be made inconstant by virtue and by vice, by too much or too little thought.' Johnson leaves this essay with a recommendation that we avoid protracted hesitation; but hesitation itself he has identified as a necessary consequence of the partly known world we live in, and the way our intelligence and our other faculties naturally work.

The deficiencies of understanding which, in one account, are made good 'by passion, and by fancy', are in another view remedied by conjecture:

> Life is not the object of science; we see a little, very little; and what is beyond we only can conjecture. If we enquire of those who have gone before us, we receive small satisfaction; some have travelled life without observation, and some willingly mislead us. (*Adventurer* 107, Vol. 2, p. 445)

In this essay, Johnson deals with the complexity and relativism of intellectual debate, and with the instability of judgement which each of us can find within himself. We disagree with each other

> not because we are irrational, but because we are finite beings, furnished with different kinds of knowledge, exerting different degrees of attention, one discovering consequences which escape another, none taking in the whole concatenation of causes and effects, and most comprehending but a very small part. (Ibid., Vol. 2, p. 441)

The ceaseless changing that takes place within ourselves tends to elude our grasp, because it occurs 'imperceptibly and gradually, and the last conviction effaces all memory of the former'. We might well ask, as readers of Johnson, what bearing this heightened awareness of relativism and mutability has upon his more general pronouncements about our mortal state. If we turn, for example, to *Rambler* 45, we find doubt attaching, not to the empirical basis of the generalization, but to the causes and palliatives of our unhappiness:

> From all our observations we may collect with certainty, that misery is the lot of man, but cannot discover in what particular condition it will find most alleviations; or whether all external appendages are not, as we use them, the causes either of good or ill. (Vol. 3, pp. 244–45)

Johnson himself addresses our question in the *Adventurer* essay. He cites contradictory views of life as offered by two Greek epigrammatists, and sustained by them 'with equal appearance of reason'. For one, life is unremittingly arduous, foolish, and unhappy. For the other, 'every state of life has its felicity'—indeed, every state seems wholly felicitous. Johnson, who translated both epigrams into Latin, finds the contrast particularly instructive: not because it will determine our view of our present state, but because it shows us that no view has absolute authority:

> In these epigrams are included most of the questions, which have engaged the speculations of the enquirers after happiness; and though they will not much assist our determinations, they may, perhaps, equally promote our quiet, by shewing that no absolute determination can ever be formed. (Vol. 2, p. 444)

Johnson himself frequently offers what appears, in its context, to be an 'absolute determination' of the happiness or misery of life. While acknowledging the inconsistency here, we should emphasize the extent to which Johnson presses for conclusions. Multiplicity and determinacy are equally attractive options for him, and are of equal interest to him as evidences of the behaviour of mind. Determinations themselves, he insists, need constant reappraisal if they are not to produce mental stagnation. And he will not settle for the evasiveness of habitual concessive relativism.

Accordingly, it is no surprise to find that Johnson sometimes celebrates our power of intellectual inquiry as convincingly as he at other times dwells on the limitations and frustrations which it encounters. We find in *Rambler* 150 an exhilarating description of the prowess of those 'great and generous' minds which, in their ranging survey of successive fields of knowledge, joyously extend the boundaries of awareness, nourished by what they come to know, and sustained by continual accessions of curiosity and hope:

> He who easily comprehends all that is before him, and soon exhausts any single subject, is always eager for new enquiries; and in proportion as the intellectual eye takes in a wider prospect, it must be gratified with variety by more rapid flights, and bolder excursions; nor perhaps can there be proposed to those who have been accustomed to the pleasures of thought, a more powerful incitement to any undertaking, than the hope of filling their fancy with new images, of clearing their doubts, and enlightening their reason. (Vol. 5, p. 34)

In the immediate context, Johnson is discussing the benefits conferred by curiosity. Being inquisitive diverts our attention from 'unmingled unabated evil' and towards 'those accidental benefits which prudence may confer on every state'. Is knowledge of calamity necessary to a true apprehension of life? Johnson replies that it is. Good and evil are relative, and in the case of evil we need the knowledge of the calamities of other people in order to measure and allay our own: 'the good of our present state is merely comparative, and the evil which every man feels will be sufficient to disturb and harrass him if he does not know how much he escapes' (Vol. 5, p. 36). However, Johnson declares elsewhere, moving once again from relative to absolute, that the ills we suffer can be total, whereas happiness cannot:

> such is the state of this world, that we find in it absolute misery but happiness only comparative; we may incur as much pain as we can possibly endure, though we can never obtain as much happiness as we might possibly enjoy. (*Adventurer* 111, Vol. 2, p. 451)

Edgar, in *King Lear*, had cause to repudiate this view of misery, though the ending of that play might perhaps corroborate it.

Rambler 150 took occasion to celebrate the gratifications of intellectual inquiry, without suggesting that these are more satisfying in prospect than in possession. This can be matched with Johnson's more general assertion that the world we live in is ideally suited to our present state, rather than causing us continuous frustration and disappointment:

> As providence has made the human soul an active being, always impatient for novelty, and struggling for something yet unenjoyed with unwearied progression, the world seems to have been eminently adapted to this disposition of the mind: it is formed to raise expectations by constant vicissitudes, and to obviate satiety by perpetual change. (*Rambler* 80, Vol. 4, pp. 55–6)

At one remove from this view of life, we find Johnson describing successive pursuits as culminating in possession and eventual satiety, each quest being succeeded by the next without an implication of absurdity or bafflement:

> such are the vicissitudes of the world, through all its parts, that day and night, labour and rest, hurry and retirement, endear each other; such are the changes that keep the mind in action; we desire, we pursue, we obtain, we are satiated; we desire something else, and begin a new persuit. (*Rambler* 6, Vol. 3, pp. 34–5)

Relatedly, curiosity 'demonstrably multiplies the inlets to happiness', and necessitates the lessening of 'the predominance of particular thoughts' (*Rambler* 5, Vol. 3, pp. 28–9). This is, once again, the activity which is 'necessary to that perfection of which our present state is capable'. By contrast, although *Rambler* 103 carries a vivid affirmation of intellectual curiosity, Johnson describes 'our present state' (quotation no. 5) with emphasis on human quests as being merely self-replenishing, unprogressive, and ultimately frustrated:

> conquest serves no purpose but that of kindling ambition, discovery has no effect but of raising expectation; the gratification of one desire encourages another, and after all our labours, studies, and enquiries, we are continually at the same distance from the completion of our schemes, have still some wish importunate to be satisfied, and some faculty restless and turbulent for want of employment. (Vol. 4, pp. 184–85)

The divergence between this assessment of our state and that quoted from *Rambler* 150 does not amount to such simple contradiction as our Greek epigrammatists provided. The discrepancy can be markedly lessened by changes of emphasis, because of the fine balances in the psychology of desire, as Johnson conceives of it. Each of us has experienced these variants within our present state.

As might be expected from these descriptions (and demonstrations) of intellectual energy, Johnson categorizes curiosity, not simply as an intellectual motive, but as a passion. As such it might, like envy, distort our view of our condition (quotation no. 9); and it is sometimes misapplied, as when we impair the 'negative security' which is all that life allows us, by indulging 'useless curiosity' about the death that may lie in wait for us (no. 10). But curiosity is persistently celebrated by Johnson, and it is the foremost exception to that general view of the passions which impugns them as distorting knowledge and obstructing reason. When curiosity falls into abeyance, it may be in consequence of the rise of some other passion to temporary predominance (*Rambler* 103, Vol. 4, p. 186). It is itself closely associated with the noble expansion of our intelligence: 'This passion is, perhaps, regularly heightened in proportion as the powers of the mind are elevated and enlarged' (*Rambler* 103, Vol. 4, p. 185). This conception of curiosity links readily with that argument by means of which Johnson finds the frustrations of our present state to be a source of knowledge of the nature of Heaven:

> I cannot but consider this necessity of searching on every side for matter on which the attention may be employed, as a strong proof of the superior and celestial nature of the soul of man. (*Rambler* 41, Vol. 3, pp. 221–22; cf. *Adventure* 120, Vol. 2, pp. 469–70)

This contrasts sharply with Johnson's more general account of our passions.

In *A Serious Call*, Law insists that it lies within our power, through the discipline of holy living, to attain 'freedom from worldly passions'. It is a claim which Johnson would not be prepared to make; but his account of the passions of our present state corresponds with Law's in many respects. Law distinguishes worldly passions from desires 'after such things as *nature* wants, and *religion* approves' (p. 164). We have very few real wants, and 'the present world is well furnish'd to supply these needs' (p. 166). Our temporal distresses are caused by our passions:

> But alas, though God, and Nature, and Reason, make human life thus free from wants, and so full of happiness, yet our passions, in rebellion against God, against *nature* and *reason*, create a new world of evils, and fill human life with imaginary wants, and vain disquiets. (p. 167)

This compares with a similarly firm assertion in *Rambler* 17, though Johnson does not think of us as naturally 'free from wants': 'The disturbers of our happiness, in this world, are our desires, our griefs, and our fears' (Yale, Vol. 3, p. 92). In Law's account of the passions, he is sometimes quite clear about the grounds of moral disapproval: we are, for instance, at fault when we live 'a life devoted to human passions, and worldly enjoyments' (p. 193). But at times Law characterizes the passions more generally, even inclusively, in pejorative terms. Passions are, in general, 'dangerous' (a central emphasis in Johnson). Having shown that pride, envy, and ambition create superfluous wants which make us the victims of self-inflicted torment, Law declares 'I could now easily proceed to shew the same effects of all our other passions' (p. 169). In Johnson, too, we can sometimes feel that the rhetoric directed against the passions in general tends to engulf discrimination among them. It is, of course, a rhetoric which both writers derive from long traditions, both Christian and classical.

It is worth noting that Law insists, as does Johnson, on the close linkages between body and soul, in this their present 'state of union': 'The soul has no thought or passion, but the body is concern'd in it' (p. 272). For Johnson, our present life is the 'complicated state' of 'incorporated mind' (*Rambler* 17 and 14: Yale, Vol. 3, pp. 97, 76). Body and mind are intricately linked and mutually dependent, the mind being—in a rather mechanistic formulation not often favoured by Johnson—'necessitated . . . to receive its informations, and execute its purposes by the intervention of the body'. it can, therefore, be clear to our minds, as they function in this 'present state of union' with 'our corporeal nature', that the body imposes limits on the attainments which the mind proposes; we observe 'how much more our minds can conceive, than our bodies can perform' (*Rambler* 151, Vol. 5, p. 39; No. 17, Vol. 3, p. 97). This is one of Johnson's many descriptions of our earthly state in terms of the inadequate realization of desire, but he does not place much emphasis on the simple categories of body and soul (or mind). Our passions are, for good or ill, motions—or commotions—of the soul. The central general definition in Johnson's *Dictionary* is 'Violent commotion of the mind'. The *Oxford English Dictionary* offers the following equivalent, with illustrative quotations drawn from texts as early as 1374, but no later than 1872:

> Any kind of feeling by which the mind is powerfully affected or moved; a vehement, commanding, or overpowering emotion. ('passion', *sb.* III. 6)

A subsidiary, but closely related, sense of the word is defined by Johnson as 'Zeal; ardour'. The *O.E.D.* defines this usage with an ardour of its own, which conveys something of the power which the word exerts for Johnson:

> An eager outreaching of the mind towards something; an overmastering zeal or enthusiasm for a special object; a vehement predilection. (Ibid., III. 10)

We still speak, of course, of having a passion *for* something.

Johnson regards the passions as the major sources of our energetic engagement with the temporal world.[2] He believes they are few in number:

> the passions of the mind, which put the world in motion, and produce all the bustle and eagerness of the busy crouds that swarm upon the earth; the passions, from whence arise all the pleasures and pains that we see and hear of, if we analize the mind of man, are very few. (*Adventurer* 95: Yale, Vol. 2, pp. 428–29)

Each of these few works similarly upon all men: 'their influence is uniform, and their effects nearly the same in every human breast: a man loves and hates, desires and avoids, exactly like his neighbour' (ibid., Vol. 2, pp. 426–27). Adventitious complications are superimposed on this simple generic base, although we can readily see through them in our pursuit of the essential human condition:

> A great part of the time of those who are placed at the greatest distance by fortune, or by temper, must unavoidably pass in the same manner: and though, when the claims of nature are satisfied, caprice, and vanity, and accident, begin to produce discriminations and peculiarities, yet the eye is not very heedful, or quick, which cannot discover the same causes still terminating their influence in the same effects, though sometimes accelerated, sometimes retarded, or perplexed by multiplied combinations. (*Rambler* 60, Vol. 3, p. 320; cf. p. 144 above)

Here again, however, Johnson can emphasise the manifold difficulties that confront our attempt to describe our present state. Our few constitutive passions

> agitated and combined, as external causes shall happen to operate, and modified by prevailing opinions and accidental

> caprices, make such frequent alterations on the surface of life, that the show while we are busied in delineating it, vanishes from the view, and a new set of objects succeeds, doomed to the same shortness of duration with the former. (*Adventurer* 95, Vol. 2, p. 429)

Johnson is prepared to devote whole essays to the working of particular passions, whether it be fear, the strongest, or envy, a 'malignant and destructive' power, or such passions as that 'for the honour of a profession' or that of 'allowing ourselves to delay what we know cannot be finally escaped'. Clearly, if the central passions are few, a wide range of strong emotional impulses can be called passions; and Johnson represents them variously, affirming them as living energies of consciousness, deprecating them as agents which disrupt our nature and deform our understanding of our present state. In *Rambler* 49 he sets himself to describe generic human development, chiefly in terms of the passions, which he sees as primary or secondary. After the simple appetitive reflexes of infancy, we develop the powers of comparison and reflection; directing these upon our widening experience, we give rise to our primary passions (in their Johnsonian binary pairings): 'hope and fear, love and hatred, desire and aversion'. These activate our growing nature, and extend their sphere of influence within us, not at this stage in a bid for absolute rule, but in accordance with the broadening of our knowledge and the strengthening of our rational powers. We school our passions according to reason and the findings of experience, in order not to act merely upon immediate impulse. The secondary passions are, like the primary, produced by the natural processes of growth, deriving from the outward direction of 'comparison', namely, the setting of our own condition alongside what we observe of the condition of others. We may note that Johnson frequently identifies the activity of 'comparison', in which reason and the passions are so closely implicated, as a fertile source of error and discouragement in our efforts to assess our present state. Error is here involved in the processes of growth. To combat such error, we should 'free our minds from the habit of comparing our condition with that of others on whom the blessings of life are more bountifully bestowed, or with imaginary states of delight and security, perhaps unattainable by mortals' (*Rambler* 186, Vol. 5, p. 211).

Secondary passions are, in themselves, relatively artificial and gratuitous, in that they stimulate strictly superfluous cravings (we recall Law's assertion that our real wants are few). This aligns them with the idea of culpable 'indulgence', which is rarely far away in Johnson's consideration of the passions:

> from having wishes only in consequence of our wants, we begin to feel wants in consequence of our wishes; we persuade ourselves to set a value upon things which are of no use, but because we have agreed to value them; things which can neither satisfy hunger, nor mitigate passion, nor secure us from any real calamity. (*Rambler* 49, Vol. 3, p. 264)

Yet the secondary passions are truly required by the self, both as palliatives 'to relieve the long intervals of inactivity', and for the more positive reason that they give our awakening faculties 'some particular direction'. They include avarice, envy, friendship, curiosity, and the love of fame.

The essays offer various criteria for judging the passions, both in themselves and in their effects. Although he values them for the way they attach us to life, Johnson chiefly uses the criterion of 'whether they tend most to promote the happiness, or increase the miseries of mankind' (ibid., Vol. 3, p. 265). Avarice and envy are 'universally condemned', friendship and curiosity 'generally praised'. But the governing emphasis, in general, falls on their distorting our awareness of 'our present state', and their working against our happiness and 'the just and rational regulation of our lives' (*Rambler* 17, Vol. 3, p. 92). The passions variously cloud, blind, discolour, deform and corrupt our judgement. Prejudice and passion bar the intellect against the intrusion of unpalatable truths. Thus, if one authoritative verdict on 'our present state' is the folly of terrestrial hopes, fears, and desires, this is tenaciously resisted, in a kind of vicious circle, by our 'appetites and passions'. Only the encounter with mortality can open the way to the sincere acknowledgement of their vanity (*Ramblers* 28, 4, 2, 160, 54).

Johnson's persistent personifying of the passions is, clearly, no mere rhetorical embellishment. They characteristically seek dominion over us, as if autonomously and from outside the reasonable self. Not only do they rebelliously 'usurp the separate command of the successive periods of life', but these successions of predominance are so native to our temporal state that 'the moral philosophers' would have done well to chart these 'climactericks of the mind' and the 'regular variations of desire' (*Rambler* 151, Vol. 5, p. 38). There is, here, some understandable oscillation between regarding turbulent passional life as normal and decrying it as deviant. However, in face of the enticements, solicitations, importunities, and depressions caused by our various passions, we propose ideals of virtuous living. Virtue, accordingly, tends to be construed as the difficult conquest, or the attempted schooling, of the passions. The fight against them requires of us vigilance, caution, the studied maintenance of morale, and strategies of timely dislodgement (*Adventurer* 108, Vol. 2, p. 450; *Rambler* 185, Vol. 5, pp. 207–8). Of 'our real state', reason and experience are 'always ready to inform us' (a statement at variance with some of Johnson's observations on our attempts to judge our true condition); the passions misinform us (*Adventurer* 108, Vol. 2, p. 450). Though Johnson recognizes some passions as virtuous, he comes close to identifying them in general with vice (*Ramblers* 49, 183). The disturbing ambivalence of their nature can be represented also in other ways: on the one hand, the passions are identified as natural; on the other, they essentially disrupt our temporal nature (*Adventurer* 108, *Rambler* 151). They can be seen as 'our lawful and faithful guides', rather surprisingly, as we exist in this our present state (*Rambler* 7, Vol. 3, p. 38). And Johnson even represents them not just as needing to be conquered but as owing us a moral duty, which is, 'not to overbear reason, but to assist it' (*Rambler* 126, Vol. 4, p. 307).

This account of Johnson the essayist's observations on the passions, though by no means exhaustive, indicates how persistently and variously he thinks about them. It is as if a passionate turbulence influences his response to the question of these intense and threatening, but indispensable, sources of our temporal energies. Inconsistencies and self-contradictions are more numerous here than in other sectors of Johnson's discussion of 'our present state'. If the passions are, on one view, intimately and educatively part of selfhood, they are, on another view, to be feared and resisted as the seditious enemies of virtue and reason (which is, of course, also a part of selfhood). If, in one light, our 'future state' is a blissful release from the disruptive effects of passions within us (*Rambler* 151, Vol. 5, p. 42), in another it is the entire gratification of those desires native to us which this temporal world never completely satisfies.

As Johnson the essayist traverses 'our present state', discursively, the reader continually finds that the difficulties, distortions, and limitations which impede clear knowledge of that state are themselves firmly identified and described. This, in its turn, constitutes knowledge. So does the persistent testing of the validity of received accounts of man's condition, in the course of which Johnson emphasizes that even perennial truths lose their value if they are not critically reappraised and genuinely meant. In this and in other ways, much of what is *demonstrated* in the processes of Johnson's thinking about our present state from (inescapably) within it, correlates with much of what he *asserts* about that state. To live is to interrogate life. His thinking is, of course, more exploratory and provisional than his habits of rhetorical emphasis, so often aspiring to the axiomatic, might suggest. He accords varying degrees of credence, on different occasions, to general verdicts on our temporal life. This variation can be seen as mirroring what he himself says about the fluctuations of human confidence as we seek to assess our lives; but there is, on the whole, a preponderant emphasis on the darker assessments. However, it would be inadequate to represent Johnson's variations of outlook as merely symptomatic of the indeterminacy of our judgement of life. Johnson characteristically recommends the virtue of active moral engagement in daily living, and the essays generally exhibit a rhetorical analogue of this virtue—the animated pursuit of the truthful communication of knowledge as it opens to the touch of curiosity and intellectual hope. This pursuit, our attempt to understand our present state, is as much the subject of inquiry as is the state itself. And it is, in the end, emphatically true that this winning of lucidity and trenchancy in face of materials that oppress us and resist definition and control, has an exemplary dimension which transcends the offered description of our present state. What the essays exemplify, at their best and over their whole range, decidedly extends our view of the creature we discuss and are.

NOTES

1. Cf. Pope, *Moral Essay I*, 19–20: 'That each from other differs, first confess;/ Next, that he varies from himself no less.'
2. Cf. Pope, *An Essay on Man*, Epistle II, 107–8: 'On life's vast ocean diversely we sail,/ Reason the card, but Passion is the gale.'

8

Rasselas and the Traditions of 'Menippean Satire'

by JAMES F. WOODRUFF

As Carey McIntosh has pointed out, *Rasselas* is 'the most problematic' of Johnson's narrative works.[1] Disagreement exists about its genre and about the effect of its style, moral, structure, plot and characterization. My aim is to suggest a context of discussion that I hope will contribute to the clarification of at least some of these controversies.

Most of the extensive and valuable discussion of the literary backgrounds of *Rasselas* has been in a biblical or relatively modern context. Occasionally Cicero and the Stoics are cited, but, as far as I am aware, the book has rarely been associated with ancient literary traditions. Earl R. Wasserman, however, has connected *Rasselas* with two Greek allegories, well known in the eighteenth century if not today: Prodicus's *Choice of Hercules* and the *Tablet* of Cebes.[2] Wasserman uses his suggestion to work out implications of a fundamental insight about *Rasselas* and its period: 'the eighteenth century . . . produced a literature that . . . questions, transforms, and undermines the established norms themselves' (3). Though Johnson must certainly have known the allegories of Prodicus and Cebes and even have been influenced by them at certain points in his work as a whole, it is hard not to share some of

Irvin Ehrenpreis's scepticism about the degree to which we should see their influence operating in *Rasselas*.[3] Yet the validity of the insight about the book's essentially subversive nature remains.

Ehrenpreis, in the concluding part of his essay, makes a series of statements that formulate precisely and elegantly many of the essential characteristics of *Rasselas* and develop the argument about the critical and ironic nature of Johnson's book. A selection of them should provide a sound starting point for further discussion.

> Rather than call the work a novel, I agree with those who classify it as a philosophical romance like More's *Utopia* and Voltaire's *Candide*. The action seems intended to illustrate a set of doctrines. What holds the reader is the author's playful substitution of ironically framed argument for exciting incident. . . . He invites us to identify ourselves with Imlac or Rasselas but then detaches himself from the person in order to smile sympathetically at him and us. . . . [Johnson] gives us a mock-romance. The story of Rasselas moves through ironic contrasts between the fantasies of traditional romance and the realities of earthly experience. (111) . . . Consistency and depth of characterization do not [lend themselves to the author's purpose of creating 'an impression that [he] has confronted all the possibilities of sublunary existence'.] (112) . . . If Johnson provides us with the superficial features of the oriental romance, he frustrates the expectations aroused by them. . . . The method is deliberate and works as comic irony. (113) . . . In the style of the speeches (as also in much of the narrative) Johnson recalls the distinctive manner of the oriental tale, but he does so in a delicate parody. . . . Even when the style is straightforward, and wisdom is offered such as the author might recommend as his peculiar teaching, it may be set in an ironic frame. (116)

These statements formulate sharply some real but difficult qualities of *Rasselas* which are certainly, as Ehrenpreis suggests, well suited to Johnson's habits as a writer, but which I propose in the following essay to associate with a somewhat wider and more enduring literary tradition than he or other writers on *Rasselas* mention.

1

A discussion has been developing in recent years, mainly outside the field of eighteenth-century studies, about a literary kind variously referred to as the anatomy, the menippea, and Menippean satire. While the genre is referred to by earlier writers, the mention is usually brief. The detailed conception of this literary kind recently developed, however, allows a new historical and critical understanding of the form of many 'problematic' works, from the eighteenth century as well as from other times. *Rasselas*, I think, is one of them, along with such a likely companion as *Candide* and such less likely associates as *Gulliver's Travels* and *Tristram Shandy*.[4] Indeed, the eighteenth-century philosophic tale may be seen as a sub-class of the genre.

To some the identification may only need to be asserted to be evident. To others one of the main focuses of objection to such a description is the word 'satire' itself. While several writers have called *Rasselas* satiric, the description has also been vigorously denied.[5] Part of the problem in using the term may lie in the conception of the Menippean genre, but part lies in the way the basic characteristics of satire *per se* are viewed. Many 'Menippean' works such as *Gulliver's Travels*, *A Tale of a Tub*, Erasmus's *Praise of Folly*, and some of Lucian's dialogues like the *Icaromenippus* or the *Vitarum auctio* are by common consent and usage 'satiric'.[6] Others, such as Boethius's *Consolation of Philosophy*, are not. It is this difficulty that has led Northrop Frye to suggest that the term 'anatomy' be substituted for the cumbersome and misleading 'Menippean satire', and Mikhail Bakhtin generally shortens the term to 'menippea'. The substitution, however, has been rejected by other writers such as Eugene Kirk and F. Anne Payne, who insist on the genre's basically satiric nature.

In the seventeenth and eighteenth centuries most attempts to understand the essential quality of satire involved placing it in an antithesis of praise and invective. Dryden uses this approach in his 'Discourse Concerning the Original and Progress of Satire' in a sentence that Johnson slightly misquotes in his *Dictionary* under the first meaning of 'invective' as a noun: 'If we take satire in the general signification of the word, as it is used in all modern languages, for an invective, 'tis certain that it is almost as old as verse.'[7] The problem, however, as Dryden recognizes, is that satire in becoming an art form becomes much more complex than its primitive original or its common modern meaning would allow. He echoes Dacier in observing

> that the word *satire* is of a more general signification in Latin than in French or English. For amongst the Romans it was not only used for those discourses which decried vice, or exposed folly, but for others also, where virtue was recommended. (II, 116)

Like most writers in the period he sees true satire as achieving general moral significance rather than remaining mere personal abuse. Johnson sums up this view in the definition of 'satire' in his *Dictionary*:

> A poem in which wickedness or folly is censured. Proper *satire* is distinguished, by the generality of the reflections, from a lampoon which is aimed against a particular person; but they are too frequently confounded.[8]

This extended conception of satire implied certain things about the satirist's character, as many writers in the eighteenth century were certainly aware.[9] An indulgence in invective can easily lead to the image of the satirist as a mean-spirited and vindictive creature who cares little for truth and real virtue in his attempts to mount an attack on his victims. Yet some satirists would rather think of themselves as noble moralists willing to suffer if necessary for the good of mankind. Pope as seen by his enemies and by himself is a good example of both images. Such a perceived conflict or tension could in turn have implications for the character satire was allowed to develop. The more scrupulous the satirist about truth and general morality the less likely he might be to indulge in violence and personal invective. But the farther the writer moves towards moral nobility and away from mere invective the less like satire his work will appear to many readers, though he may still think of himself as working within satiric traditions. In the end it comes to a matter both of the real character of the writer and of the rhetorical character he wishes to project in his works. It has been observed, most notably by W. Jackson Bate in his influential discussion of 'Johnson and Satire Manqué', that Johnson seems to have felt acutely both the impulse of the satirist and the need to mute that impulse because of compassion and, one might add, a concern for truth.[10] Several of the illustrative quotations he gives for 'satire' and its derivatives in the *Dictionary*, particularly for the word 'satirist' itself, reiterate a need to mute the violence of satire and to stress positive moral concerns. They bring out the tension we have noted between the character of satire and that of the good satirist. Two examples must serve, though at least eight out of the sixteen quotations used to illustrate these words have a similar thrust.

> Wycherly, in his writings, is the sharpest *satyrist* of his time; but, in his nature, he has all the softness of the tenderest dispositions: in his writings he is severe, bold, undertaking; in his nature gentle, modest, inoffensive.
>
> *Granville.*

> Yet soft his nature, though severe his lay;
> His anger moral, and his wisdom gay:
> Blest *satyrist*! who touch'd the mean so true,
> As show'd vice had his hate and pity too.
>
> *Pope.*

Taken together, the quotations Johnson selects bring out the responsibilities of the satirist and the dangers inherent in using a powerful weapon irresponsibly, the sort of points that Addison before him had reiterated many times. They caution by implication against the temptation satire too readily offers of indulging ill nature, and they suggest the controls we should expect to find operating when Johnson himself worked in a satiric mode or genre.

The complex nature of satire, involving tensions between the personal and the general, invective and exposure, raillery and morality, makes it difficult to simplify its definition in terms of a single characteristic such as attack or ridicule. A satiric writer experiencing the compunctions just suggested would be likely, I think, to de-emphasize the more personal, more violent aspects—the mere decrying of vice—and to emphasize the exposure of folly and the recommending of virtue. When this aspect of satire is stressed it begins to sound more and more like one of Johnson's usual modes. This stripping bare from the encrustations of pretence and wish-fantasy is perhaps satire's most universal though not its sole aim. The fictions of satire force the fresh look that leads to such exposure. Satire intends not only to rob the shameless of honour but, in a famous phrase, to clear the mind of cant, of what we take for granted and mindlessly repeat. Satire is the mode of 'reality', of the actual, of things as they are. At base it is the opposite of romance, which is the mode of wishes and their fulfilment and of the ideal rather than the actual. Sometimes to show or suggest this difference satire stresses the anti-romantic.

Irony becomes another way of establishing the actual through implied contrast, for it is a trope that is constantly bringing out a sense of difference. In the most general sense irony depends on a perception of discrepancy within moral structures. In itself it does not necessarily imply moral judgement, only difference. Though such judgement is frequent in satire and the ironic discrepancy is between an actual and an ideal (as in Juvenal), there may be ironies where right (and wrong) rests on both sides and our primary awareness is of the discrepancy between different perspectives. This latter kind of irony is, in fact, frequent in Johnson's writing. Other kinds of irony, like 'dramatic irony' or even much 'tragic' or 'comic irony', depend on discrepancies in knowledge or in point of view—between different characters, between audience and characters, or even between knowledge of a part and of the whole. Irony, then, can be employed as a ready means to the satiric end of exposure. Similarly, ridicule in satire is perhaps more means than end. In a good deal of satire at least, the underlying intention, as we have noted, is to expose a truth or reality concealed or ignored by the assumptions or fictions or wilful misrepresentations of everyday living and converse. The ridicule is one of the techniques used to effect the exposure of falsity and discovery of truth.[11]

When satire is viewed thus *Rasselas* appears much more convincingly to belong within the mode. The point has already been made succinctly by Arieh Sachs:

> The method of *Rasselas* is the method of satire, in the sense that it involves an ironical exposé of human delusions which is

> intended to make us confront unpleasant realities. By means of its irony, it makes us see the absurdity of many 'luscious falsehoods' and feeds us the salutary 'bitterness of truth'.[12]

The conception of the 'Menippean satire' allows a good deal more to be said about *Rasselas* seen in this way and also allows us to incorporate into our view many of the characteristics of the book noted by Ehrenpreis and others.

2

Not only does it make sense to see *Rasselas* as Menippean satire in a modern critical context, but there is a good possibility that Johnson himself might have looked on it as connected with that kind of work. Thus there is some point in looking both at how the genre was viewed in Johnson's time and how it has been described by recent critics. The principal source of theoretical and historical knowledge about Menippean satire in the seventeenth and eighteenth centuries was Isaac Casaubon's *De Satyrica Graecorum Poesi et Romanorum Satira* originally published in 1605.[13] Later writers who touch on the genre, such as Dacier, Dryden (in his 'Discourse . . .' prefixed to the translation of Juvenal and Persius, 1693[14]), and Joseph Trapp add very little. Dryden's few pages are a good summary from an important writer who saw his own 'MacFlecknoe' and 'Absalom and Achitophel' as being of this kind.[15] He follows Casaubon in preferring the term 'Varronian satire', though he notes that the Roman satirist Varro himself, whose works survive only in fragments, called it Menippean after the Cynic philosopher Menippus of Gadara, who later appears as a character in the dialogues of Lucian. One essential characteristic of Menippean satire for these writers rests in the root meaning of satire in *satura*, a mixture, a point first established by Casaubon. Dryden notes: 'This sort of satire was not only composed of several sorts of verse, like those of Ennius, but was also mixed with prose; and Greek was sprinkled amongst the Latin' (113). Varro, 'one of those writers whom they called *spoudogeloioi*, studious of laughter' (114), had commented on the mixture of mirth and philosophy in his own writings. Dryden observes Menippus's reputation for cynical impudence, obscenity, and parody, but notes that 'Varro, in imitating him, avoids his impudence and filthiness, and only expresses his witty pleasantry. . . . As [Varro's] subjects were various, so most of them were tales or stories of his own invention' (115). The writers and works that for Dryden define the continuation of this tradition are the *Satyricon* of Petronius Arbiter, many of Lucian's dialogues, particularly his *Vera Historia*, the *Golden Ass* of Apuleius, the *Apocolocyntosis* of Seneca, the *Symposium* of the Emperor Julian the Apostate, Erasmus's *Praise of Folly*, John Barclay's *Euphormionis Lusinini Satyricon*, a German work (probably, according to W. P. Ker, the *Epistolae Obscurorum Virorum*), Spenser's *Mother Hubbard's Tale*, and his own works mentioned above. In these remarks, many of the characteristics listed in recent accounts of the genre are already present, though its satiric ethos is assumed rather than explicitly articulated. Central to Dryden's and the seventeenth-century view is a notion of medley that breaks through ordinary literary decorums, brings together mirth and philosophic seriousness, and is usually embodied in dialogue or at least quasi-narrative forms, often fragmentary and digressive.

Modern criticism spells out much more fully the notion of medley central to older views, and often seeks the *raison d'être* behind the mixtures. Considerable scholarship has touched on the subject of Menippean satire in classical literature. A rather full summary in relation to Lucian is given by J. Bompaire in his *Lucien Ecrivain*, and Eugene P. Kirk has recently published *Menippean Satire: An Annotated Catalogue of Texts and Criticism*, a useful account of texts and scholarship that follows the genre to 1660.[16] Kirk emphasizes the genre's Protean character, how writers looking to the same models can be led by their own concerns to emphasize very different characteristics so that both Boethius and Erasmus can be seen as imitators of Lucian. Such diversity makes definition difficult. Kirk arrives at a statement of 'family resemblances' that appears to grow from a sense of the genre similar to Dryden's, and emphasizes diversity of language, variety of structure, and a concentration in theme on subjects dealing with problems of right learning or right belief.

Even more suggestive of aspects of Johnson's work are the analyses of this genre by Northrop Frye, Mikhail Bakhtin and F. Anne Payne. Frye outlined his view in *Anatomy of Criticism*.[17]

He distinguishes the kind of characterization typically found in these works from more 'novel-centred' conceptions.

> The Menippean satire deals less with people as such than with mental attitudes. Pedants, bigots, cranks, parvenus, virtuosi, enthusiasts, rapacious and incompetent profesional men of all kinds, are handled in terms of their occupational approach to life as distinct from their social behaviour. . . . [Its characterization] is stylized rather than naturalistic, and presents people as mouthpieces of the ideas they represent. . . . A constant theme in the tradition is the ridicule of the *philosophus gloriosus*. . . . The novelist sees evil and folly as social diseases, but the Menippean satirist sees them as diseases of the intellect, as a kind of maddened pedantry which the *philosophus gloriosus* at once symbolizes and defines. (309)

The characterization in *Rasselas*, frequently described as wooden yet in context somehow right, is suggested by such an account. The book also contains a whole procession of *philosophi gloriosi* from the would-be flyer to the astronomer. Many other characteristics of Menippean satire noted by Frye could readily be illustrated from *Rasselas*: its loose-jointed narrative is often confused with romance but differs significantly from it; 'at its most concentrated the Menippean satire presents us with a vision of the world in terms of a single intellectual pattern' (310)[18]; 'the form is not invariably satiric in attitude, but shades off into more purely fanciful or moral discussions' (310); the dialogue and the *cena* or symposium often appear; piling up of erudition and jargon are common and authors of this sort of work have frequently been encyclopaedic compilers. Frye adds to writers and works already mentioned not only Rabelais and Swift but Burton's *Anatomy of Melancholy*, the work which Johnson said 'was the only book that ever took him out of bed two hours sooner than he wished to rise'.[19]

Before Frye wrote, the Russian scholar Mikhail Bakhtin had analysed the menippea in his book *Problems of Dostoevsky's Poetics*, which originally appeared in the late 1920s but was not widely known in the West until recent years.[20] For Bakhtin the concept of the menippea is deeply connected with his notion of the carnivalization of literature. He sees the 'carnival spirit' holding together and making coherent the disparate characteristics of the genre. Bakhtin posits a large class of ancient serio-comical literature including 'Menippean satire' and 'Socratic dialogue' with several other forms, and notes the difficulties of establishing distinct and stable boundaries within its realm. He suggests three basic characteristics for all the serio-comic genres. (1) 'Their starting point for understanding, evaluating, and formulating reality is the *present*' (88). I understand this to mean that they make a sense of things-as-they-are reality their basis rather than introducing a vision of epic or tragic distance. (2) These genres are *consciously* based on *experience* and on *free imagination* rather than on *legend*. They are often explicitly critical of previous formulations of experience such as are found in myth. (3) They exhibit deliberate multifariousness and discordance. Stylistically self-conscious, they reject the stylistic unity of the established genres. Bakhtin proceeds next to the Socratic dialogue, pointing out how it is set up to undermine the claims of those who profess to possess the truth, which 'does not reside in the head of an individual person; it is born of the dialogical intercourse *between people* in the collective search for the truth' (90). Thus juxtaposed points of view are characteristic of the serio-comic genres.

Bakhtin's listing of specific traits of the menippea is also relevant to *Rasselas*. The weight and nature of the comic element can vary widely from the burlesque of Varro and Lucian to the contemplative irony and 'reduced laughter' of Boethius.[21] Recent writers, beginning with Clarence Tracy and Alvin Whitley, have found a comic element in *Rasselas*, though the precise way to read it remains a problem.[22] The genre also shows great freedom of invention and fantasy. However, it creates

> *extraordinary situations* in which to provoke and test a philosophical idea—the word or the *truth*, embodied in the image of the wise man, the seeker after this truth. We emphasize that the fantastic serves here not in the positive *embodiment* of the truth, but in the search after the truth, its provocation and, most importantly, its *testing*. (94)

Rather than developing complex argument like the Socratic dialogue, the Menippean dialogue tests ultimate philosophical positions, and makes us aware of the human dimensions of ideas. These are the characteristics of *Rasselas*.

Bakhtin's statement is a precise formulation of the way in

which *Rasselas* differs from the simple, Aesop's-fable type of apologue or from allegory as conventionally conceived; many passages such as the encounter with the stoic in Chapter 18 or with the philosopher of nature in Chapter 22 show the testing of ultimate positions in their human terms. The positions tested are characteristically of an 'ethico-practical inclination' rather than more clearly 'academic' ones. Characteristic too is the juxtaposition of stripped-bare positions (for example, the happiness of solitude set against the happiness of various kinds of society, or the sensual indulgence of young men set against the stoic denial of an old man). There are only hints in *Rasselas* of the tri-level construction (heaven, earth, hell) often found, but they may be important, as is the characteristic of observation from an unusual point of view—here wealthy outsiders from the happy valley look at the ordinary world. Significantly, Johnson brings his characters to the level of the real world for most of their work of observation. The whole element of the fantastic is muted in *Rasselas* compared with many works in the genre. However, 'the representation of man's unusual, abnormal moral and psychic states—insanity of all sorts . . . unrestrained day-dreaming . . . etc.' (96) appears in the astronomer or the daydreaming of Rasselas and later of all the young people. Of other elements identified by Bakhtin, *Rasselas* includes sharp contrasts and oxymoronic combinations (the happy valley as paradise and prison, for example), elements of a social Utopia usually involving a journey to another land (the happy valley again, and perhaps the Arab's harem, but with some interesting—though not unprecedented—reversals), inserted genres intensifying the variety of styles and tones, parody, etc. (the elements of anti-romance and of the oriental tale, as well as summaries of several philosophical positions, dissertations, dialogues, etc. and various life stories which are in a way mock-aretology, another ancient aspect of the genre), and finally a topical quality (not prominent in Johnson though he does address some current philosophical issues). The element most obviously omitted from *Rasselas* is the scandalous, the 'underworld naturalism' that has given so many Menippean works the reputation of dirty books. The omission is typical of Johnson. But Boethius omits it too and in so doing, as Casaubon pointed out, emulates Varro who effectively established the genre.[23]

F. Anne Payne offers the most extensive and probing analysis of Menippean satire I have yet encountered.[24] Her discussions of Lucian and Boethius are extremely suggestive in relation to Johnson's work, though eighteenth-century literature is not her concern. She maintains that the genre should continue to be viewed in the context of satire, but that it is satire of a special kind whose ultimate aim is to set the mind free. While ordinary satire is frequently seen as setting up some ideal standard and criticising deviations, she sees at this genre's centre a questioning of the very possibility of ideal standards.[25] Consequently interest centres on freedom of will and the dominance of choice in human action as well as in thought. The conventions found in the satires are 'merely aids to the dramatization of this fundamental assumption' (6). Johnson's exploration of the 'choice of life' obviously has this kind of focus, and the end, if seen only as a demonstration that the travellers should abandon their search for the answer to an impossible question and get on 'with living an ordinary life in an everyday world' (202), sounds very much like one of Lucian's terminal positions. Johnson, however, superimposes the Christian perspective of eternity on the position typically taken by the pagan writer, thus transforming its meaning.

Several of the characteristics Payne adds to Bakhtin's list have an obvious applicability to *Rasselas*: a central dialogue between a 'know-it-all' and a 'neophyte'; one character involved in an endless quest, 'helped' by the comments of the other, but with any norm which tries to provide an end satirized; freedom to think, frequently imaged as freedom of action, seen as a gift and a burden; characters who 'exhibit a courteous intention to continue conversing no matter what happens and no matter what must be given up'; and the radiation of 'an unquenchable hope and titanic energy for whatever the problem is' (10). Payne stresses that the genre is to be recognized not by the occurrence of particular characteristics—many occur at least singly in other kinds of work—but by the totality and by the domination of themes like freedom of will, choice, and the questioning of the possibility of ideal standards.

To consider *Rasselas*'s affinities to this genre leads to certain emphases, especially on the anti-establishment dimension which it shares with most of Johnson's writings. The genre works towards questioning things. It lets nothing rest easy. Ultimately a grasp on reality is aimed at—just the opposite of the world of wishes that dominates in romance. In *Rasselas* the stress is always on the presence of alternatives and the uncertainty of final answers. All truths except the final and ultimately unknowable divine truth are partial, but the undercurrent of hope and elation which many readers sense in this book as in other Menippean works (despite the temptation rationally to label the book pessimistic) comes from the vision of the world without forced answers, the emphasis on discovery and on the continuing effort to know rather than the subsidence into easy decision or agnosticism. The Menippean satirist is 'too restless for settled schools'.[26] Johnsonians will surely echo with 'Nullius addictus jurare in verba magistri . . .'.[27] In *Rasselas* Johnson has created frequent difficulties for readers by undercutting in some way speakers of obvious wisdom, as he does with Imlac at the end of Chapter 10. This does not mean that we are to reject the speaker. It is part of the creation of a dialogical way of thinking. We are neither to accept or reject on the basis of authority but to weigh thoughtfully in context. Above all Johnson does not want his readers to relax into merely following authority in earthly matters. Only in the other dimension which Robert G. Walker has argued lies behind most of *Rasselas*, that dimension of spiritual immortality suggested by the mind's unsatisfiable yearning and which in its fullness always keeps behind the surface of the work, is there a prospect of certainty.[28] In this respect Johnson has modified some of the genre's tendency as described by Payne. While he questions the possibility of ideal earthly and temporal standards he holds out the possibility of eternity where the hope for enduring happiness may be fulfilled. The constant irony remains, however, of the separation between this dimension and the temporal, living and changing world where inevitably unsatisfied human beings find themselves.

3

Having established the relationship of *Rasselas* to Menippean satire, we are left with two further lines of questioning: what was Johnson's likely knowledge of and attitude to works of this kind, and what are the significant affinities between *Rasselas* and major earlier works from the genre?

Johnson's acquaintance throughout his life with works from this tradition can be demonstrated. Often he can be shown not merely to have known them but to have liked and admired them. During his first interview as a new undergraduate at Pembroke College, Oxford, he quoted Macrobius, and, though this could have been the *Commentary on the Dream of Scipio*, Charles G. Osgood has suggested that it may have been the *Saturnalia*, a compendium of learning in the Menippean tradition.[29] Other Menippean works appear in the list of his undergraduate library left behind at Oxford in 1729: More's *Utopia*, the *Colloquies* of Erasmus, and the *Satyricon* of John Barclay, the early-seventeenth-century Franco-Scottish neo-Latin writer, whose allegorical romance *Argenis* was also in Johnson's collection. The works of Seneca are included in the list too.[30]

Works of this kind are part of the schemes of education Johnson drew up during the 1730s.[31] Among Greek authors for pre-University study (along with the allegory of Cebes, mentioned by Wasserman) is 'Lucian by Leeds', a collection of the dialogues prepared for school use originally published in the mid-1670s.[32] Its motto from Horace's *De Arte Poetica* (ll. 343–44), 'Omne tulit punctum, qui miscuit utile dulci/ Lectorem delectando pariterque movendo [*sic*]', a significant hint of Johnson's and the eighteenth century's dominant attitude towards this kind of work, is close in sentiment to the passage from Phaedrus that Johnson used as a motto for the collected *Idlers*. Leedes's collection contained several of the dialogues of the gods along with some of the other shorter dialogues and the *Judicium Dearum*, *Somnium sive Gallus*, and *Vitarum Auctio*. The sale catalogue of Johnson's library (far from a complete listing, of course, of the books he owned) includes works by several Menippean authors: the Emperor Julian, Boethius, Lucian (three editions), Macrobius, Erasmus, More, Cervantes (two editions), Swift, Burton, Seneca and Lipsius.[33]

Other connections with writers whose works have at least sometimes been looked on as Menippean appear throughout Johnson's life. We have evidence of his admiring Chaucer, Burton, Cervantes and Boileau.[34] Lucian was not only included in his scheme of education (a usual thing at the time) but was once noticed as his reading during a stagecoach journey, and in 1776 he alluded to the *Juppiter Tragoedus* in a way suggesting he had been struck by how Lucian shows a sense of character and emotion operating in 'intellectual' argument.[35] His interest in Boethius was also enduring. On several occasions he was involved with the *Consolation of Philosophy* in the context of translation, and he drew from it in the *Rambler* and *Adventurer*.[36] Not all these writers and works are equally relevant to *Rasselas*. In many of them, however, are found a tone or stance that seems to be echoed or deliberately built on by Johnson. The sense many of them try to establish of the value, even the necessity, of giving up attractive but ultimately impossible delusions and resting content with freshly apprehended ordinary reality is in harmony with one dominant strain in Johnson's own thought, as is the rather consistent strain of anti-romance that runs through them. The odd mixtures and complex ironies characteristic of much of this work suggest another important side of his writing.

The connection of Johnson's work with the traditions of Menippean satire is not simple. It is often a good example of what is now fashionably referred to as intertextuality, a condition where works 'have meaning in relation to other texts which they take up, cite, parody, refute, or generally transform'.[37] Sometimes the affinities between *Rasselas* and earlier works connected with this tradition go so far that they suggest an association specific as well as general; here I can only present a few of these. Some works already mentioned offer one striking point of resemblance—Barclay's *Euphormio* presents the story of a young man who comes from a Utopia to the ordinary world and in the course of his adventures exhaustively surveys it—as well as some general stylistic resemblance in the use of balance and parallel. Similarities of vision occur fairly often in other works, and similarities of design can be found. However, some of the writings of Lucian of Samosata and Boethius's *Consolation of Philosophy* are of particular interest.

4

Evidence of Johnson's knowledge of Lucian has already been mentioned. Like Johnson Lucian is fundamentally devoted to getting at the basic realities which lie under the structure of human illusions, though as a pagan he rests, unlike Johnson, in the here and now. Lucian sometimes uses allegories rather like those Johnson included in his periodical essays, reminding us that Prodicus and Cebes are not the only classical models for allegory.[38] An element of anti-romance also runs throughout Lucian, most apparent perhaps in the *Vera historia* but more directly reminiscent of Johnson in *De morte Peregrini* or *Alexander*, whose mock-aretology deflates, by realistic presentation, the forms and illusion of exemplary biography. Beyond general similarities of vision and treatment particular works by Lucian more closely resemble *Rasselas*. For example, the *Vitarum auctio* presents the weakness in practice of all philosophies through an auction of their founders or practitioners, and the *Somnium sive Gallus* contains a kind of Pythagorean 'choice of life' in the cock's accounts of the various transmigrations he has lived through from high to low, male to female, human to animal.[39] The stimulus to the survey is Micyllus's desire to find out the relative happiness of the different lives (21), and on the whole animals come out best. As the cock says, 'there is no existence that did not seem to me more care-free than that of man, since the others are conformed to natural desires and needs alone' (27; II, 227). The perception is like the one that Rasselas arrives at in Chapter 2.

Anyone who reads through the works of Lucian will find, I think, more interesting points of contact with Johnson's work. Obviously it is Lucian the moralist, '*Lucian*, severe, but in a gay disguise'[40] as seen in the seventeenth and eighteenth centuries, rather than Lucian the entertainer of modern scholarship, that engages Johnson. Johnson's Lucian is not the Lucian of Fielding or even of Swift. In some respects it is as if Johnson sees him through Boethius's eyes. But the Greek writer provides many examples of ways to embody brilliantly an ironic, questioning world view that in important respects is consonant with Johnson's own, and poses issues that Johnson engages in his turn. Two of Lucian's dialogues in particular show interesting affinities with *Rasselas*.

The first is the *Navigium seu vota*. In this dialogue a trip to see a ship that had landed at Piraeus after a peculiarly trouble-ridden voyage suggests the perception that human wishes are as uncertain and as subject to misfortune and fatality as the voyage. Each of three companions tells of his wishes during their walk back to Athens, and in turn the Lucian figure helps show the vanity of these wishes for wealth, for power, and for more than man's mortal and imperfect bodily state allows. The themes, of course, are favourites with Johnson. The final wish, particularly, suggests *Rasselas* and is what the would-be flier in Chapter 6 tries to put into practice. One of the *Navigium*'s wishes, in fact, involves the magically granted ability to fly. 'I alone would know the source of the Nile and how much of the earth is uninhabited and if people live head-downwards in the southern half of the world', says Lucian's Timolaus (44; VI, 483). 'How easily shall we then trace the Nile through all his passage; pass over to distant regions, and examine the face of nature from one extremity of the earth to the other!' says Johnson's philosopher.[41] A desire to fly is a recurrent symbol in Lucian of aspiration to more than the human state permits,[42] and this could easily have been a source for Johnson's similar use of the image, along with all the more modern contexts so illuminatingly set out by Gwin Kolb and Louis Landa.[43] Johnson certainly modifies the motif in introducing it into 'realistic' action, but the essential point is the same.

Lucian's long dialogue *Hermotimus* also suggests *Rasselas* in certain ways. Its subject is the failings of all specialized philosophies as guides to happiness, with particular reference to Hermotimus's Stoic master but with the moral extended to other philosophies as well. Like *Rasselas*, it contains in passing the deflation of a Stoic who acts passionately in response to the ordinary contingencies of life (though on a different scale of magnitude from the calamity Johnson introduces). But it is focused throughout on an obsessive pursuit of happiness and the single philosophical way of life that will be most likely to lead to it. One of the problems considered is how, with limited experience, to make an intelligent choice of such a philosophy. Choice can only be valid if the full range of choices is known. Lycinus imagines the problem posed this way:

> 'Tell me this, Lycinus: suppose an Ethiopian, a man who had never seen other men like us, because he had never been abroad at all, should state and assert in some assembly of the Ethiopians that nowhere in the world were there any men white or yellow or of any other colour than black, would he be believed by them? Or would one of the older Ethiopians say to him: "Come now, you are very bold. How do you know this? You have never left us to go anywhere else, and indeed you have never seen what things are like among other peoples?" . . .
>
> 'Let us make a comparison, Lycinus, and posit a man who knows only the Stoic tenets, like this friend of yours, Hermotimus; he has never gone abroad to Plato's country or stayed with Epicurus or in short with anyone else. Now, if he said that there was nothing in these many lands as beautiful or as true as the tenets and assertions of Stoicism, would you not with good reason think him bold in giving his opinion at all, and that when he knows only one, and has never put one foot outside Ethiopa?' (31–2; VI, 317–19)

One can imagine that such a passage may have jogged Johnson's imagination towards the construction of his own tale. 'What if we were to examine the experience of an Ethiopian who does examine all the choices of life open?', Johnson may have asked himself. At least the passage strongly suggests the situation in Chapter 3 of *Rasselas* where the old man's reminder that he has not seen the miseries of the world gives the prince a motive for wanting to escape the happy valley.[44]

Other details in *Hermotimus* also resemble elements of Johnson's book. One passage (71), for example, elaborates on the seductiveness of daydreaming and the difficulty of coming back to reality afterwards—a mental state noted in both Chapters 4 and 43 of *Rasselas*. Throughout Lucian's dialogue one observes a constant concern more with the human factor than with the philosophical doctrine. There is, moreover, a basic perception, as Lycinus says, 'that virtue lies in action, in acting justly and wisely and bravely' (79; VI, 405). His final advice is 'you will do better in the future to make up your mind to join in the common life. Share in the city life of everyday, and give up your hopes of the strange and puffed-up' (84; VI, 413). There are also ironic dimensions to the work's ending, though Hermotimus's final response recalls Gulliver more clearly than *Rasselas*. In throwing off what he now calls his madness he proposes to change his appearance as much as his mind. Unlike Imlac and the astronomer who are content 'to be driven along the stream of life' he thanks Lycinus for coming and pulling him out 'when I was being carried away by a rough, turbid torrent, giving myself to it and going with the stream' (86; VI, 415). These elements, some though not all specific to *Hermotimus*, suggest a special relationship between it and *Rasselas* that is more than the merely generic and may even be genetic.

Johnson reinterprets and goes beyond positions found in Lucian, but in many respects he seems in *Rasselas* to be carrying on a dialogue with him. They work over the same themes and subjects with similar aims and techniques. In his analysis of Lucian's satires Ronald Paulson makes statements that could up to a point apply to Johnson.[45]

> Aristophanes focused on the solution; Lucian focuses on the quest and on the witnesses and their testimony. He is interested in the separate encounters, knowing that there is no solution but only the people who offer false solutions. (32)

Paulson analyses Lucian's basic techniques as a writer of anti-romance and shows how he works to expose the evil of illusion and reduce things to the plane of reality which if not ideal is at least real. Lucian's 'purpose', he concludes, 'is the very general one of discomfiting his reader, shaking up his cherished values, disrupting his orthodoxy' (41). Johnson is also concerned with disrupting the orthodoxies of a too easy optimism. But always in Johnson behind this view of man's earthly life is a Christian sense of the immortality of the soul and of the new perspective that the prospect of eternity can give to the inconclusiveness and ordinariness of terrestrial and temporal life.

5

Boethius's *Consolation of Philosophy*, Menippean though not obviously comic or satiric, engages, like the works by Lucian just discussed, some of the same central themes as *Rasselas*; it leads to a specifically Christian conclusion; and to a greater extent than Lucian, I think, its style frequently suggests Johnson's strikingly balanced, ironic dignity. In many respects it is very different from *Rasselas*. It is not a tale but a dialogue between the imprisoned Boethius and the allegorical figure of the Lady Philosophy, its passages of prose alternate with passages of verse, and much of the time it is concerned less with practical moral problems than with rather technical questions of philosophy and theology. The search for happiness becomes an exploration of the problem of the *summum bonum*. Yet there are underlying similarities that suggest Johnson may have been transferring some of Boethius's problems and themes to another context. The two works complement each other; Boethius treats at length the philosophical and theological issues that Johnson mutes and Johnson brings into the foreground the practical moral dimensions unexplored in Boethius. Most of the ground they share is covered in the first three books of the *Consolation*, particularly the second, the book of fortune (which examines and rejects worldly conditions, such as wealth, power and fame, as possible sources of enduring happiness), and the third, the book of the *summum bonum* (which examines the nature of happiness). It is, by the way, from these two books especially that Johnson drew mottoes and quotations for the *Rambler* and *Adventurer*, and it was mainly the metres from these two books that Johnson and Mrs. Thrale translated week by week.

The underlying thematic structure of the *Consolation* is in broad outline like that used by Johnson. It begins with one who is disillusioned with what had been taken to be happiness (I, i). Boethius is concerned that righting wrongs and doing good in a position of power (one of Rasselas's favourite aspirations) has not brought him earthly happiness (I, iv). In this first book a strong image of man's condition as imprisonment is developed, just as Johnson develops the image of the happy valley as an imprisonment, mental as well as physical, from which Rasselas seeks to escape. Also developed in this first book is a sense of human alienation. Man finds himself surrounded by the order in God's natural world expressed in ordered and balanced images and statements. Only man's acts do not seem to participate in this order (I, v). Rasselas too finds himself in the happy valley in a natural world (expressed in its completeness in a highly ordered set of images), from which he apprehends his difference (9; 14–16; 23–4).

Boethius proceeds in the second book to consider the constant vicissitudes of fortune. The deepest poetic sense of this part lies perhaps in a realization of the inevitable transience and change of things in this world and of man's yearning in such a context for permanence, a quality of vision shared with *Rasselas*. After the refutation of false ideas of how happiness may be obtained, the third book proceeds to an exploration of what constitutes true happiness and the supreme good, concluding that God is happiness itself. These books are close to the middle section of *Rasselas*. The final conclusion is also the same, that man is led by the immortality of his soul, the yearning of the mind to find again its proper place which it cannot quite locate in the order of nature, to realize that true and lasting happiness is only to be found with God in the realm of eternity.[46] Although Johnson's presentation of a 'choice of life' gives his work a different emphasis, its wisdom is consonant with that of Boethius.

Boethius's fourth and fifth books go on among other things to explore the rôle of evil in the scheme proposed and to affirm the freedom of the human will, the final freedom of the mind that transcends the imprisonment of the body. Only in the most general terms are these parts echoed by Johnson. More akin to the tone of *Rasselas* is the ironic view of human weaknesses and insufficiencies in the face of the cosmic scheme perceptible in the verses that conclude the books of the *Consolation*, the account of Orpheus in III, xii, for instance, where the power of human love leads to disaster on the upward way and the sense of ironic discrepancy is perhaps at its strongest and most poignant,[47] or the distinctly ambiguous accounts of ancient heroes in IV, vii.

Boethius's Menippean dialogue takes up some of the commonplaces which Lucian treated ironically—the vain pursuit of happiness, the vanity of wishes, the power of fortune—with a heightened sense of the discrepancy between the position of the human sufferer and the transcendent capabilities personified in Philosophy which though still human are able to lead man to the divine. He goes beyond Lucian's here-and-now reality to focus on the status of the human mind and the affirmation of its freedom. While Johnson shares this central interest in the mind, he recognizes more clearly the delusions to which reason can be subject. He also affirms the value of a grasp on here-and-now reality, but with the important qualification that while freed from delusion it must be put in the perspective of the transcendent.

This perspective is in Boethius especially the gift of Philosophy. It does not take away melancholy or imperfection, but allows it to be seen in a larger context and thus transformed in significance. A similar gift of perspective occurs at the end of *Rasselas*. The wishing mortals continue with their wishing though now they know they will not get what they want. It is only those without such perspective who fall prey to disillusion or even madness. The difference is that between Swift and the Gulliver at the end of the fourth voyage[48]; with considerable variations of tone, the ends of many Menippean satires present something similar. This gift of perspective is an important reason why, I think, *Rasselas* does not seem ultimately to most readers a sad or nihilistic book. As Philosophy says, 'Talia sunt quippe quae restant, ut degustata quidem mordeant, interius autem recepta dulcescant.'[49]

6

The affiliation of *Rasselas* with the tradition of Menippean satire and with specific works from that tradition suggests an important dimension of the environment within which Johnson's imagination was operating when he wrote the book. Much recent scholarship on *Rasselas* deals, in fact, with aspects of its 'Menippean' character, even though the term is not used.[50] The 'Lucianic' strain in Johnson is not confined to *Rasselas*. This quality of vision has for long been recognized as part of the essential Johnson even if this name has not been applied to it, and it is strong in the periodical essays. I have argued elsewhere that the *Idler*, written at the same time as *Rasselas*, can profitably be associated with works of this kind.[51] In *Rasselas* Johnson takes up themes basic to Lucian and Boethius and seems even to engage specific works and passages by them, but he transforms the ancient commonplaces into something Johnsonian and of the eighteenth century. There is no single 'source' for *Rasselas* (like the undiscovered source of the Nile), but a confluence of many streams. He goes beyond Lucian in a specifically Christian way and gives to Boethius a more directly practical, here-and-now thrust. He casts his work as a 'tale' in compliance, no doubt, with the taste of his time and the model of the contemporary *conte philosophique* (though narrative of one kind or another had always been common enough in the genre), and he brings in not only Abyssinian and Biblical background but suggestions of a popular genre, the oriental tale, and elements of other forms and genres. He gives every indication of writing with awareness not only of a vast philosophic and theological background which he distills to its essentials but also of how things were done in this *kind* of work and of the sort of emphases it usually gave.

At the core of *Rasselas* is an exploration of the psychology and environment of choice, which is equally important with the idea of the search for happiness as the controlling principle of the book (though the two can scarcely be separated). Johnson produced a work which generates all sorts of meaningful patterning in terms not only of ideas *per se* but of structures of thought, imagery and human situation. It is a technique and a structure calculated to raise questions, stimulate thought, and undermine orthodox illusions rather than to provide answers. Truths always exist in human contexts. A reader needs consequently to cultivate an awareness not only of obvious pattern but, as Ehrenpreis suggests, a sensitivity to variations in tone and style and to complex and subtle ironies which, while they do not undercut the main thrust of the work, may qualify it. This constant possibility of irony and allusion means that a reader must further cultivate an awareness of the impact of differences as well as similarities within the larger controlling patterns which he perceives in the book. In this context the final direction of the book is not to the disillusioning proof of a thesis but to a satiric sense that we should discover reality by whatever means and learn to rest with the impossibilities and imperfections of the world in the context of a larger knowledge that inoculates us against disillusion and in Christian terms sanctifies and transforms the ordinary.

NOTES

1. *The Choice of Life* (New Haven: Yale University Press, 1973), p. 163.
2. 'Johnson's *Rasselas*: Implicit Contexts', *Journal of English and Germanic Philology*, LXXIV (1975), 1–25. Page references to this and other works cited will after the first citation be included in parentheses in the text.
3. Irvin Ehrenpreis, '*Rasselas* and Some Meanings of "Structure" in Literary Criticism', *Novel*, XIV (1981), 101–17. See pp. 112–13.
4. Johnson himself in 1778 observed to Boswell the similarity in plan and conduct between *Candide* and *Rasselas*. See *Life*, Vol. 1, p. 342. For a comparison see James L. Clifford, 'Some Remarks on *Candide* and *Rasselas*' in *Bicentenary Essays on* Rasselas, ed. Magdi Wahba, Supplement to *Cairo Studies in English*, 1959, pp. 7–14, and McIntosh, pp. 209–12.
5. E.g. see Alvin Whitley, 'The Comedy of *Rasselas*', *E.L.H.*, XXIII (1956), 48–70 (who blunts his argument by making little distinction between satire and comedy); Arieh Sachs, *Passionate Intelligence* (Baltimore: Johns Hopkins Press, 1967), pp. 98–9; Clifford, p. 10; George F. Butterick, 'The Comedy of Johnson's *Rasselas*', *Studies in the Humanities*, II (1971), 25–31. Vs. Sheldon Sacks, *Fiction and the Shape of Belief* (Berkeley and Los Angeles: University of California Press, 1964), especially pp. 49–60; Patrick O'Flaherty, 'Dr. Johnson as Equivocator: The Meaning of *Rasselas*', *Modern Language Quarterly*, XXXI (1970), 195–208.
6. In the absence of agreed-on English names I follow the convention of referring to Lucian's works by the Latin names common since the Renaissance. A table of equivalent names appears in Christopher Robinson, *Lucian and His Influence in Europe* (London: Duckworth, 1979), pp. 239–41.
7. John Dryden, *Of Dramatic Poesy and Other Critical Essays*, ed. George Watson (London: Everyman, 1962), Vol. 2, p. 97.
8. In this and other citations I refer to the fourth edition of Johnson's *Dictionary* (London, 1773), two volumes folio. For an extended discussion of meanings of and attitudes to satire in this period see P. K. Elkin, *The Augustan Defence of Satire* (Oxford: Clarendon Press, 1973).
9. See Elkin, Chapters 6 and 7.
10. Originally in *Eighteenth-Century Studies in Honor of Donald F. Hyde*, ed. W. H. Bond (New York: Grolier Club, 1970), pp. 145–60. The argument is repeated in Bate's *Samuel Johnson* (New York: Harcourt Brace Jovanovich,

1977), pp. 489–97. Cf. Johnson's 'Life of Akenside', para. 7 (*Lives*, Vol. 3, p. 413).

11. It will be noted that in this discussion I have in mind the treatments of satire by Edward W. Rosenheim, *Swift and the Satirist's Art* (Chicago: University of Chicago Press, 1963), especially pp. 11–13, and Sheldon Sacks, especially pp. 7 and 26. The latter uses his definition of satire to differentiate it from the apologue, of which he uses *Rasselas* as an example. While I respect the theoretical rigour and literary perception of these writers I cannot completely accept their arguments on this point.
12. Sachs, pp. 98–9.
13. *De Satyrica Graecorum Poesi et Romanorum Satira* (1605; rept. Delmar, N.Y.: Scholar's Facsimiles and Reprints, 1973, intro. Peter E. Medine). Parts of Casaubon's discussion are translated in Eugene P. Kirk, *Menippean Satire: An Annotated Catalogue of Texts and Criticism* (New York: Garland, 1980), pp. 231–33.
14. This book was in Johnson's undergraduate library. See Aleyn Lyell Reade, *Johnsonian Gleanings: Part V. The Doctor's Life 1728–1735* (1928; repr. New York: Octagon, 1968), p. 225.
15. Dryden, Vol. 2, pp. 113–15.
16. J. Bompaire, *Lucien Ecrivain* (Paris: Boccard, 1958), pp. 550–62; Kirk, n. 13, above, especially his description of the genre, p. xi.
17. N. Frye, *Anatomy of Criticism* (Princeton, N.J.: Princeton University Press, 1957), pp. 308–12.
18. Cf. the tendency of most recent discussions of structure in *Rasselas*. See, for example, Gwin J. Kolb, 'The Structure of *Rasselas*', *P.M.L.A.*, LXVI (1951), 698–717; Emrys Jones, 'The Artistic Form of *Rasselas*', *Review of English Studies*, n.s. XVIII (1967), 387–401; and Eric Rothstein, *Systems of Order and Inquiry in Later Eighteenth-Century Fiction* (Berkeley and Los Angeles: University of California Press, 1975), pp. 23–61. Rothstein lists other studies on p. 37.
19. Boswell, *Life*, Vol. 2, p. 121.
20. M. Bakhtin, *Problems of Dostoevsky's Poetics*, tr. R. W. Rotsel (Ann Arbor: Ardis, 1973). See Ch. 4, especially pp. 87–113.
21. See ibid., p. 296 n. 91.
22. Tracy, 'Democritus, Arise! A Study of Johnson's Humour', *Yale Review*, XXXIX (1950), 294–310; Whitley, 'The Comedy of *Rasselas*'; Butterick, 'The Comedy of Johnson's *Rasselas*'.
23. Casaubon, *De . . . Satira*, p. 270. A translation is in Kirk, p. 233.
24. *Chaucer and Menippean Satire* (Madison: University of Wisconsin Press, 1981). See especially Chapters 1–3.
25. Cf. Ronald Paulson's contrast of Juvenal and Lucian, *The Fictions of Satire* (Baltimore: Johns Hopkins Press, 1967), p. 32.
26. In this paragraph I paraphrase Payne, p. 11.
27. Motto of the *Rambler* from Horace, *Epistles*, I, i, 14.
28. *Eighteenth-Century Arguments for Immortality and Johnson's 'Rasselas'*, English Literary Studies Monograph Series No. 9 (Victoria, B.C.: University of Victoria, 1977).

29. Charles G. Osgood, 'Johnson and Macrobius'. *Modern Language Notes*, LXIX (1954), 246. Osgood associates the text he proposes from Macrobius with *Rasselas*.
30. See Reade, *Johnsonian Gleanings*, Part V, Appendix K, pp. 213–29.
31. Boswell, *Life*, Vol. 1, pp. 99–100.
32. *Nonnulli e Luciani Dialogis selecti, Et Scholiis illustrati ab Edwardo Leedes . . . In usum eorum, Qui dum Graecari student, non metuunt interim ridere* (London, 1678). There were later editions.
33. Donald Greene, *Samuel Johnson's Library: An Annotated Guide*, and J. D. Fleeman (ed.), *The Sale Catalogue of Samuel Johnson's Library: A Facsimile Edition*, English Literary Studies Monograph Series Nos. 1 and 2 (Victoria, B.C.: University of Victoria, 1975).
34. For Chaucer, *Life*, Vol. 4, p. 381. For Cervantes and Boileau, William Shaw and Hester Lynch Piozzi, *Memoirs and Anecdotes of Dr. Johnson*, ed. Arthur Sherbo (London: Oxford University Press, 1974), pp. 152–53. See also Johnson's 'Life of Butler', paras. 22, 23, 25 (*Lives*, Vol. 1, pp. 209–10). Cf. Stuart Tave's account of eighteenth-century readings of *Don Quixote* as primarily satiric, *The Amiable Humorist* (Chicago: University of Chicago Press, 1960), pp. 151–63.
35. Anecdote from Croker's Boswell in *Johnsonian Miscellanies*, ed. G. B. Hill (1897; rept. New York: Barnes and Noble, 1966), Vol. 2, p. 405; *Life*, Vol. 3, p. 10.
36. He suggested a translation to Elizabeth Carter, 1738 (*Life*, Vol. 1, p. 102) and undertook one with Mrs. Thrale in the mid-1760s (Samuel Johnson, *Poems*, ed. David Nichol Smith and Edward L. McAdam, 2nd edn. (Oxford: Clarendon Press, 1974), pp. 169–77). See also *Idler* 69 (11 August 1759) on previous English translations. See *Ramblers* 6, 7, 96, 143, 178, *Adventurer* 10.
37. Jonathan Culler, *The Pursuit of Signs* (Ithaca, N.Y.: Cornell University Press, 1981), p. 38.
38. See e.g. *De mercede conductis*, 42; *Somnium sive vita*, 5–16; *Prometheus es in verbis*, 6. The extended metaphor of scaling the heights in *Hermotimus* 5 is also reminiscent of one of Johnson's allegorical images. Parenthetical references in the text will be to the marginal chapter numbers in the Loeb edition (as above in this note) followed by volume and page for quotations. Lucian, ed. with English transl. by A. M. Harmon, K. Kilburn, and M. D. Macleod (London: Heinemann, 1913–67), 8 vols.
39. Cf. also *Menippus* and perhaps *Charon, Icaromenippus*, and *Piscator*.
40. Walter Harte, *An Essay on Satire, Particularly on the Dunciad* (1730), Augustan Reprint Society, Publication Number 132 (Los Angeles, 1968), p. 18.
41. *The History of Rasselas Prince of Abissinia*, ed. R. W. Chapman (Oxford: Clarendon Press, 1927), p. 30.
42. Cf. not only *Navigium* and *Icaromenippus* but *Somnium sive Gallus*, 23, and *Hermotimus*, 71.
43. Gwin J. Kolb, 'Johnson's "Dissertation on Flying" and John Wilkins' *Mathematical Magick*', *Modern Philology*, XLVII (1949), 24–31; Louis Landa, 'Johnson's Feathered Man: "A Dissertation on the Art of

Flying" Considered' in *Eighteenth-Century Studies in Honor of Donald F. Hyde*, ed. W. H. Bond (New York: Grolier Club, 1970), pp. 161–78.

44. In the original the elder addresses the one of limited experience as *thrasutate*, a noun formation related to the adjective *thrasus* meaning in a good sense 'bold, spirited, resolute' and in a bad sense 'rash, venturous, presumptuous', and it is tempting to speculate that some residual memory of the word may have influenced Johnson's choice of an Abyssinian name for his prince, whose character its meaning certainly touches. Johnson had formed many names in the *Rambler* on Greek roots. One may add that '*Nekuia*' is the title of a dialogue by the real Menippus thought to lie behind Lucian's *Menippus* and apparently involving a descent to the underworld and an exploration of the vanity of human wishes. Does Pekuah suggest *peko* meaning to comb or to card wool, perhaps the occupations of a lady's companion? Or does Imlac, another real Abyssinian name, suggest *elake*, 'he spoke loud, shouted forth' or 'he sang', activities not inappropriate to a rhetorician and poet? It may be added that the subtitle of *Hermotimus* is '*peri haireseōn*', translated in the Loeb as 'concerning the Sects [of philosophy]'. It could also be translated 'concerning choices'. *Rasselas*, of course, in Johnson's letter to William Strahan of 20 January 1759, was titled 'The Choice of Life'. The title of *Vitarum auctio* (Philosophies for Sale) is '*Biōn prasis*', 'the sale of lives', or, as the Loeb editor points out, 'of various types of the philosophic life' as they are embodied in their practitioners—a meaning close to Johnson's usage here. Cf. also J. P. Hardy's note on the 'choice of life' topos in ancient literature in his edition of *Rasselas* (London: Oxford University Press, 1968), pp. 141–42.
45. *The Fictions of Satire*, pp. 31–42.
46. The pattern may be a frequent Menippean one in so far as there is a final movement to the divine.
47. Johnson not only translated these verses with Mrs. Thrale but alluded to them in *Ramblers* 143 and 178. The lines he quotes in the latter are not far in tone (and even form), especially in the Latin, from the opening paragraph of *Rasselas*, and the paragraph following in *Rambler* 178 suggests the context of the search for happiness and its relation to the life of faith. Cf. especially ll. 52–4.
48. Cf. Swift's letter to Pope, 26 November 1725: 'I tell you after all that I do not hate Mankind, it is vous autres who hate them because you would have them reasonable Animals, and are Angry for being disappointed' (*Correspondence*, ed. Harold Williams (Oxford: Clarendon Press, 1963), Vol. 3, p. 118).
49. 'Those remedies that are left now are like those that sting on the tongue, but sweeten once taken within' (III, i: *The Theological Tractates and The Consolation of Philosophy*, ed. H. F. Stewart, E. K. Rand, and S. J. Tester, Loeb Classical Library (Cambridge, Mass.: Harvard University Press, 1973), pp. 228–29).
50. Among critical discussions, for example, Carey McIntosh anticipates several Menippean qualities in his description of the form of *Rasselas*. See *The Choice of Life*, e.g. pp. 201, 206, and other parts of his discussion.

Among others see also Ehrenpreis, '*Rasselas* and Some Meanings of "Structure" in Literary Criticism'; Whitley, 'The Comedy of *Rasselas*'; Sheridan Baker, '*Rasselas*: Psychological Irony and Romance', in *Essays in English Neoclassicism in Memory of Charles B. Woods: Philological Quarterly*, XLV (1966), 249–61. The need for studies of large and complex backgrounds is typical of Menippean works. There are many of the backgrounds of *Rasselas*.

51. James F. Woodruff, 'Johnson's *Idler* and the Anatomy of Idleness', *English Studies in Canada*, VI (1980), 21–38, especially 36–7.

9

Johnson and Commemorative Writing

by MARY LASCELLES

Commemorative writing—what does this expression denote? Certain literary forms, of course: the epitaph, whether an inscription or 'inscriptional in form and feeling'[1]; the elegy, in its restricted modern sense of lament for the dead; and, as we draw near the present day, the memoir and obituary notice. Beyond these established forms, however, something is to be discerned; and that *something* is happily exemplified in Johnson's writings.

To confine reflections on any part of Johnson's literary theory and practice within the narrow compass of an essay entails some arbitrary limitation. I propose to leave out his formal epitaphs, in Latin, preferring to dwell rather on what may be called his *occasional* commemorative writing: those occasions which he grasps and turns to one opportunity after another for commemorating friend or benefactor.

This practice must be set against a background of his theory. His interest in the epitaph as a distinct form was of long duration and constancy. It was first declared in 1740, when he contributed *An Essay on Epitaphs* to *The Gentleman's Magazine*.[2] Here he takes up an uncompromising position; the epitaph has not received the critical attention due to it on the score of its antiquity and—this runs through the argument—its moral usefulness: 'Nature and reason have dictated to every nation, that to preserve good actions from oblivion, is both the interest and the duty of mankind.'[3] The function of the epitaph is didactic.

The *Essay* offers recommendations in which we hear the common sense of the eighteenth century: brevity, fitness. But there are other intimations; the reader must not expect to be told all the achievements of a famous man. A traditional epithet should serve to distinguish one Caesar from another, these few words to recall what we ought to know about Newton: '*Isaacus Newtonus, naturae legibus investigatis, hic quiescit.*'[4] Are these the tones of the proud, disappointed scholar?

An abrupt interjection announces Johnson's abiding interest in the traditions of the mediaeval church. He claims that 'in the monkish ages, however ignorant and unpolished, the epitaphs were drawn up with far greater propriety than can be shown in those which more enlightened times have produced.' He quotes a typical example—'*Orate pro anima miserrimi peccatoris*'—calling it 'an address, to the last degree, striking and solemn, as it flowed naturally from the religion then believed, and awakened in the reader sentiments of benevolence for the deceased, and of concern for his own happiness.'[5] He may think poorly of mediaeval Latinity, but he is free from the contemporary prejudice which dismissed all medieval religious practices as 'superstition'.

More resoundingly, the first shot is fired in what will be a long and hard-fought battle.

> In writing epitaphs, one circumstance is to be considered, which affects no other composition; the place in which they are now commonly found restrains them to a particular air of solemnity, and debars them from the admission of all lighter or gayer ornaments. In this it is, that the style of an epitaph necessarily differs from that of an elegy. . . . All allusions to the heathen mythology are, therefore, absurd.[6]

Not only will Johnson maintain his prohibition of these 'ornaments'; he will extend it to the elegy.

Presently, he returns to the subject, with a difference. In his *Dissertation on the Epitaphs written by Pope*,[7] he is concerned with the application of these principles. The epitaph is still to be judged by its capacity for edification; its effect on the reader should be a desire to emulate the virtues recorded—and this is most likely to be effectual when they were exercised in private life. The *Dissertation* does not much advance our knowledge of Johnson's deeper convictions. He was evidently repelled by Pope's glittering paradoxes, but contents himself with taking the antithetical couplets apart, one by one, and exposing the logical fallacy in them. 'Where is the relation between the two positions, that he *gained no title* and *lost no friend*?' 'There is no opposition between an *honest courtier* and a *patriot*.'[8] We miss the light-house beam of his generalizations, except where he shakes off his preoccupation with particulars, as in the reflection:

> It will not always happen that the success of a poet is proportionate to his labour. The same observation may be extended to all works of imagination, which are often influenced by causes wholly out of the performer's power, by hints of which he perceives not the origin, by sudden elevations of mind which he cannot produce in himself, and which sometimes rise when he expects them least.[9]

For the most part, however, Johnson is content to apply and develop rules which he had propounded in the *Essay*. A fanciful expression in the epitaph on Rowe provokes an outburst, seemingly disproportionate to the offence:

> To wish *Peace to thy shade* is too mythological to be admitted into a christian temple: the ancient worship has infected almost all our other compositions, and might therefore be contented to spare our epitaphs. Let fiction, at least, cease with life, and let us be serious over the grave.[10]

To inveigh against *fiction*—associated in the *Dictionary* with *intent to deceive*—may seem a severe reprimand for a mere figure of speech. It is clear that Johnson is extending his censure of mythological allusion from situation to context; it is not only in a church, where commemorative inscriptions are likely to be found, that these 'ornaments' provoke him, but in the very language of reflections upon death.

The occasions on which Boswell teazed Johnson by importuning him to expatiate on this subject are notorious[11]; but, to be quite fair, even to Boswell, a great many of Johnson's friends would press him with such questions, as though they thought he must be forced to speak out. They were mistaken.

The sermon he wrote for his wife's funeral is an outspoken discourse on death, in the spirit of the seventeenth-century preachers, in whose work he was widely read.[12] In it he develops the argument that philosophy will not suffice to fortify man against his natural and proper fear of death. Revealed religion alone can testify to the immortality of the soul, and the divine mercy it will need.

Johnson, it is clear, was perturbed not only by the mythology but also by the philosophical assumptions of that pagan world which dominated poetic convention, as his comment on a passage in *Measure for Measure* testifies. The Duke, in his supposed office as religious counsellor, assures Claudio that

> Thy best of rest is sleep,
> And that thou oft provok'st; yet grosly fear'st
> Thy death, which is no more.

Here Warburton had quoted Cicero, adding that the Epicurean 'insinuation' had been judiciously omitted. Johnson retorts:

> Here Dr. Warburton might have found a sentiment worthy of his animadversion. I cannot without indignation find Shakespeare saying that 'death is only sleep,' lengthening out his exhortation by a sentence which in the Friar is impious, in the reasoner is foolish, and in the poet trite and vulgar.[13]

He is provoked alike by the airy pagan assurance and Warburton's unctuous comment.

The thunder rumbles on through the *Lives of the Poets*. Even Dryden is not allowed to sport with mythological allusion, either in formal panegyric—'He had not yet learned, indeed he never learned well, to forbear the improper use of mythology'—or, more understandably, in elegy: 'nor was he serious enough to keep heathen fables out of his religion'.[14] At last the storm breaks in the notorious denunciation of *Lycidas*: 'Where there is leisure for fiction there is little grief.'[15] There is no need to quote at length from this well known and much discussed passage. Indeed, it seems foolhardy to enter an arena where Titans have encountered[16]; but I think there is one particular hitherto unremarked. The word *myth* is not in Johnson's *Dictionary*, and the *N.E.D.* has no instance of its use until well into the nineteenth century. What should this signify? Surely, that to our age belongs an interest, deepening into awe, at what can be divined of early man's endeavours to express his sense of his own predicament. Thus, there is more than one frontier to be crossed if we are to understand Johnson's repugnance to joining in a game which his fellow poets enjoyed. We must reckon with the playfulness which they, and he, took for granted in allusions to classical mythology.

There is not a great deal to be learned about Johnson's theory from the *Lives of the Poets*—least of all from his commendation of particular elegies, though he mentions several. Edmund Smith's *Poem on the Death of Mr. John Phillips*, for example, is characterized as one 'which justice must place among the best elegies which our language can shew'. Presently, however, an awkward recollection seems to halt him—'There are some passages too ludicrous'—but he takes it in his stride: 'Every human performance has its faults.'[17] Was he speaking from memory? And can we account for the praise allotted to Cowley's elegy on Sir Henry Wotton and Tickell's on Addison,[18] by surmising that Johnson made it a rule not to condemn what he had not re-read? On firm ground with a well remembered author, he is ready to condemn outright. Here is his verdict on Dryden's *Threnodia Augustalis*: 'It has neither tenderness nor dignity, it is neither magnificent nor pathetick. . . . He is, he says, "petrified with grief", but the marble sometimes relents, and trickles in a joke.'[19] *Tenderness* and *dignity*—if these indeed lie at the heart of commemorative writing, then we have come a long way from the epitaph as an instructive record.

Something has intervened. In all this tale of what epitaph and elegy ought to do, we have heard much of the reader's claims, but no whisper on behalf of the dead man. Johnson's practice is, however, less predictable than his theory, and therefore of far greater interest.

What may the dead man ask of his commemorator? In the first place, guardianship of his reputation. This is not always easy within the confines of so brief and formal a tribute. Reflecting on the bland uniformity of Pope's eulogies, Johnson had admitted: 'The difficulty in writing epitaphs is to give a particular and appropriate praise.'[20] Given the scope of a memoir, however, this may be done, as he shows in his own lives of Savage and Collins, which are in effect memoirs, with biographical information attached.

The *Life of Savage*[21] is surely one of those *performances* (to borrow a favourite Johnsonian word) in which imaginative insight transcends what may fairly be expected. Line by line, the image is built up of that extraordinary character who had power to charm such a diversity of friends and benefactors—until he fell out with them and had to seek more. In his heyday,

> he was courted by all who endeavoured to be thought men of genius, and caressed by all who valued themselves upon a refined taste. To admire Mr. Savage was a proof of discernment, and to be acquainted with him was a title to poetical reputation.[22]

Opportunity was invariably thrown away on him; not only his own gifts and advantages, but also the time, patience and resources of those who befriended him, were squandered. Johnson's maxim seems to be

> Nothing extenuate,
> Nor set down aught in malice—

but the need for extenuation is almost limitless. Johnson meets it by making us believe that a conjunction of circumstances and temperament weighted the scales against Savage, and he does this with an assumption of authority whose source is disclosed only towards the end. When Savage left for Wales, he 'parted from the author of this narrative with tears in his eyes'.[23] Might not a contemporary reader, outside the Johnsonian circle and still unacquainted with Boswell, at this point exclaim: 'So this is why the story rings with the authentic tones of experience!'

And so the road winds downhill, all the way to the miserable end, dependence on the charity of the gaoler in a debtors' prison; and Johnson challenges the reader to consider what his own conduct would have been in all the circumstances of Savage's life.

This, however, is not the whole tale of Johnson's concern with a dead man's reputation. As much again can be read in that memoir of another hapless friend, William Collins.

Comparison between these two lives brings to light a crucial distinction. A man solicitous about another's memory may be facing either of two questions: how he will be remembered, or whether he will be remembered at all.

Johnson shared his solicitude for Collins while he was still alive with the Wartons.

> I knew him a few years ago full of hopes and full of projects, versed in many languages, high in fancy, and strong in retention. This busy and forcible mind is now under the government of those who lately would not have been able to comprehend the least and most narrow of its designs.[24]

His endeavours to ensure that this promise, though unfulfilled, should not be forgotten were spread over eighteen years, beginning with his contribution to the *Poetical Character* published by Francis Fawkes and William Woty in 1763,[25] and ending only with his completion of the *Lives of the Poets* in 1781. That first signal of his commitment may be likened to a personal obituary notice in a modern literary journal. It was inserted after a brief account of Collins's life,[26] and ascribed to an eminent man of letters 'who knew him intimately well'. It does something to offset, though not to contradict, the sad observation in the memoir: 'For a man of such an elevated genius, Mr. Collins has wrote but little.'[27] Convinced as he was of the *genius*, when it came to achievement Johnson could find no more than this to say: 'He wrote now and then odes and other poems, and did something, however little.'[28]

When he came to write the *Life*, Johnson reprinted this *Character*, explaining that it had been written when the subject was still fresh in his mind. There it stands between a short biography and two lines of moving valedictory: 'Such was the fate of Collins, with whom I once delighted to converse, and whom I yet remember with tenderness.'[29] A few critical afterthoughts serve to conclude an account of the melancholia in which he died.

In the meanwhile, however, Johnson had done something remarkable—indeed, singular; I have found no parallel to it. In his edition of Shakespeare he had attached this note to the dirge which her brothers chant over Imogen: 'For the obsequies of Fidele, a song was written by my unhappy friend, Mr.

William Collins of Chichester, a man of uncommon learning and abilities. I shall give it a place at the end in honour of his memory.'[30] And there indeed it stands, at the close of the play.

There is a vein of irony in all this. Johnson evidently thought that, whereas Savage would always stand high as a poet, his conduct required some apology. Collins, on the other hand, though remembered for his amiable qualities, would hardly be credited with poetic gifts, unless one who knew him were to vouch for them. And yet, if an anthology of eighteenth-century poetry were now to appear without so much as one of his odes, there would be consternation; but who would protest at the omission of Savage?

So much for the reader and the subject of epitaph or elegy. But there is a third person to be considered: has the writer no voice? What if he is indeed not a hireling but a true mourner?

Johnson's voice as mourner is pitched so low that its message may be mistaken. Professor Bertrand Bronson calls the elegy on Levet 'an expression of deep personal loss, but stated in language so general that we merely infer the private grief as a natural part of the common experience'.[31] This is equally applicable to the sermon for his wife's funeral. In the heart of this meditation on death is set a delineation, hardly less general, of the mourner's condition:

> He who suffers one of the sharpest evils which this life can shew, amidst all its varieties of misery; he that has lately been separated from the person whom a long participation of good and evil had endeared to him: he who has seen kindness snatched from his arms, and fidelity torn from his bosom; he whose ear is no more to be delighted with tender instruction, and whose virtue shall be no more awakened by the seasonable whispers of mild reproof

will find consolation in religion.[32] These words might express no more than sympathetic general observation of the state of bereavement, if it were not for their resemblance to some that Johnson was prompted by Dodsley's loss of his wife to write to Thomas Warton:

> I hope he will not suffer so much as I yet suffer for the loss of mine. . . . I have ever since seemed to myself broken off from mankind, a kind of solitary wanderer in the wild of life, without

> any certain direction, or fixed point of view. A gloomy gazer on a World to which I have little relation.[33]

Although no candid reader can miss the tenderness and dignity of Johnson's private record of his sorrow *On the Death of Dr. Robert Levet*, yet such is the reticence of expression that it is possible to underrate its poignancy. I fear I have formerly done so, and therefore take this opportunity of quoting a better authority:

> The sense of loss is shot through every line of this earnest record of the virtues of an awkward friend who had employed well 'the single talent,' and makes the whole poem glow with the warmth of natural sentiment.[34]

Yet another kind of loss is commemorated in the tribute paid to a fellow craftsman lately dead. When he has been a writer, it may be regarded as a salute to the craft they both practise. Johnson had composed a formal epitaph for Goldsmith in Westminster Abbey—and had got his way about the language. He was hindered from writing something ampler and more familiar: copyright difficulties stood in the way of a Life.[35] So he brought into play his own kind of opportunism, and wrote an *occasional* tribute. He opened the *Life of Parnell* with a disclaimer: it was

> a task which I should very willingly decline, since it has been lately written by Goldsmith; a man of such variety of powers and such felicity of performance that he always seemed to do best that which he was doing; a man who had the art of being minute without tediousness, and general without confusion; whose language was copious without exuberance, exact without constraint, and easy without weakness.

He will give the gist of his life of Parnell, glad of the opportunity of paying tribute to his memory.[36]

For Johnson it was not necessary that the fellow craftsman should be a writer. He was ready to call on his professionalism whenever help was wanted with an epitaph. Of Claudy Phillips he knew only that he was a musician and died poor; but, in talk with Garrick, he revised *extempore* the feeble lines written by Wilkes and, calling on those traditional makers of music, the angelic host, provided four of his own:

Rest here distrest by poverty no more,
Find here that calm thou gav'st so oft before;
Sleep undisturb'd within this peaceful shrine,
Till angels wake thee with a note like thine.[37]

Johnson's part in commemorating Hogarth is another story, worth recalling; Garrick, having been asked by Mrs. Hogarth to write an epitaph for her husband's tomb, sent what he had drafted to Johnson for correction. Johnson corrected it, drastically. Apart from an outright condemnation of the third stanza, his objections and alterations are verbal; he was as attentive to regularity and sweetness in this as in any other kind of verse. '*Learn* and *mourn* cannot stand for rhymes. *Art and Nature* have been seen together too often.' And here the guardian of the language is roused: '*Feeling* for *tenderness* or *sensibility* is a word merely colloquial of late introduction, not yet [sure] enough of its own existence to claim a place upon a stone.'[38] These censures are softened by praise of Garrick's phrase *pictured Morals*, 'a beautiful expression, which I would wish to retain', by insistence on the difficulty of this kind of writing, and by the companionable offer—'Suppose you worked upon something like this'—followed by two stanzas which refine upon Garrick's draft. So, originally preserved in a letter of tentative suggestions, we have the splendid lines:

Here death has clos'd the curious eyes
That saw the manners in the Face.

Can Johnson have been thinking of Hogarth's portraits of Captain Coram, and Simon Fraser Lord Lovat?

In the event, Garrick compromised, and two stanzas, the first his own, the second based on Johnson's, were inscribed on the monument in Chiswick churchyard.[39]

Thus far, I have been considering tributes, whether initiated by Johnson or no, which expressed, if not personal grief, at least personal regard. There is still the expression of gratitude by a community to a public benefactor. This is the voice we hear in Johnson's tribute to Laud, in *The Vanity of Human Wishes*.

The choice of illustrations, for this *imitation* of Juvenal's tenth satire, is remarkable. Juvenal had said, in his first satire, that, regardful of his own safety, he must draw his illustrations from past history. As this literary game developed and flourished, with an inclination towards Horace in eighteenth-century England, insults and compliments were tossed to and fro with little fear of the consequences. Johnson alone, and only in this poem, casts back to the recent past and through the years of our own civil war to the sixteenth century. He is known to have been interested in the career of 'Swedish Charles'; he was clearly inspired to choose Wolsey by Shakespeare's picture of his fall; about one at least of his seventeenth-century characters he must have felt he had something to say. What he said about Laud, in the context he selected, laid him open to attack by Macaulay, who, gathering up Oxford, Laud and Johnson in a rhetorical gesture, cast them on a bonfire to be consumed by his righteous indignation.[40] It is time to ask what Johnson had in fact done. Where he prefers his own historical illustrations to Juvenal's, he softens the glaring colours of the original picture with tragic shadows. Here he goes further; for the ignoble ambitions of the orator he substitutes the worthy aims of the scholar. Faithful, however, to Juvenal's main intention, he makes the achievement of those aims in itself a disaster. Academic excellence brings William Laud, Archbishop of Canterbury, to a dangerous, and, as it proves, a fatal eminence. This, compressed into six lines, is certainly elliptical; but surely the train of thought is clear. Laud is mourned, not by church or state,[41] but by his own University, to which he had been a notable benefactor: Art and Genius, what can and what cannot be taught (according to the *Dictionary*), represent the commonwealth of scholarship. This is Clarendon's Laud, but without the impetuous acrimony in controversy. Was Johnson under any obligation to include this? Though he doubtless thought Laud right and his adversaries wrong, yet he draws, elsewhere, no idealized portrait of him as a controversialist. This is how he appears, locked in conflict with Cheynel: 'They were both, to the last degree, zealous, active, and pertinacious'[42]—pugilists, both.

Writing of biography in *The Idler* (84), Johnson admits the likelihood of partisanship: 'The zeal of gratitude, the ardour of patriotism, fondness for an opinion, or fidelity to a party, may easily overpower the vigilance of a mind habitually well disposed, and prevail over unassisted and unfriended veracity.' His assumption that a man's life may be written either by friend or enemy would have shocked his favourite, Izaak Walton, for whom biography *was* commemoration; but whatever change has come over the literary scene leaves the epitaph untouched. It must not, Johnson wrote, ascribe fictitious virtues to a man, but 'whoever is curious to know his faults must inquire after them in other places'.[43] Or, more trenchantly: 'In lapidary inscriptions a man is not upon oath.'[44] In this respect, at least, he may claim kinship with the composer of a tribute to a benefactor. I leave the last word, on what lies behind that vexed passage in *The Vanity of Human Wishes*, with G. M. Young: 'Will the imagination ever be neutral? I doubt it. But if it can, then it had better keep clear of the seventeenth century.'[45]

I have kept to the end an example of Johnson's commemorative writing which I hold to be the most spontaneous, the most deeply characteristic—though this entails a final bend in the road: the return to personal engagement with a benefactor. What led up to it needs a little disentangling. Here is the sequence of events, in so far as this can be indicated briefly. In 1702–4, the Oxford University Press published Clarendon's massive *History of the Rebellion*. His insertion, from a subsequent composition, of autobiographical material, and the want of a single authoritative manuscript, gave an opening for John Oldmixon, in his *History of England* (1730), to impugn the good faith of the University and its Press. In 1759 the publication of the *Life*—the word autobiography had not yet been coined—with the intricate negotiations between Clarendon's heirs and the University and the complexity of the manuscript material, gave fresh occasion for suspicion.[46] Taking as his theme the hazards of posthumous publication, with particular reference to memoirs, Johnson launched a vehement attack on Oldmixon and his confederate, Duckett. In *Idler* 65 (14 July 1759) he opens with a cordial welcome to Clarendon's *Life*, calling it the 'sequel' of the *History*; glances at ill-fated posthumous works, notably Burnet's narrative, suspect for want of a manuscript, and points triumphantly to Clarendon's *History*, which,

> tho' printed with the sanction of one of the first universities of the world, had not an unexpected manuscript been happily

> discovered, would, with the help of factious credulity, have been brought into question by the two lowest of all human beings, a scribbler for a party, and a commissioner of excise.

The two were recognizable as Oldmixon and Duckett, both now dead. In the second—that is, the first collected—edition of *The Idler* (1761), Johnson was to ask that the manuscript of the *Life* should be exhibited, to avert suspicion.[47] Presently the political climate changed, passions subsided, and, in the event, the verdict has gone against the detractors. Some nineteen to twenty years later, however, Johnson was again involved in this controversy. Writing the Life of Edmund Smith, he had to deal with the old allegation that Smith had forged passages for insertion into Clarendon's *History*. Here he could call as witness one who had known both Smith and Duckett: Gilbert Walmsley. Though, as a 'virulent' Whig, Walmsley might not be concerned to vindicate the *History*, yet he had exonerated Smith from the charge of forgery, calling him 'a man of great veracity'.[48]

So, by crooked and miry ways, we come to a name which evoked from Johnson that glowing tribute of gratitude:

> Of Gilbert Walmsley, thus presented to my mind, let me indulge myself in the remembrance. I knew him very early; he was one of the first friends that literature procured me, and I hope that at least my gratitude made me worthy of his notice.

Despite difference of age and opposition in politics, 'I honoured him, and he endured me'. Presently, we come to the core of the matter:

> His studies had been so various that I am not able to name a man of equal knowledge. His acquaintance with books was great; and what he did not immediately know he could at least tell where to find. Such was his amplitude of learning and such his copiousness of communication that it may be doubted whether a day now passes in which I have not some advantage from his friendship.

I dwell on this passage, not presuming to suppose that other readers of Johnson have overlooked it, but in the hope of separating it from an *accretion*. In acknowledging his own obligation, Johnson had associated with himself that other beneficiary of Walmsley's kindly help, David Garrick,[49] 'whom I hoped to have gratified with this character of our common friend: but what are the hopes of man! I am disappointed by that stroke of death, which has eclipsed the gaiety of nations and impoverished the publick stock of harmless pleasure.' On 24 April 1779, with the first set of *Lives* newly published and Garrick scarcely three months dead, Boswell chose to tax Johnson with too high an estimate of Garrick's worth. This drew a defence of Garrick's life and conduct; but Boswell did not know where to stop. 'I presumed to animadvert on his eulogy on Garrick in his "Lives of the Poets".' Johnson answered with temperate warmth: Garrick's death had eclipsed, not extinguished, the gaiety of nations. 'BOSWELL. "But why nations?" JOHNSON. "Why, Sir, some exaggeration must be allowed. Besides, nations may be said—if we allow the Scotch to be a nation, and to have gaiety,—which they have not." ' Boswell, still unabashed, then forced him to defend *harmless pleasure*. He replied that, pleasure being 'a word of dubious import . . . to be able therefore to furnish pleasure that is harmless, pleasure pure and unalloyed, is as great a power as man can possess.'[50] So Boswell got from him one of his happiest maxims. Boswell makes us laugh both at him and with him, and this uncommon gift earns him our gratitude; but I wish he had not chosen to *animadvert* on that particular passage, for the laughter drowns a voice I would rather hear—Johnson's own, unprompted and unprovoked, cherishing remembrance of past benefits.

Those few, short paragraphs devoted to Walmsley's memory comply with Johnson's demands of commemorative writing—appropriate praise, singling out what is due—but they go far beyond this in reaching out to grasp fleeting opportunity for the recall to life of a long past friendship. How far beyond may be divined in a distinction he makes elsewhere, between words that 'fill the ear' and 'ideas that slumber in the heart'.[51]

There is a better way of conveying insight and appreciation than by critical commentary: delicate and apt citation. Serving in Salonika in the Royal Garrison Artillery, and leading a 'nomadic and semi-barbarous existence . . . in camps and dugouts and troop-trains', R. W. Chapman commemorated his friendship with Ingram Bywater in 'The Portrait of a Scholar',[52] and chose as motto that passage from Johnson's tribute to Gilbert Walmsley which I have just quoted. The circumstances were not alike; but this kind of comparison need not run on parallel lines. Present and future might differ widely, but not the retrospect. That lost world of scholarship in which, though the temporary soldier might himself return to it, he would not find his old friend waiting,[53] is luminous with the same glow which had lit Johnson's memory of Walmsley. 'It is to be doubted whether a day now passes, in which I have not some advantage from his friendship.' That theme recurs in the essay.

Mutatis mutandis—I in my turn cherish the recollection of that not uncritical but long-suffering and large-hearted friend, R. W. Chapman, to whom I owe any capacity I may possess for reading Johnson truly.

NOTES

1. R. W. Ketton-Cremer, *Lapidary Verse*, in *Proceedings of the British Academy*, XLV (1959) 246.
2. It was printed in the third edition of *The Idler*, 1767.
3. Johnson, *Works* (Oxford, 1825), Vol. 5, p. 260.
4. Ibid., p. 261.
5. Ibid., p. 264.
6. Ibid., p. 262.
7. Contributed to *The Universal Visiter* in 1756; included in the third edition of *The Idler*, and appended to the *Life of Pope*, *Lives*, Vol. 3, pp. 254–72, from which I quote.
8. Ibid., pp. 260, 258.
9. Ibid., p. 268.
10. Ibid., p. 261.
11. E.g., *Lives*, Vol. 2, p. 107; a notorious example.
12. See Yale, Vol. 14, pp. 261–71. The editors are at pains to demonstrate Johnson's familiarity with the homiletic tradition of the seventeenth century.
13. Yale, Vol. 7, pp. 192–93. According to modern scene-division, III. i. 17–19.
14. *Lives*, Vol. 1, p. 427, on *Astraea Redux*, and 439, on *Threnodia Augustalis*.
15. Ibid., Vol. 1, p. 163.
16. Notably, Walter Raleigh, Robert Bridges and R. W. Chapman. See, for

example, R. W. Chapman, *Johnson on Poetry*, in *Johnsonian and Other Essays and Reviews* (Oxford, 1953).

17. *Lives*, Vol. 2, pp. 16–17. The problem is to decide which of those 234 lines is more absurd than the rest.
18. Ibid., Vol. 1, p. 36, and Vol. 2, p. 117.
19. Ibid., Vol. 1, p. 438.
20. *Dissertation*, pp. 263–64.
21. First published 1744; again in 1748, and (with other lives) in 1767; finally, in *Lives*, Vol. 2, from which I quote. But see *Early Biographical Writings of Dr. Johnson*, ed. J. D. Fleeman (Farnborough, 1973), for Johnson's revisions of the text; also edition by C. Tracy (Oxford, 1971).
22. *Lives*, Vol. 2, p. 358.
23. Ibid., pp. 413–14.
24. *Letters*, number 51, to Joseph Wharton, 8 March 1754.
25. See *Early Biographical Writings*, pp. 513–16.
26. Birkbeck Hill suggests that Johnson may have used this. See *Lives*, Vol. 3, p. 334, note 1.
27. *Early Biographical Writings*, p. 515.
28. *Lives*, Vol. 3, p. 335.
29. Ibid., p. 339.
30. Yale, Vol. 8, p. 899. According to modern scene-division, IV. ii. 281. The Yale editors do not reprint Collins's poem.
31. 'Personification Reconsidered', in *New Light on Dr. Johnson* (New Haven: Yale, 1959), p. 190.
32. Yale, Vol. 14, p. 266.
33. *Letters*, number 56, 21 December 1754.
34. David Nichol Smith, 'Johnson's Poems', in *New Light*, p. 15.
35. *O.H.E.L.*, *The Mid-Eighteenth Century*, by John Butt and Geoffrey Carnall (Oxford: Clarendon, 1979), p. 47.
36. *Lives*, Vol. 2, p. 49.
37. For the circumstances, and evidence of Johnson's authorship, see Johnson, *Poems*, David Nichol Smith and Edward L. McAdam (Oxford: Clarendon, 1941, 2nd edn. 1974), pp. 89–91.
38. *Letters*, number 269, 12 December 1771.
39. For the poem, the circumstances, variants and Garrick's final version, see *Poems*, pp. 181–82.
40. Thomas Babington Macaulay, article on Johnson in the *Encyclopaedia Britannica*.
41. Compare Cleveland's 'The state in Strafford fell, the Church in Laud'.
42. Life of Francis Cheynel, first published in *The Student* (1751). See *Works*, 1825, Vol. 6, pp. 413–28.
43. *Essay*, p. 265.
44. *Life*, Vol. 2, p. 407: told by Burney to Boswell.
45. 'No Servile Tenure', in *Daylight and Champagne* (London, 1937), p. 45.
46. For the long and complicated history of this affair, see Ian Green, 'The Publication of Clarendon's Autobiography, and the Acquisition of his Papers by the Bodleian Library', in *Bodleian Library Record*, X (1982), 349–67.

47. Yale, Vol. 2, p. 203, note 7.
48. *Lives*, Vol. 2, p. 20, and Appendix A.
49. For Walmsley's help to the two young men, see *Life*, Vol. I, p. 102.
50. Ibid., Vol. 3, pp. 387–88.
51. *Lives*, Vol. 1, p. 459.
52. The essay (written in 1917) was first published in 1919. It may be found in *The Portrait of a Scholar and Other Essays written in Macedonia* (Oxford, 1921).
53. Bywater did not live to see the end of the war.

Index

Abingdon, Bertie Willoughby, Earl of, 104–5
Adams, William, 32–3
Addison, Joseph, 43, 45, 47, 162, 190
Aesop, 168
Aix-la-Chapelle, Treaty of, 131, 132
Akenside, Mark, 118, 130
Aldrovandus, 56
Alexander the Great, 40, 132
America, South, 93
American War of Independence, 108
Amhurst, Nicholas, 90
Anderson, Robert, 57
Anderton, William, 121
Anne, Queen, 109
Apuleius, Lucius, 165
Arbiter, Petronius, 165
Arbuthnot, John, 89
Argyll, Archibald Campbell, 3rd Duke of, 95
Argyll, John Campbell, 2nd Duke of, 104–5
Aristophanes, 176
Aristotle, 27, 38, 58
Arnold, Matthew, 43
Athens, 174
Atterbury, Francis, 126
Austen, Jane, 20

Bacon, Francis, Viscount St. Albans, 22
Bakhtin, Mikhail, 160, 165, 166–68, 169
Balmerino, Arthur Elphinstone, Lord, 113, 128
Barber, Francis, 70
Barclay, John, 165, 171, 172
Baronius, Caesar, 58
Bate, Walter Jackson, 161–62
Bath, Earl of, *see* Pulteney
Beattie, James, 39
Bedford, John Russell, Duke of, 104–5
Bembo, Pietro, 65
Bender, 131
Benn, Tony, 102
Bentham, Jeremy, 67
Bentley, Richard, 53, 63, 65, 67
Berkeley, George, 39–40
Bernouilli family, 67
Beza, Theodore, 51
Bible, The, 53, 55–6
Birch, Thomas, 58
Blackstone, Sir William, 38
Blake, William, 14, 15
Blakeway, Edward, 121
Bodin, Jean, 117
Boerhaave, Hermann, 56
Boethius, 160, 165–73 *passim*, 178–79, 180
Boileau-Despreaux, Nicolas, 172
Bolingbroke, Henry St. John, Viscount, 90, 95, 105, 111, 129
Bompaire, J., 165
Boothby, Hill, 34
Boswell, James, 44, 46, 70; *Correspondence*, 33; *Life of Johnson*, 52, 60, 61, 87, 107, 108, 188, 191, 199; (quoted) 13, 28, 33–46 *passim*, 50, 52, 63, 64, 72–8 *passim*, 82, 110–20 *passim*, 166, 191, 197; projected work on 1745 rebellion, 115–16, 119
Boucher, Leon, 44
Bouffier, Claude, *see* Buffier
Boulton, James T., 45
Boyer, Abel, 89, 91
Bracciolini, Poggio, 65
Bradley, A. C., 78
Bradshaigh, Lady, 80
Bridges, Robert, 189
Britain, politics of, 89, 120, 125, 126, 127–28
Bronson, Bertrand, 193
Buchanan, George, 51
Buckingham, John Sheffield, Duke of, 121
Buenos Aires, 44
Buffier, Claude, 39
Buffon, Georges Louis Leclerc, Comte de, 56
Burke, Edmund, 38
Burnet, Gilbert, 197
Burney, Charles, 31, 41, 55, 66, 77
Burney, Frances, 71, 76
Burton, Robert, 166, 172
Bute, John Stuart, Earl of, 121, 122, 123
Butler, Samuel, 54, 60
Butterfield, Sir Herbert, 108
Byrom, John, 113, 118, 121, 130, 131
Bywater, Ingram, 199

Caesar, Mrs. Charles, 187
Cambridge, 121
Cameron, Archibald, 112–13
Camus, Albert, 101
Carlisle, Henry Howard, Earl of, 104–5
Carlisle, Cumbria, 130
Carlyle, Thomas, 48
Caroline of Ansbach, Queen, 92, 93
Carter, Elizabeth, 67, 183

Carteret, John, later Earl Granville, 92, 96
Casaubon, Isaac, 65, 164, 169
Cave, Edward, 87, 92, 97, 105
Cebes, 158, 171, 173
Cervantes Saavedra, Miguel de, 75, 171–72
Chambers, Ephraim, 34–5
Chambers, Robert, 38
Chapman, R. W., 189, 199–200
Charles XII of Sweden, 131, 132, 135–36, 196
Charles, Prince of Wales, 31
Charles Edward, 'Young Pretender', 113, 114, 118, 127–36 *passim*
Chatterton, Thomas, 53, 66
Chaucer, Geoffrey, 172
Chesterfield, Philip Dormer Stanhope, Earl of, 45–6
Cheynel, Francis, 196
Chilo of Lacedemon, 59
Chiswick, 195
Cholmondeley, George, Earl of, 97
Chrysostom, St., 58
Churchill, Charles, 44, 45, 123
Cicero, Marcus Tullius, 52, 82, 158, 189
Clarendon, Edward Hyde, Earl of, 196, 197–98
Clarke, Samuel, 63–4
Clenardus, Nicholas, 52, 54
Cleobolus the Lindian, 59
Clifford, James L., 46, 123
Club, The, 43, 46
Cobbett, William, 101
Cobbett's Parliamentary History of England, 105
Coleridge, Samuel Taylor, 25, 43, 78
Collins, William, 191–93
Columbus, Christopher, 132
Congreve, William, 131
Constantinople, 41
Convention with Spain, 93, 94
Cooper, Thomas, 123–24
Cope, Sir John, 130
Coram, Captain Thomas, 195
Cornwall, 93, 100
Cowley, Abraham, 32, 190
Cowper, William, 44
Coxe, William, 98, 105
Craftsman, 90, 92, 105, 125
Croker, John Wilson, 66
Cromwell, Oliver, 89
Culler, Jonathan, 172
Culloden, Battle of, 114, 131
Cumming, Alexander, 31

Dacier, André, 161, 164
Daily Gazetteer, 87, 90–1
Defoe, Daniel, 70, 131
Derby, 115, 132
Derwentwater, Lord, *see* Radcliffe
Descartes, René, 38, 39, 57
Diaz, Alberto Franco, 44
Diderot, Denis, 40, 57
Dies Irae, 80
Diodorus Siculus, 59
Diogenes Laertius, 49–50, 59
Dodsley, Robert, 193
Dryden, John, 19–20, 43, 45, 131, 160–61, 164–65, 189, 190
Duckett, George, 197–98

Edinburgh, 93, 127
Edward I and II, 131
Edwards, Oliver, 38
Edwards, Thomas, 78
Ehrenpreis, Irvin, 159, 164, 180
Eliot, George, 15, 16–17, 25, 28, 29, 30
Eliot, T. S., 31, 43, 44, 47
Elphinston, James, 25
Elstob, Elizabeth, 67
Empson, William, 82
Encyclopaedia Britannica, 196
English satire, 161
Ennius, Quintus, 164
Epictetus, 59
Epicurus, 175
Epistolae Obscurorum Virorum, 165
Erasmus, Desiderius, 62, 160, 165, 171
Erskine, Thomas, 73
Ethiopia, 175
Euclid, 59
Euler, Leonhard, 67
Europe, 89
Excise Bill, 92

Faber, Jacques, 57
Fallopius, Gabriele, 56
Falmouth, Hugh Boscawen, Viscount, 100
Farmer, Richard, 54, 67, 121–22, 123
Fawkes, Francis, 192
Fenton, Elijah, 42
Fielding, Henry, 70–83 *passim*, 173
Fleury, André Hercule de, 129
Flood, Henry, 101
Florida, 94
Ford, Cornelius, 49
France, 92, 96, 109, 131; academy, 32, 33, 34–5; Johnson in, 35, 41; satire in, 161
Frederick, Prince of Wales, 93, 100
Freemasons, 41
Frye, Northrop, 160, 165–66
Funus linguae Hellenisticae, 65

Garrick, David, 33, 78, 194, 195, 199
Gay, John, 22, 89
Gazetteer, see Daily Gazetteer
Gentleman's Magazine, 86, 87, 110, 113, 186
George I, 92, 120
George II, 92, 94, 95, 96, 100, 112, 120–29 *passim*
George III, 31, 41, 42, 108–22 *passim*, 133
Georgia, 93
Gibbon, Edmund, 43
Giddings, Robert, 123
Gin Act, 92
Goldsmith, Oliver, 7, 14–15, 32, 43, 48, 56, 194
Gower, John Leveson-Gower, Earl, 128–29, 134

Index

Graevius, Johann Georg, 54
Granville, George (Lord Lansdown), 162
Gray, Thomas, 44, 77
Greek Anthology, 59, 146–47, 149
Greek language, 52, 62, 65; literature, 62, 158, 164, 171
Greene, Donald J., 105, 107, 108, 110, 112, 117, 120–21, 123, 133
Greenwich, 87
Greville family, 93
Grey, Zachary, 60
Gronovius, Jacobus, 54
Gross, John, 13
Gwynn, John, 31

Hales, Stephen, 56
Halifax, George Montagu Dunk, Earl of, 104–5
Hallett, H. F., 39
Handel, George Frederick, 41
Hannibal, 127, 131–32
Hanover, 120, 121, 126, 131
Hardwicke, Philip Yorke, Duke of, 94, 96, 97
Harleian Library, 51, 55, 58
Harley, Edward, 100
Harte, Walter, 173
Hawkins, Sir John, 42, 64, 71, 87–8, 105, 121–30 *passim*
Hazlitt, William, 15, 24, 101
Hebrides, 41, 119
Heidegger, Martin, 39
Heinsius, Nicholas, 51
Herodotus, 59
Herschel, William, 36
Hervey, John, Lord, 97
Hickes, George, 55
Highlands, 127, 129
Hill, George Birkbeck, 66, 88
Historians, 107–10, 133–34
Hitler, Adolf, 53
Hogarth, Jane, 195
Hogarth, William, 195
Holland, 126
Homer, 64, 73
Honduras, 93
Hooker, Richard, 58
Horace, 22, 75, 86, 171, 196
Housman, A. E., 65
Huet, Pierre Daniel, 65
Humboldt, Friedrich, Heinrich Alexander, Baron von, 67
Hume, David, 38
Hyde, Mary, 35

Indian languages, 54
Ireland, 92, 94
Italy, 32, 34, 41, 51

Jacobite rebellion of 1745, 114–15, 129, 130, 131
Jacobitism, 90, 93, 100, 103, 104, 109–35 *passim*
James II, 114, 123, 124, 131
James, Henry, 76
James, Robert, 34, 55
James Edward, 'Old Pretender', 112–17 *passim*, 124, 128, 130, 131–32
Jenkins, Robert, 93
Johnson, Elizabeth, 189, 193
Johnson, Michael, 35, 51, 58

Johnson, Samuel: and aphorisms, 13–29, 142, 144, 156, 199; and the arts, 42–3; on biography, 196–97; and bookbinding, 35; and canonicity, 53; and classical authors, 158–85; and commemorative writing, 186–200; and compilation, 55; as 'dictator', 43–8; and editing, 54; and elegy, 187; and languages, 41–2; and Latin, 70, 187; and law, 37–8; and liberty, 171–72; his literary projects, 33, 61–2, 135; and medicine, 34; monument to, 64; and music, 40–1; his nicknames, 48; and non-juring, 117, 118, 122, 124, 133; and the novel, 70–83; and old age, 42; and painting, 42–3; and the passions, 137–57; his pension, 41, 113, 121–23; and philology, 54–5; and philosophy, 38–40; and politics, 38, 86–135; and publishers, 67; and satire, 160–64; scholarship, 51–67; and schoolteaching, 36, 171; and science, 34, 35, 56–7; his 'scope', 31–48; his style, 13–29; his talk, 13, 28, 33–41 *passim*, 70–4, 76, 78, 81–2, 101, 110–20 *passim*, 166, 181, 188, 199; and theology, 55–6; his topicality, 87; his travels, 35, 41; and truisms, 13–29, 142, 144, 156; Yale edition of, 20; Writings: *The Adventurer*, 172, 177, (No. 67) 23, (No. 95) 152–3, (No. 99) 132, (No. 102) 132, (No. 107) 143, 144, 146–47, (No. 108) 155, (No. 111) 148, (No. 119) 40, (No. 120) 138, 139, 140, 150; biographies, 58; *A Compleat Vindication of the Licenser of the Stage*, 87; criticism, 70–83; debates in parliament, 18, 86–101, 110; dedications and prefaces, 31, 36, 41, 42, 43, 60, 67; *A Dictionary of the English Language*, 13–14, 16–17, 32–3, 34, 36–7, 45–6, 54, 58, 59, 61, 67, 71, 110, 111, 112, 113, 134, 151, 160–61, 162, 188, 189, 196; *A Dissertation on the Epitaphs written by Pope*, 187–88, 190; epitaphs, 32, 186, 193–94; *An Essay on Epitaphs*, 186–87, 197; essays, 22, 23, 25, 28, 29, 137–57, 179; *The False Alarm*, 28, 110–11; *Gentleman's Magazine* contributions, 18, 33, 86–101, 110; Harleian Library catalogue, 51, 55, 58; *The Idler*, 17, 22, 171, 180, 200, (No. 2) 25, (No. 6) 20, (No. 10) 39, (No. 13) 20, (No. 14) 40, (No. 23) 17, (No. 40) 20, (No. 45) 43, (No. 58) 17, (No. 65) 197–98, (No. 80) 24, (No. 84) 196–97, (No. 87) 17, (No. 102) 17; 'Introduction to The Political State of Great Britain', 110, 123, 124; *Irene*, 93; Jenyns review, 59; journalism, 86–101 *passim*, 104, 105, 108; *A Journey to the Western Islands of Scotland*, 41, 119–20; Latin translations, 147; letters, 20, 35–6, 42, 45, 46, 119, 133, 192, 193–94, 195; life of Frederick the

Johnson, Samuel (*contd.*)
Great, 104; *The Life of Richard Savage*, 26–7, 48, 78, 133, 191–93; *The Lives of the English Poets*, 13, 35, 55, 60, 61, 70, 110, 133, 180, 189, 199, (Addison) 129, 133, 190, (Akenside) 118, 130, 133, (Butler) 133, (Collins) 191–93, (Cowley) 32, 190, (Dryden) 189, (Fenton) 133, (Gray) 77, (Milton) 14, 20, 36, 77, 133, 189, (Pope) 77, (Prior) 133, (Rowe) 79–80, (Smith) 190, 198–200, (Swift) 82, 133, (Waller) 133, (Yalden) 133; Lobo translation, 58; *Literary Magazine* contributions, 59; *London*, 21–2, 24, 26, 86–7, 110, 125–27, 128, 129, 133; *Marmor Norfolciense*, 87, 120–21, 123, 126–27; *Medicinal Dictionary* entries, 34; *Miscellaneous Observations on Macbeth*, 58, 60; 'On the Death of Dr. Robert Levet', 125, 193–94; pamphlets, 123, 133; *Preceptor* preface, 33, 58, 60; *The Rambler*, 22, 24, 58–9, 172, 177, (No. 1) 23, 25, (No. 2) 18–19, 23, 25, 26, 29, 154, (No. 3) 25, (No. 4) 70–2, 74–5, 77, 78, 80–1, 83, 154, (No. 5) 22, 149, (No. 6) 22, 149, (No. 7) 59, 139, 155, (No. 9) 22, (No. 11) 22, 59, (No. 13) 59, (No. 14) 23, 59, 137, 140, 143, 151, (No. 17) 22, 59, 150, 151, 154, (No. 18) 23, (No. 19) 143, (No. 21) 22, (No. 24) 22, 59, (No. 28) 154, (No. 29) 23, 142, 143, (No. 31) 143, (No. 32) 59, (No. 36) 35, 59, (No. 37) 59, (No. 38) 59, 143, (No. 40) 137, (No. 41) 142, 150, (No. 45) 144, 146, (No. 47) 13, (No. 49) 153, 154, 155, (No. 54) 139, 154, (No. 60) 144, 152, (No. 63) 138, 140, 144–46, (No. 71) 27, 28, 142, (No. 75) 16, (No. 78) 28, 137, 139, 140, (No. 80) 148, (No. 85) 137, 144, (No. 86) 47–8, 59, (No. 88) 59, (No. 90) 59, (No. 92) 47, 59, (No. 94) 59, (No. 97) 73, (No. 103) 137, 140, 149, 150, (No. 109) 24, (No. 111) 137, (No. 126) 138, 140, 149, 155, (No. 127) 132, (No. 128) 138, 140, (No. 137) 37, (No. 139) 59, (No. 140) 59, (No. 143) 184, (No. 150) 147–48, 149, (No. 151) 151, 155, 156, (No. 156) 47, (No. 160) 154, (No. 178) 184, (No. 180) 138, 140, 141, 149, (No. 181) 20, (No. 183) 155, (No. 185) 155, (No. 186) 138, 140, 153–54, (No. 189) 23, (No. 203) 40, (No. 206) 40, (No. 208) 47; *Rasselas*, 13, 18, 19, 20, 25, 32, 35–6, 37, 52–3, 59, 67, 75–6, 80, 137, 140, 158–85; reviews, 59; sermons, 63, 139, 189, 193; Shakespeare edition, 59–60, 63, 77, (notes) 70, 77, 78–9, 80, 189, 192–93, (preface) 13, 28, 47, 70, 75, 77, 91, (proposals) 59; *Taxation no Tyranny*, 108, 110, 133; *The Vanity of Human Wishes*, 18, 26, 32, 80, 110, 125, 127–32, 133, 137, 195–96, 197
Johnson, Sarah, 34
Jones, Emrys, 20
Jones, Sir William, 67
Jonson, Ben, 35, 43
Julian the Apostate, 165, 171
Junius, Francis, 33
Juvenal, 22, 25, 86–7, 126, 127, 129, 131, 133, 163, 164, 195–96

Keats, John, 28
Keene, Sir Benjamin, 93, 94
Kennedy, John, 31
Kenrick, William, 44–5
Ker, W. P., 165
Ketton-Cremer, R. W., 186
Kilmarnock, William Boyd, Earl of, 113, 128
Kircher, Athanasius, 56
Kirk, Eugene, 160, 165
Kolb, Gwin J., 174

Landa, Louis, 174
Langton, Bennet, Snr., 114
Langton, Bennet, 38, 52, 63, 114
Lascelles, Mary, 76
Latin, 52, 62, 161, 164, 187
Laud, William, 195–96
Lauder, William, 53, 66
Law, William, 141, 150–51, 154
LeClerc, Jean, 51, 65
Leedes, Edward, 171
Lennox, Charlotte, 75
Levet, Robert, 193–94
Licensing Act, 89, 92
Lichfield, George Henry Lee, Earl of, 37
Lichfield, Staffs., 37
Linnaeus, Charles, 56, 67
Lipsius, Richard Adalbert, 52, 62, 66, 69, 172
Literary Magazine, 59, 124
Lloyd, 67
Locke, John, 38, 108
Lomond, Loch, 70
London, 13, 21, 22, 58, 87, 93, 132; Bolt Court, 101; Buckingham Palace, 31; Mermaid Tavern, 43; Royal Academy, 42–3; St. John's Gate, 92; St. Paul's Cathedral, 64; Society of Arts (later Royal Academy), 42–3; the Tower, 128, 130; Tyburn, 126; Vauxhall, 43; Westminster Abbey, 194; Will's Coffee House, 43
London Magazine, 91
Lort, Michael, 67
Lovat, Simon Fraser, Lord, 113, 128, 195
Lucan, Charles Bingham, Earl of, 35
Lucian, 160–84 *passim*
Lye, Edward, 55
Lysons, Samuel, 67

Macaulay, Thomas Babington, 24, 38, 196
Machiavelli, Niccolo, 129
McIntosh, Carey, 158
Macpherson, James, 53, 66
Macrobius, Ambrosius Aurelius Theodorus, 51, 171
Madrid, 93
Maittaire, Michael, 58, 64
Malebranche, Nicholas, 39
Malone, Edmond, 53
Manchester, 113, 130, 131
Martial, 60
Mary, Queen, 109
Maxwell, William, 112, 124
Memoirs of Martinus Scriblerus, 120

Index

Menippean satire, 158–85
Menippus, 164–65
Middle English Dictionary, 55
Milton, John, 14, 36, 40, 44, 47, 53, 60, 64, 77, 107, 189
Modena, 52
Montfaucon, Bernard de, 54
Moore, Robert Etheridge, 74, 77
More, Hannah, 73–4, 81
More, Thomas, 159, 171
Morgan, David, 121
Morgann, Maurice, 78
Morhof, Daniel, 57, 65
Murray, Lord George, 114

N.E.D., see O.E.D.
Namier, Sir Lewis, 108–9, 110, 119
Newcastle, Thomas Pelham-Holles, Duke of, 90, 94, 95, 97
Newton, Sir Isaac, 64, 67, 187
Nile, River, 174, 180
Non-juring, 117, 118, 122, 124, 133
North, Frederick, Lord, 123
Novel, Johnson and the, 70–83

O.E.D., 151–52, 189
Odysseus, 75
Oldmixon, John, 197–98
Oldys, William, 51, 58, 67
Olympiodorus, 58
Onslow, Arthur, 95
Orford, Earl of, *see* Walpole, Sir Robert
Oriental languages, 54
Oriental romance, 159
Orwell, George, 9
Osborne, Thomas, 45
Osgood, Charles G., 171
Ossian, 53
Owen, J. B., 108
Oxford, 32, 38, 51, 58, 171, 196
Oxford Latin Dictionary, 55

Paracelsus, 56
Paris, 44, 132
Parliament, 86–106 *passim*, 108
Parnell, Thomas, 194
Parr, Samuel, 53, 64–6
Parrhasiana, 61
Parties, political, 86–136, *passim*
Paulson, Ronald, 176
Payne, F. Anne, 160, 165, 169–70
Pelham family, 96
Pennsylvania, 34
Penrith, 130
Percy, Thomas, 33, 60, 66, 122
Periander of Corinth, 22, 59
Perotti, Niccolo, 60
Persius, 164
Peter, Czar, 132
Phaedrus, 171
Philadelphia, 34
Phillips, Claudy, 194
Phillips, John, 190
Photius, 58
Piraeus, 174
Pitt, Thomas, 100
Pitt, William, the elder, 93, 94, 97–8
Pitt, William, the younger, 109
Plato, 175
Plutarch, 59
Pococke, Richard, 41–2
Poetical Character, 192
Poggiana, 61
Politian, 60, 62, 65, 69
Political State of Great Britain, 89, 91
Pope, Alexander, 22, 24, 33, 43, 77, 86, 89, 90–1, 95, 121, 129, 131, 143, 152, 161, 162, 187–88, 190
Porson, Richard, 64, 67
Potter, Robert, 44
Prestonpans, Battle of, 127
Prior, Matthew, 44
Prodicus, 158, 173
Pulteney, William (later Earl of Bath), 92, 95, 98, 99, 100, 105

Quintus Curtius, 59

Rabelais, François, 166
Radcliffe, Charles, titular Earl of Derwentwater, 113
Raleigh, Walter, 189
Reade, Aleyn Lyell, 66
Reed, Isaac, 67
Reid, Thomas, 39
Religion, non-Christian, 55–6
Rembrandt van Rijn, 32
Renaissance, scholarship of, 51–67 *passim*
Reynolds, Frances, 73
Reynolds, Sir Joshua, 31, 32, 36, 38, 42
Richards, Thomas ('a Welch gentleman'), 33
Richardson, Samuel, 70–83
Roman satire, 161
Rome, 87, 132
Rosenheim, Edward W., 182
Rowe, Nicholas, 188
Rowley poems, 53
Royal Society, 56
Rush, Benjamin, 34
Rymer, Thomas, 55

Sachs, Arieh, 163–64
Sacks, Sheldon, 182
Salisbury, Bishop of, *see* Sherlock
Salmasius, Claudius, 51, 65
Salonika, 199
Sandby, William, 105
Sandys, Samuel, 96, 97
Sarpi, Father Paul, 61–2, 69
Satire, Johnson and, 160–64
Satyr, In French and English, A, 132
Savage, Richard, 26–7, 48, 191–93
Saxony, 120
Scaliger, Joseph Justus, the younger, 51, 58, 62, 65
Scaliger, Julius Caesar, the elder, 51, 57

Scaligerana, 61
Schwartz, Delmore, 43–4
Scotland, 41, 95, 100, 127, 130
Scots, 199
Scott, Sir Walter, 45
Scott, Sir William, 37
Scriblerians, 120
Sedgwick Romney, 108, 109, 133
Sejanus, 127, 129, 131
Seneca, 165, 171, 172
Shakespeare, William, 14, 31, 53, 54, 70–83 *passim*, 100, 148, 189, 192–93, 196
Shaw, William, 55
Shenstone, William, 33
Sheridan, Richard Brinsley, 14
Sherlock, Thomas, 97
Shippen, William, 100
Sholokov, Mikhail, 53
Sigonio, Carlo, 51–2
Simon, Richard, 56
Skinner, Stephen, 33
Smith, David Nichol, 77, 194
Smith, Edmund, 190, 198
Smollett, Tobias, 48, 70, 71, 104
Socrates, 14, 167
South Sea Scheme, 89
Spain, war with, 87, 93–4, 96, 98–9, 129
Spectator, 38
Spenser, Edmund, 54, 60, 165
Stamp Act, 89
Stanhope, James, Earl, 92
Star Chamber, 89
Steevens, George, 67
Stephanus, Byzantinus, 54
Stephen, Leslie, 44
Sterne, Lawrence, 70, 71, 82, 83, 160
Stoics, 158, 174–75
Stuart kings, 89, 112ff.
Suffolk, Henrietta Howard, Countess of, 92
Sunderland, Charles Spencer, Earl of, 92
Swift, Jonathan, 22, 33, 82, 89, 94, 96, 120, 160, 166, 172, 173, 176, 179

Taylor, John, 114–15, 116
Temple, Sir William, 34
Terence, 40
Thackeray, William Makepeace, 46, 74
Theobald, Lewis, 54
Thrale, Harry, 41
Thrale, Henry, 35, 41
Thrale, Hester, 41, 60, 66, 73, 119, 133, 177, 183
Thrale, Hester Maria ('Queeney'), 41
Thrale, Susannah, 35
Thuanus (or de Thou), Jacques, 62–3
Tickell, Thomas, 190
Timberland, Ebeneezer, 105
Torbuck, John, 105
Townshend, George, 46
Tracy, Clarence, 167
Trapp, Joseph, 164
True Briton, 126–27
Twain, Mark, 101
Tyers, Thomas, 34

U.S.A., 108
Universal Visiter, The, 200
Upton, John, 54

Varro, Marcus Terentius, 164–65, 167, 169
Vida, Girolamo, 51
Voltaire, 159, 160

Wales, 19, 35, 41, 87, 126
Walmsley, Gilbert, 198–200
Walker, Robert G., 170
Waller, William, 42
Walpole, Horace, 100
Walpole, Horatio, 95, 100
Walpole, Sir Robert, 85–106 *passim*, 123, 125, 127, 129, 131
Walpole, Robert, Lord (Prime Minister's son), 92
Walton, Izaak, 197
Warburton, William, 43, 78, 189
Warton, Joseph, 54, 192
Warton, Thomas, 192, 193–94
Wasserman, Earl R., 158, 171
Werenfels, Samuel, 65
West Indies, 93
Wharton, Philip, Duke of, 126
Whitaker's Tables of Precedency, 15
Whitley, Alvin, 167
Wilkes, John, 101, 194
William III, 109, 126
William the Conqueror, 131
Wittgenstein, Ludwig, 39
Wolfius, 58
Wolf, Friedrich August, 67
Wolsey, Thomas, 129, 130, 131, 196
Woolf, Virginia, 14, 15
World, The, 45–6
Wotton, Sir Henry, 190
Woty, William, 192
Wowerus, Joannes, 65
Wycherley, William, 162
Wyndham, Sir William, 94, 96

Yeats, William Butler, 28
Young, G. M., 197

Zouch, Thomas, 58